Course **Business Skills and Environment**

The Ohio State University

http://create.mheducation.com



ISBN-10: 125928610X    ISBN-13: 9781259286100

# Contents

# Credits

# Rodek

# Organizing the Enterprise: Which Form Is Best for You?

EXCERPTED FROM

*Entrepreneur's Toolkit: Tools and Techniques to Launch and Grow Your Business*

Harvard Business School Press
*Boston, Massachusetts*

ISBN-10: 1-4221-0530-X
ISBN-13: 978-1-4221-0530-6
5306BC

**Grow Your New Business**



This chapter was originally published as chapter 3 of *Entrepreneur's Toolkit,*
copyright 2005 Harvard Business School Publishing Corporation.

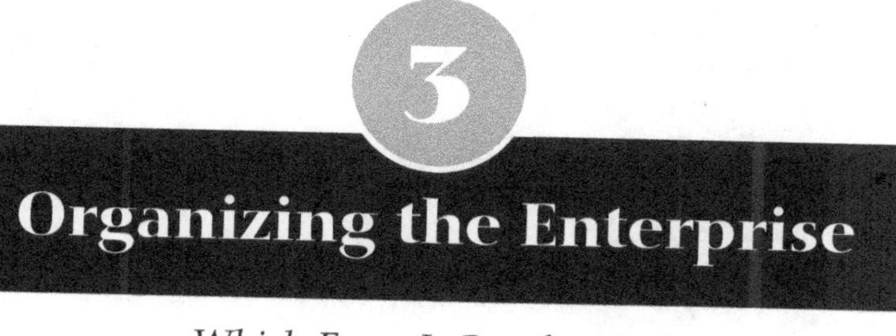

# 3 Organizing the Enterprise

*Which Form Is Best for You?*

## Key Topics Covered in This Chapter

- *the various legal forms of organization available to U.S. businesses*
- *the advantages and disadvantages of each form*
- *determining which form is best for your business*

ONE KEY ISSUE that every entrepreneur must address at the onset of a new venture is the legal form the enterprise will adopt. Should it be a sole proprietorship, a partnership, a corporation, a limited liability company?

This decision is driven chiefly by the objectives of the entrepreneur and the firm's investors. But taxation and legal liabilities also play a part. The choice is made difficult by the trade-offs built into the law. To get the most favorable tax treatment, a business must often give up some protection from liability, some flexibility, or both. This chapter provides a brief overview of the choices available to the new enterprise and summarizes the advantages and disadvantages of each.

## Sole Proprietorship

The *sole proprietorship* is the oldest, simplest, and most common form of business entity. It is a business owned by a single individual. For tax and legal liability purposes, the owner and the business are one and the same. The proprietorship is not taxed as a separate entity. Instead, the owner reports all income and deductible expenses for the business on Schedule C of the personal income tax return. Note that the earnings of the business are taxed at the individual level, whether or not they are actually distributed in cash. There is no vehicle for sheltering income.

### A Note About Legalities

The information given in this chapter is based on U.S. law but should not be considered as legal advice. Always consult with an attorney on these matters. Readers located outside the United States should consult their own legal and tax sources.

For liability purposes, the individual and the business are also one and the same. Thus, legal claimants can pursue the personal property of the proprietor and not simply the assets used in the business.

### Advantages of a Sole Proprietorship

Perhaps the greatest advantage of this form of business is its simplicity and low cost. You are not required to file with the government, although some businesses, such as restaurants and child day care centers, must be licensed by local health or regulatory authorities. Nor is any legal charter required. The owner can simply begin doing business.

The sole proprietorship form of business has other advantages:

- The owner or proprietor is in complete control of business decisions.
- The income generated through operations can be directed into the proprietor's pocket or reinvested as he or she sees fit.
- Profits flow directly to the proprietor's personal tax return; they are not subject to a second level of taxation. In other words, profits from the business will not be taxed at the business level.
- The business can be dissolved as easily and informally as it was begun.

These advantages account for the widespread adoption of the sole proprietorship in the United States. Any person who wants to set up shop and begin dealing with customers can get right to it, in most cases without the intervention of government bureaucrats or lawyers.

### Disadvantages of the Sole Proprietorship

This legal form of organization, however, has disadvantages:

- The amount of capital available to the business is limited to the owner's personal funds and whatever funds can be borrowed. This disadvantage limits the potential size of the business, no matter how attractive or popular its product or service.
- Sole proprietors have unlimited liability for all debts and legal judgments incurred in the course of business. Thus, a product liability lawsuit by a customer will not be made against the business but rather against the owner.
- The business may not be able to attract high-caliber employees whose goals include a share of business ownership. Sharing the benefits of ownership, other than simple profit-sharing, would require a change in the legal form of the business.
- Some employee benefits, such as owner's life, disability, and medical insurance premiums, may not be deductible—or may be only partially deductible—from taxable income.
- The entity has a limited life; it exists only as long as the owner is alive. Upon the owner's death, the assets of the business go to his or her estate.
- As you will see later in this book, venture capitalists and other outside investors of equity capital will not participate in a sole proprietorship business.

## Partnership

A *partnership* is a business entity having two or more owners. In the United States a partnership is treated as a proprietorship for tax and liability purposes. Earnings are distributed according to the partner-

## Tips for Starting a Sole Proprietor Business

You can start a sole proprietorship by simply going to it: by offering your services as a consultant, buying and reselling merchandise, writing a subscription newsletter, and so forth. It's simple. Here are some useful tips:

- Keep your household and business finances separate. You can do that by setting up a separate bank account for your business; run all the business's checks and receipts through that account.
- Use Quicken or a computer spreadsheet to keep track of the many business expenses you'll encounter during the tax year. If you track them under the same categories used in the business expenses section of IRS form Schedule C, it will be simple to itemize these expenses and deduct them from taxable income. And save every receipt!
- If you run the business under a name other than your own—e.g., Surfside Management Consulting—you may need to file a "fictitious name" or "doing business as" certificate in the city where the business is domiciled. And make sure that the name is not already taken by another business.
- Most U.S. states prohibit the use of the words *Corporation*, *Corp.*, *Incorporated*, *Inc.*—and even *Company* and *Co.*—after the business's name if it is not incorporated.

ship agreement and are treated as personal income for tax purposes. Thus, like the sole proprietorship, the partnership is simply a conduit for directing income to its partners, as in this example:

> *Bill and Bob formed a partnership and started a restaurant called The Billy-Bob Café. By agreement, they split the profits of the business equally, the total of which amounted to $140,000 last year. Bill, who had no other source of earnings last year, reported $70,000 in income on his personal tax return. Bob, who earned another $20,000 from a*

*part-time job, had to report $90,000 on his personal income tax return ($70,000 in partnership income plus $20,000 from his other job).*

Partnerships have a unique liability situation. Each partner is jointly and severally liable. Thus, a damaged party can pursue a single partner or any number of partners—and that claim may or may not be proportional to the invested capital of the partners or the distribution of earnings. This means that if Bill did something to damage a customer, that customer could sue both Bill *and* Bob even though Bob played no part in the problem.

Organizing a partnership is not as effortless as with a sole proprietorship. The partners must determine, and should set down in writing, their agreement on a number of issues:

- The amount and nature of their respective capital contributions (e.g., one partner might contribute cash, another a patent, and a third property and cash)
- How the business's profits and losses will be allocated
- Salaries and draws against profits
- Management responsibilities
- The consequences of withdrawal, retirement, disability, or the death of a partner
- The means of dissolution and liquidation of the partnership

## Advantages of a Partnership

Partnerships have many of the same advantages of the sole proprietorship, along with others:

- Except for the time and the legal cost of crafting a partnership agreement, it is easy to establish.
- Because there is more than one owner, the entity has more than one pool of capital to tap in financing the business and its operations.

- Profits from the business flow directly to the partners' personal tax returns; they are not subject to a second level of taxation.
- The entity can draw on the judgment and management of more than one person. In the best cases, the partners will have complementary skills.

## Disadvantages of a Partnership

As mentioned earlier, partners are jointly and severally liable for the actions of the other partners. Thus, one partner can put other partners at risk without their knowledge or consent. Other disadvantages include the following:

- Profits must be shared among the partners.
- With two or more partners being privy to decisions, decision making may be slower and more difficult than in a sole proprietorship. Disputes can tie the partnership in knots.
- As with a sole proprietorship, the cost of some employee benefits may not be deductible from income taxation.
- Depending on the partnership agreement, the partnership may have a limited life. Unless otherwise specified, it will end upon the withdrawal or death of any partner.

## The Limited Partnership

The type of partnership entity described thus far is legally referred to as a general partnership. It is what we normally think of when describing a partnership. There is another partnership form, however, that you should understand: the *limited partnership*. This is a hybrid form of organization having both limited and general partners. The general partner (there may be more than one) assumes management responsibility and unlimited liability for the business and must have at least a 1 percent interest in profits and losses. The limited partner (or partners) has no voice in management and is legally liable only for the amount of his or her capital contribution plus any other debt obligations specifically accepted.

The usual motive behind a limited partnership is to bring together individuals who have technical or management expertise (the general partners) and well-heeled investors who know little about the business—or who lack the time to participate—but who wish to participate in an opportunity for financial gain.

Note that in a limited partnership, profits and losses can be allocated differently among the partners. That is, even if profits are allocated 20 percent to the general partner and 80 percent to the limited partners, the limited partners may get 99 percent of the losses. (Well-heeled limited partners often favor this arrangement when they can use the partnership's losses to offset taxable earnings from other sources.) Losses, however, are deductible only up to the amount of capital at risk. The distribution of profit is subject to all sorts of creative structuring, such as those observed in certain venture capital and real estate partnerships. In some of those arrangements, the limited partners get 99 percent of the profits until they have gotten back an amount equal to their entire capital contributions, at which point the general partner begins to receive 30 percent and the limited partners' share drops to 70 percent.

## C Corporations

The *C corporation* is synonymous with the common notion of a corporation. When a business incorporates, it becomes a C corporation unless it makes a special election to become an S corporation, which is described later in this chapter. C corporations in the United States are vastly outnumbered by sole proprietorships, and yet they account for almost 90 percent of all U.S. sales. This is because the vast majority of the nation's major companies are corporations.

In the United States, a corporation is an entity chartered by the state and treated as a person under the law. This means that it can sue and be sued; it can be fined and taxed by the state; and it can enter into contracts. The C corporation can have an infinite number of owners. Ownership is evidenced by shares of company stock. The entity is managed on behalf of shareholders—at least indirectly—by a board of directors.

The corporate form is appealing to entrepreneurs for several reasons. First, in contrast to the sole proprietorship, the C corporation's owners are personally protected from liability. To appreciate this protection, consider the case of the massive oil spill of the oil tanker *Exxon Valdez* in 1989. Even if the damages against Exxon had exceeded the company's net worth, the courts could not have pursued the company's individual shareholders for further damages. An individual owner's liability is limited to the extent of his or her investment in the firm. This corporate shell, or veil, can be pierced only in the event of fraud.

Another appealing feature is the corporation's ability to raise capital. Unlike the sole proprietorship and partnership, which must rely on a single owner or small number of partners for equity capital, a corporation has the potential to tap the capital of a vast number of investors: individuals as well as institutions, such as pension funds and mutual funds. Equity (or ownership) capital is contributed by shareholders when they purchase stock issued directly from the company. In return they receive a fractional ownership share in the assets and future fortunes of the company. A successful and growing company can often raise capital through successive public offerings of its stock. The corporation can also borrow money.

## Advantages of the C Corporation

The advantages of the C corporation, then, can be summarized as follows:

- Shareholders have limited liability for the corporation's debts and judgments against it. Officers, however, can be held personally liable for their actions, such as the failure to withhold and pay corporate taxes.
- Corporations can raise funds through the sale of stock.

- Corporations can deduct the cost of certain benefits they provide to officers and employees.
- Theoretically, a corporation has an unlimited life span.
- Because a corporation can compensate employees with company shares, it is in a better position than proprietorships and partnerships to attract and retain talent.
- Ownership shares are transferable. Shareholders can sell some or all of their interests in the company (assuming that there's a market for them). They can also give their shares to family members or charities.

### Disadvantages of the C Corporation

As if to remind us that we cannot have our cake and eat it, the C corporation has several clear disadvantages. Perhaps the greatest is the problem of double taxation. The C corporation is taxed on its earnings (profits). Whatever is left over after taxes can be distributed to shareholders in the form of dividends or can be retained in the business to finance operations or growth. But consider what happens to after-tax dividends that are distributed to shareholders. These dividends must be reported by shareholders as taxable dividend income. Thus, earnings are taxed twice: once at the corporate level and again at the shareholder level.

(Note: Dividend income is taxed in the United States at a lower rate than in the past. Beginning in 2003, qualified dividends are subject to the same 5 percent or 15 percent maximum tax rate that applies to net capital gain. Before 2003, all dividends were taxed at the higher tax rates that applied to ordinary income.)

To understand this double-taxation problem, consider this example:

> *Amalgamated Hat Rack earned $647,500 before taxes and paid a little more than 46 percent of this ($300,000) in state and federal corporate income taxes, leaving it with $347,500 in after-tax profit. If the company paid $10,000 of that in the form of a dividend to Angus McDuff, its founder and CEO, McDuff would be required to add that amount to his personal taxable income, which might be taxed by both the state and*

*the federal government. Thus, the same income is taxed twice. (Note: There is a minor exception to this double-taxation issue in the case of corporations that receive dividend income from other corporations.)*

Other disadvantages include the following:

- The process of incorporation is often costly. The corporation must create a set of rules for governing the entity, including stockholder meetings, board of directors meetings, the election of officers, and so forth.
- Corporations are monitored by federal, state, and some local agencies. Public corporations must publish their results quarterly.

For the entrepreneur, adoption of the corporate form is a way to "liquefy" his or her personal equity in the company; paper wealth can be turned into real money. And it is a great way to raise the capital needed for growth. But every share sold dilutes the entrepreneur's ownership and personal control.

## S Corporations

The *S corporation* is another creature of U.S. tax law. It is a closely held corporation whose tax status is the same as the partnership's, but its participants enjoy the liability protections granted to corporate shareholders. In other words, it is a conduit for passing profits and losses directly to the personal income tax returns of its shareholders, whose legal liabilities are limited to the amount of their capital contributions.

In exchange for these favorable treatments, the law places a number of restrictions on the types of corporations that can elect S status. To qualify for S corporation status, an organization must meet the following requirements:

- Have only one class of stock, although differences in voting rights are allowed
- Be a domestic corporation, owned wholly by U.S. citizens, and derive no more than 80 percent of its revenues from non-U.S. sources

- Have thirty-five or fewer stockholders (husbands and wives count as one stockholder)
- Derive no more than 25 percent of revenues from passive sources, such as interest, dividends, rents, and royalties
- Have only individuals, estates, and certain trusts as shareholders (i.e., no corporations or partnerships)

The last provision excludes venture capitalists as potential shareholders because most venture-capitalist firms are partnerships.

## The Limited Liability Company

The limited-liability company (LLC) is a relatively new type of entity designed to afford the same benefits as does the S corporation. The LLC is similar to an S corporation in that it enjoys the tax advantages of a partnership and the liability protections of a corporation. Although state laws differ somewhat, an LLC is like an S corporation but with none of the restrictions on the number or type of participants. Owners are neither proprietors, partners, nor shareholders; instead, they are "members."

The LLC is similar to a partnership in that the LLC's operating agreement (the equivalent of a partnership agreement) may distribute profits and losses in a variety of ways, not necessarily in proportion to capital contributions. Law firms are often organized as LLCs.

Aside from its taxation and limited liabilities protections, the LLC is simple to operate; like a sole proprietorship, for example, there is no statutory requirement to keep minutes, hold meetings, or make resolutions—requirements that often trip up corporation owners.

## Which Form Makes Sense for You?

As you have no doubt gathered, tax implications are an important factor in the choice of a business entity. Indeed, the incentives of the U.S. tax code give rise to certain tactics that can be risky. For example, the aforementioned double taxation of a corporation's distributed earnings provides an incentive for owner-employees to pay all profits to themselves as compensation. Unlike dividends, compensation is deductible as an expense to the corporation and thus is not taxed twice. However, the Internal Revenue Service (IRS) has certain rules on what is considered reasonable compensation; these rules are designed to discourage just such behavior.

Note too that the tax on individuals in so-called flow-through entities such as partnerships and LLCs is on the income *earned* and not on the actual cash distributed. The income of the partnership is taxed at the personal level of the partners, whether or not any cash is actually distributed. Thus, earnings retained in the business to finance growth or to create a monetary nest egg are taxed even though they are not distributed to the owners.

If the venture is projected to create large losses in the early years, then there may be some benefit to passing those losses through to investors, assuming that the investors are in a position to use them to offset other income and thus reduce their taxes. This situation would favor the partnership or LLC. Similarly, if the business intends to generate substantial cash flow and return it to investors as the primary means of creating value for investors, then a partnership or LLC is still attractive. If, however, the business will require cash investment over the long term and if value is intended to be harvested through a sale or public offering, then a C corporation is the most attractive option.

Of course, a business may move through many forms in its lifetime. A sole proprietorship may become a partnership and finally a C corporation. A limited partnership may become an LLC and then a C corporation. Each transition, however, requires considerable legal work and imposes an administrative burden on the management and owners of the firm. The advantages of the right form of organization at each stage certainly may warrant these burdens. On the other hand, high-potential ventures on the fast track should avoid losing time and focus by jumping through these hoops. For them, the corporate form is almost always best. As corporations, they can use stock and options to lure an experienced management team and to conserve cash. They can even use stock in lieu of all-cash arrangements in paying for consulting services. Also, venture capitalists (VCs) may not take them seriously if they are not incorporated, because VCs will want a block of ownership.

Consequently, if you are an entrepreneur, consider the likely evolution of your business before selecting a particular form of organization, and consult with a qualified tax attorney or accountant before making this important choice.

## Summing Up

Table 3-1 summarizes this chapter by outlining the types of businesses discussed here.

TABLE 3-1

## Forms of Business

| Form of Business | Key Benefits | Key Disadvantages |
|---|---|---|
| Sole proprietorship | • Simple to organize and operate<br>• One level of taxation | • Full liability of the owner<br>• Cannot raise outside equity capital, thus limiting potential size of the business |
| Partnership | • Can bring in additional talent and personal capital<br>• One level of taxation | • Full liability of partners<br>• Capital limited to the pockets of the partners and their ability to borrow<br>• Unless addressed through the partnership agreement, dissolves with the death or withdrawal of any partner |
| C corporation | • Theoretically capable of attracting equity capital through share ownership<br>• Preferred form of venture capitalists<br>• Able to deduct many benefit payments to employees<br>• Shareholders enjoy limited liability | • Complex to set up and operate<br>• Income subject to double taxation |
| S corporation | • Like a proprietorship and partnership, subject to only one level of taxation<br>• Shareholders enjoy limited liability | • Complex to set up and operate<br>• Limited in the number of shareholders<br>• Venture capitalists cannot be shareholders |
| Limited partnership | • Limited liability<br>• One level of taxation | • Complex to set up |
| Limited liability company | • Simpler to set up and operate than a corporation<br>• Limited liability for members<br>• One level of taxation<br>• Infinite number of possible members | • Cannot attract outside equity capital |

## Harvard Business Essentials

*The New Manager's Guide and Mentor*

The Harvard Business Essentials series is designed to provide comprehensive advice, personal coaching, background information, and guidance on the most relevant topics in business. Drawing on rich content from Harvard Business School Publishing and other sources, these concise guides are carefully crafted to provide a highly practical resource for readers with all levels of experience, and will prove especially valuable for the new manager. To assure quality and accuracy, each volume is closely reviewed by a specialized content adviser from a world-class business school. Whether you are a new manager seeking to expand your skills or a seasoned professional looking to broaden your knowledge base, these solution-oriented books put reliable answers at your fingertips.

Books in the Series:

*Business Communication*
*Coaching and Mentoring*
*Creating Teams with an Edge*
*Crisis Management*
*Decision Making*
*Entrepreneur's Toolkit*
*Finance for Managers*
*Hiring and Keeping the Best People*
*Manager's Toolkit*
*Managing Change and Transition*
*Managing Creativity and Innovation*
*Managing Employee Performance*
*Managing Projects Large and Small*
*Marketer's Toolkit*
*Negotiation*
*Power, Influence, and Persuasion*
*Strategy*
*Time Management*

Harvard Business Review
www.hbr.org

*It's a dirty little secret: Most executives cannot articulate the objective, scope, and advantage of their business in a simple statement. If they can't, neither can anyone else.*

# Can You Say What Your Strategy Is?

by David J. Collis and Michael G. Rukstad

Reprint R0804E

*It's a dirty little secret: Most executives cannot articulate the objective, scope, and advantage of their business in a simple statement. If they can't, neither can anyone else.*

# Can You Say What Your Strategy Is?

by David J. Collis and Michael G. Rukstad



Can you summarize your company's strategy in 35 words or less? If so, would your colleagues put it the same way?

It is our experience that very few executives can honestly answer these simple questions in the affirmative. And the companies that those executives work for are often the most successful in their industry. One is Edward Jones, a St. Louis–based brokerage firm with which one of us has been involved for more than 10 years. The fourth-largest brokerage in the United States, Jones has quadrupled its market share during the past two decades, has consistently outperformed its rivals in terms of ROI through bull and bear markets, and has been a fixture on *Fortune*'s list of the top companies to work for. It's a safe bet that just about every one of its 37,000 employees could express the company's succinct strategy statement: Jones aims to "grow to 17,000 financial advisers by 2012 [from about 10,000 today] by offering trusted and convenient face-to-face financial advice to conservative individual investors who delegate their financial decisions, through a national network of one-financial-adviser offices."

Conversely, companies that don't have a simple and clear statement of strategy are likely to fall into the sorry category of those that have failed to execute their strategy or, worse, those that never even had one. In an astonishing number of organizations, executives, frontline employees, and all those in between are frustrated because no clear strategy exists for the company or its lines of business. The kinds of complaints that abound in such firms include:

- "I try for months to get an initiative off the ground, and then it is shut down because 'it doesn't fit the strategy.' Why didn't anyone tell me that at the beginning?"
- "I don't know whether I should be pursuing this market opportunity. I get mixed signals from the powers that be."
- "Why are we bidding on this customer's business again? We lost it last year, and I thought we agreed then not to waste our time chasing the contract!"

• "Should I cut the price for this customer? I don't know if we would be better off winning the deal at a lower price or just losing the business."

Leaders of firms are mystified when what they thought was a beautifully crafted strategy is never implemented. They assume that the initiatives described in the voluminous documentation that emerges from an annual budget or a strategic-planning process will ensure competitive success. They fail to appreciate the necessity of having a simple, clear, succinct strategy statement that everyone can internalize and use as a guiding light for making difficult choices.

Think of a major business as a mound of 10,000 iron filings, each one representing an employee. If you scoop up that many filings and drop them onto a piece of paper, they'll be pointing in every direction. It will be a big mess: 10,000 smart people working hard and making what they think are the right decisions for the company—but with the net result of confusion. Engineers in the R&D department are creating a product with "must have" features for which (as the marketing group could have told them) customers will not pay; the sales force is selling customers on quick turnaround times and customized offerings even though the manufacturing group has just invested in equipment designed for long production runs; and so on.

If you pass a magnet over those filings, what happens? They line up. Similarly, a well-understood statement of strategy aligns behavior within the business. It allows everyone in the organization to make individual choices that reinforce one another, rendering those 10,000 employees exponentially more effective.

What goes into a good statement of strategy? Michael Porter's seminal article "What Is Strategy?" (HBR November–December 1996) lays out the characteristics of strategy in a conceptual fashion, conveying the essence of strategic choices and distinguishing them from the relentless but competitively fruitless search for operational efficiency. However, we have found in our work both with executives and with students that Porter's article does not answer the more basic question of how to describe a particular firm's strategy.

It is a dirty little secret that most executives don't actually know what all the elements of a strategy statement are, which makes it impossible for them to develop one. With a clear definition, though, two things happen: First, formulation becomes infinitely easier because executives know what they are trying to create. Second, implementation becomes much simpler because the strategy's essence can be readily communicated and easily internalized by everyone in the organization.

## Elements of a Strategy Statement

The late Mike Rukstad, who contributed enormously to this article, identified three critical components of a good strategy statement—objective, scope, and advantage—and rightly believed that executives should be forced to be crystal clear about them. These elements are a simple yet sufficient list for any strategy (whether business or military) that addresses competitive interaction over unbounded terrain.

Any strategy statement must begin with a definition of the ends that the strategy is designed to achieve. "If you don't know where you are going, any road will get you there" is the appropriate maxim here. If a nation has an unclear sense of what it seeks to achieve from a military campaign, how can it have a hope of attaining its goal? The definition of the objective should include not only an end point but also a time frame for reaching it. A strategy to get U.S. troops out of Iraq at some distant point in the future would be very different from a strategy to bring them home within two years.

Since most firms compete in a more or less unbounded landscape, it is also crucial to define the scope, or domain, of the business: the part of the landscape in which the firm will operate. What are the boundaries beyond which it will not venture? If you are planning to enter the restaurant business, will you provide sit-down or quick service? A casual or an upscale atmosphere? What type of food will you offer—French or Mexican? What geographic area will you serve—the Midwest or the East Coast?

Alone, these two aspects of strategy are insufficient. You could go into business tomorrow with the goal of becoming the world's largest hamburger chain within 10 years. But will anyone invest in your company if you have not explained how you are going to reach your objective? Your competitive advantage is the essence of your strategy: What

**David J. Collis** (dcollis@hbs.edu) is an adjunct professor in the strategy unit of Harvard Business School in Boston and the author of several books on corporate strategy. He has studied and consulted to Edward Jones, the brokerage that is the main example in this article, and has taught in the firm's management-development program. **Michael G. Rukstad** was a senior research fellow at Harvard Business School, where he taught for many years until his untimely death in 2006.

your business will do differently from or better than others defines the all-important means by which you will achieve your stated objective. That advantage has complementary external and internal components: a value proposition that explains why the targeted customer should buy your product above all the alternatives, and a description of how internal activities must be aligned so that only your firm can deliver that value proposition.

Defining the objective, scope, and advantage requires trade-offs, which Porter identified as fundamental to strategy. If a firm chooses to pursue growth or size, it must accept that profitability will take a back seat. If it chooses to serve institutional clients, it may ignore retail customers. If the value proposition is lower prices, the company will not be able to compete on, for example, fashion or fit. Finally, if the advantage comes from scale economies, the firm will not be able to accommodate idiosyncratic customer needs. Such trade-offs are what distinguish individual companies strategically.

## Defining the Objective

The first element of a strategy statement is the one that most companies have in some form or other. Unfortunately, the form is usually wrong. Companies tend to confuse their statement of values or their mission with their strategic objective. A strategic objective is *not*, for example, the platitude of "maximizing shareholder wealth by exceeding customer expectations for _______ [insert product or service here] and providing opportunities for our employees to lead fulfilling lives while respecting the environment and the communities in which we operate." Rather, it is the single precise objective that will drive the business over the next five years or so. (See the exhibit "A Hierarchy of Company Statements.") Many companies do have—and all firms should have—statements of their ultimate purpose and the ethical values under which they will operate, but neither of these is the strategic objective.

The mission statement spells out the underlying motivation for being in business in the first place—the contribution to society that the firm aspires to make. (An insurance company, for example, might define its mission as providing financial security to consumers.) Such statements, however, are not useful as strategic goals to drive today's business decisions. Similarly, it is good and proper that firms be clear with employees about ethical values. But principles such as respecting individual differences and sustaining the environment are not strategic. They govern how employees should behave ("doing things right"); they do not guide what the firm should do ("the right thing to do").

Firms in the same business often have the same mission. (Don't all insurance companies aspire to provide financial security to their customers?) They may also have the same values. They might even share a vision: an indeterminate future goal such as being the "recognized leader in the insurance field." However, it is unlikely that even two companies in the same business will have the same strategic objective. Indeed, if your firm's strategy can be applied to any other firm, you don't have a very good one.

It is always easy to claim that maximizing shareholder value is the company's objective. In some sense all strategies are designed to do this. However, the question to ask when creating an actionable strategic statement is, Which objective is most likely to maximize shareholder value over the next several years?

## A Hierarchy of Company Statements

Organizational direction comes in several forms. The mission statement is your loftiest guiding light—and your least specific. As you work your way down the hierarchy, the statements become more concrete, practical, and ultimately unique. No other company will have the same strategy statement, which defines your competitive advantage, or balanced scorecard, which tracks how you implement your particular strategy.

**MISSION**
Why we exist

**VALUES**
What we believe in and how we will behave

**VISION**
What we want to be

**STRATEGY**
What our competitive game plan will be

**BALANCED SCORECARD**
How we will monitor and implement that plan

**The BASIC ELEMENTS of a Strategy Statement**

**OBJECTIVE** = Ends

**SCOPE** = Domain

**ADVANTAGE** = Means

getting specific

(Growth? Achieving a certain market share? Becoming the market leader?) The strategic objective should be specific, measurable, and time bound. It should also be a single goal. It is not sufficient to say, "We seek to grow profitably." Which matters more—growth or profitability? A salesperson needs to know the answer when she's deciding how aggressive to be on price. There could well be a host of subordinate goals that follow from the strategic objective, and these might serve as metrics on a balanced scorecard that monitors progress for which individuals will be held accountable. Yet the ultimate objective that will drive the operation of the business over the next several years should always be clear.

The choice of objective has a profound impact on a firm. When Boeing shifted its primary goal from being the largest player in the aircraft industry to being the most profitable, it had to restructure the entire organization, from sales to manufacturing. For example, the company dropped its policy of competing with Airbus to the last cent on every deal and abandoned its commitment to maintain a manufacturing capacity that could deliver more than half a peak year's demand for planes.

Another company, after years of seeking to maximize profits at the expense of growth, issued a corporate mandate to generate at least 10% organic growth per year. The change in strategy forced the firm to switch its focus from shrinking to serve only its profitable core customers and competing on the basis of cost or efficiency to differentiating its products, which led to a host of new product features and services that appealed to a wider set of customers.

At Edward Jones, discussion among the partners about the firm's objective ignited a passionate exchange. One said, "Our ultimate objective has to be maximizing profit per partner." Another responded, "Not all financial advisers are partners—so if we maximize revenue per partner, we are ignoring the other 30,000-plus people who make the business work!" Another added, "Our ultimate customer is the client. We cannot just worry about partner profits. In fact, we should start by maximizing value for the customer and let the profits flow to us from there!" And so on. This intense debate not only drove alignment with the objective of healthy growth in the number of financial advisers but also ensured that every implication of that choice was fully explored. Setting an ambitious growth target at each point in its 85-year history, Edward Jones has continually increased its scale and market presence. Striving to achieve such growth has increased long-term profit per adviser and led the firm to its unique configuration: Its only profit center is the individual financial adviser. Other activities, even investment banking, serve as support functions and are not held accountable for generating profit.

## Defining the Scope

A firm's scope encompasses three dimensions: customer or offering, geographic location, and vertical integration. Clearly defined boundaries in those areas should make it obvious to managers which activities they should concentrate on and, more important, which they should not do.

The three dimensions may vary in relevance. For Edward Jones, the most important is the customer. The firm is configured to meet the needs of one very specific type of client. Unlike just about every other brokerage in the business, Jones does not define its archetypal customer by net worth or income. Nor does it use demographics, profession, or spending habits. Rather, the definition is psychographic: The company's customers are long-term investors who have a conservative investment philosophy and are uncomfortable making serious financial decisions without the support of a trusted adviser. In the terminology of the business, Jones targets the "delegator," not the "validator" or the "do-it-yourselfer."

The scope of an enterprise does not prescribe exactly what should be done within the specified bounds. In fact, it encourages experimentation and initiative. But to ensure that the borders are clear to all employees, the scope should specify where the firm or business will not go. That will prevent managers from spending long hours on projects that get turned down by higher-ups because they do not fit the strategy.

For example, clarity about who the customer is and who it is not has kept Edward Jones from pursuing day traders. Even at the height of the internet bubble, the company chose not to introduce online trading (it is still not available to Jones customers). Unlike the many brokerages that committed hundreds of millions of dollars and endless executive hours to debates over whether to introduce online trading (and if so, how to price and position it in a way that did not cannibalize or conflict with traditional offerings), Jones wasted no money or time on that decision because it had set clear boundaries.

Similarly, Jones is not vertically integrated into proprietary mutual funds, so as not to violate the independence of its financial advisers and undermine clients' trust. Nor will the company offer penny stocks, shares from IPOs, commodities, or options—investment products that it believes are too risky for the conservative clients it chooses to serve. And it does not have metropolitan offices in business districts, because they would not allow for the convenient, face-to-face interactions in casual settings that the firm seeks to provide. Knowing not to extend its scope in these directions has allowed the firm to focus on doing what it does well and reap the benefits of simplicity, standardization, and deep experience.

### Defining the Advantage

Given that a sustainable competitive advantage is the essence of strategy, it should be no surprise that advantage is the most critical aspect of a strategy statement. Clarity about what makes the firm distinctive is what most helps employees understand how they can contribute to successful execution of its strategy.

As mentioned above, the complete definition of a firm's competitive advantage consists of two parts. The first is a statement of the customer value proposition. Any strategy statement that cannot explain why customers should buy your product or service is doomed to failure. A simple graphic that maps your value proposition against those of rivals can be an extremely easy and useful way of identifying what makes yours distinctive. (See the exhibit "Wal-Mart's Value Proposition.")

The second part of the statement of advantage captures the unique activities or the complex combination of activities allowing that firm alone to deliver the customer value proposition. This is where the strategy statement draws from Porter's definition of strategy as making consistent choices about the configuration of the firm's activities. It is also where the activity-system map that Porter describes in "What Is Strategy?" comes into play.

As the exhibit "Edward Jones's Activity-System Map" shows, the brokerage's value proposition is to provide convenient, trusted, personal service and advice. What is most distinctive about Jones is that it has only one financial adviser in an office, which allows it to have more offices (10,000 nationally) than competitors do. Merrill Lynch has about 15,000 brokers but only 1,000 offices. To make it easy for its targeted customers to visit at their convenience—and to provide a relaxed,

## Wal-Mart's Value Proposition

Wal-Mart's value proposition can be summed up as "everyday low prices for a broad range of goods that are always in stock in convenient geographic locations." It is those aspects of the customer experience that the company overdelivers relative to competitors. Underperformance on other dimensions, such as ambience and sales help, is a strategic choice that generates cost savings, which fuel the company's price advantage.

If the local mom-and-pop hardware store has survived, it also has a value proposition: convenience, proprietors who have known you for years, free coffee and doughnuts on Saturday mornings, and so on.

Sears falls in the middle on many criteria. As a result, customers lack a lot of compelling reasons to shop there, which goes a long way toward explaining why the company is struggling to remain profitable.

*in approximate order of importance to Wal-Mart's target customer group

Source: Jan Rivkin, Harvard Business School

personable, nonthreatening environment—Jones puts its offices in strip malls and the retail districts of rural areas and suburbs rather than high-rise buildings in the central business districts of big cities. These choices alone require Jones to differ radically from other brokerages in the configuration of its activities. With no branch-office management providing direction or support, each financial adviser must be an entrepreneur who delights in running his or her own operation. Since such people are an exception in the industry, Jones has to bring all its own financial advisers in from other industries or backgrounds and train them, at great expense. Until 2007, when it switched to an internet-based service, the firm had to have its own satellite network to provide its widely dispersed offices with real-time quotes and allow them to execute trades. Because the company has 10,000 separate offices, its real estate and communication costs are about 50% higher than the industry average. However, all those offices allow the financial advisers who run them to deliver convenient, trusted, personal service and advice.

Other successful players in this industry also have distinctive value propositions

## Edward Jones's Activity-System Map

This map illustrates how activities at the brokerage Edward Jones connect to deliver competitive advantage. The firm's customer value proposition appears near the center of the map—in the "customer relationship" bubble—and the supporting activities hang off it. Only the major connections are shown.

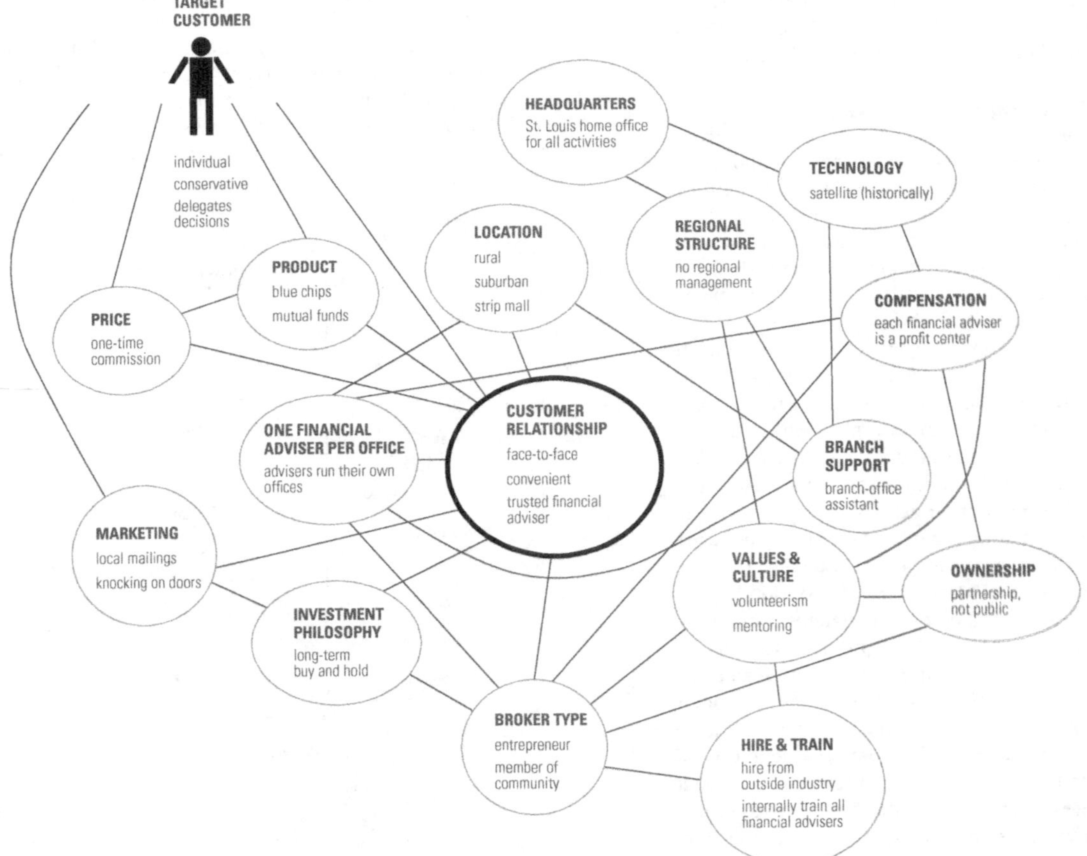

and unique configurations of activities to support them.

**Merrill Lynch.** During the five-year tenure of former CEO Stan O'Neal, who retired in October 2007, Merrill Lynch developed an effective strategy that it called "Total Merrill." The company's value proposition: to provide for all the financial needs of its high-net-worth customers—those with liquid financial assets of more than $250,000—*through retirement*. While a lot of brokerages cater to people with a high net worth, they focus on asset accumulation *before retirement*. Merrill's view is that as baby boomers age and move from the relatively simple phase of accumulating assets to the much more complex, higher-risk phase of drawing cash from their retirement accounts, their needs change. During this stage, they will want to consolidate their financial assets with a single trusted partner that can help them figure out how to optimize income over their remaining years by making the best decisions on everything from annuities to payout ratios to long-term-care insurance. Merrill offers coherent financial plans for such customers and provides access to a very wide range of sophisticated products based on a Monte Carlo simulation of the probabilities of running out of money according to different annual rates of return on different categories of assets.

How does Merrill intend to deliver this value to its chosen customers in a way that's unique among large firms? First, it is pushing brokers—especially new ones—to become certified financial planners and has raised internal training requirements to put them on that road. The certified financial planner license is more difficult for brokers to obtain than the standard Series 7 license, because it requires candidates to have a college degree and to master nearly 100 integrated financial-planning topics. Second, Merrill offers all forms of insurance, annuities, covered calls, hedge funds, banking services, and so on (unlike Edward Jones, which offers a much more limited menu of investment products). Since several of these products are technically complex, Merrill needs product specialists to support the client-facing broker. This "Team Merrill" organization poses very different HR and compensation issues from those posed by Edward Jones's single-adviser offices. Merrill's compensation system has to share income among the team members and reward referrals.

**Wells Fargo.** This San Francisco bank competes in the brokerage business as part of its tactic to cross-sell services to its retail banking customers in order to boost profit per customer. (It aims to sell each customer at least eight different products.) Wells Fargo's objective for its brokerage arm, clearly stated in a recent annual report, is to triple its share of customers' financial assets. The brokerage's means for achieving this goal is the parent company's database of 23 million customers, many of them brought into the firm through one particular aspect of the banking relationship: the mortgage. Wells Fargo differs from Edward Jones and Merrill Lynch in its aim to offer *personalized*, rather than *personal*, service. For example, the firm's IT system allows a bank clerk to know a limited amount of information about a customer (name, birthday, and so on) and appear to be familiar with him or her, which is quite different from the ongoing individual relationships that Jones and Merrill brokers have with their clients.

## The Strategic Sweet Spot

The strategic sweet spot of a company is where it meets customers' needs in a way that rivals can't, given the context in which it competes.

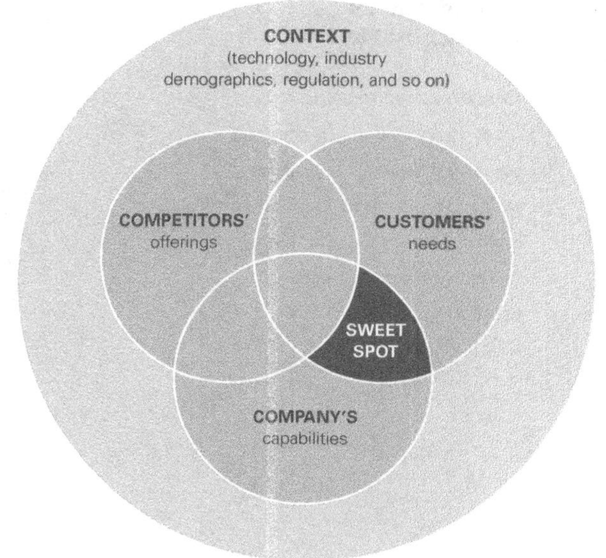

**LPL Financial.** Different again is LPL Financial, with offices in Boston, San Diego, and Charlotte, North Carolina. LPL sees its brokers (all of whom are independent financial advisers affiliated with the firm) rather than consumers as its clients and has configured all of its activities to provide individualized solutions and the highest payouts to its brokers. This means that the vast majority of the activities performed by the corporate headquarters staff are services, such as training, that brokers choose and pay for on an à la carte basis. As a result, LPL's headquarters staff is very small (0.20 people per broker) compared with that of Edward Jones (1.45 people per broker). Low overhead allows LPL to offer a higher payout to brokers than Jones and Merrill do, which is its distinctive value proposition to its chosen customer: the broker.

By now it should be apparent how a careful description of the unique activities a firm performs to generate a distinctive customer value proposition effectively captures its strategy. A relatively simple description in a strategy statement provides an incisive characterization that could not belong to any other firm. This is the goal. When that statement has been internalized by all employees, they can easily understand how their daily activities contribute to the overall success of the firm and how to correctly make the difficult choices they confront in their jobs.

### Developing a Strategy Statement

How, then, should a firm go about crafting its strategy statement? Obviously, the first step is to create a great strategy, which requires careful evaluation of the industry landscape.

## Leaving No Room for Misinterpretation

Executives at Edward Jones have developed a detailed understanding of every element of the firm's strategy. Here is an example.

**Edward Jones's Strategy Statement**

To grow to 17,000 financial advisers by 2012 by offering trusted and convenient face-to-face financial advice to **conservative individual investors who delegate their financial decisions**, through a national network of one-financial-adviser offices.

**"conservative"**

Our investment philosophy is long-term buy and hold. We do not sell penny stocks, commodities, or other high-risk instruments. As a result we do not serve day traders and see no need to offer online trading.

We charge commissions on trades because this is the cheapest way to buy stocks (compared with a wrap fee, which charges annually as a percentage of assets) when the average length of time the investor holds the stock or mutual fund is over 10 years.

**"individual"**

We do not advise institutions or companies.

We do not segment according to wealth, age, or other demographics. The company will serve all customers that fit its conservative investment philosophy. Brokers will call on any and every potential customer. Stories abound within Jones of millionaires who live in trailers—people all the other brokerages would never think of approaching.

**"investors"**

Our basic service is investment. We do not seek to offer services such as checking accounts for their own sake, but only as part of the management of a client's assets.

**"who delegate their financial decisions"**

We do not target self-directed do-it-yourselfers, who are comfortable making their own investment decisions. We are also unlikely to serve validators, who are merely looking for reassurance that their decisions are correct.

This includes developing a detailed understanding of customer needs, segmenting customers, and then identifying unique ways of creating value for the ones the firm chooses to serve. It also calls for an analysis of competitors' current strategies and a prediction of how they might change in the future. The process must involve a rigorous, objective assessment of the firm's capabilities and resources and those of competitors, as described in "Competing on Resources: Strategy in the 1990s," by David J. Collis and Cynthia A. Montgomery (HBR July–August 1995)—not just a feel-good exercise of identifying core competencies. The creative part of developing strategy is finding the sweet spot that aligns the firm's capabilities with customer needs in a way that competitors cannot match given the changing external context—factors such as technology, industry demographics, and regulation. (See the exhibit "The Strategic Sweet Spot.") We have found that one of the best ways to do this is to develop two or three plausible but very different strategic options.

For example, fleshing out two dramatically different alternatives—becoming a cheap Red Lobster or a fish McDonald's—helped executives at the Long John Silver's chain of restaurants understand the strategic choices that they had to make. They had been trying to do a bit of everything, and this exercise showed them that their initiatives—such as offering early-evening table service and expanding drive-through service—were strategically inconsistent. (Competing on the basis of table service requires bigger restaurants and more employees, while drive-through service requires high-traffic locations and smaller footprints.) As a result, they chose to be a fish McDonald's, building smaller restaurants with drive-through service in high-traffic locations.

The process of developing the strategy and then crafting the statement that captures its essence in a readily communicable manner should involve employees in all parts of the company and at all levels of the hierarchy. The wording of the strategy statement should be worked through in painstaking detail. In fact, that can be the most powerful part of the strategy development process. It is usually in heated discussions over the choice of a single word that a strategy is crystallized and executives truly understand what it will involve.

The end result should be a brief statement that reflects the three elements of an effective strategy. It should be accompanied by detailed annotations that elucidate the strategy's nuances (to preempt any possible misreading) and spell out its implications. (See the exhibit "Leaving No Room for Misinterpretation.")

When the strategy statement is circulated throughout the company, the value proposition chart and activity-system map should be attached. They serve as simple reminders of the twin aspects of competitive advantage that underpin the strategy. Cascading the statement throughout the organization, so that each level of management will be the teacher for the level below, becomes the starting point for incorporating strategy into everyone's behavior. The strategy will really have traction only when executives can be confident that the actions of empowered frontline employees will be guided by the same principles that they themselves follow.

• • •

The value of rhetoric should not be underestimated. A 35-word statement can have a substantial impact on a company's success. Words do lead to action. Spending the time to develop the few words that truly capture your strategy and that will energize and empower your people will raise the long-term financial performance of your organization.

---

Reprint R0804E
To order, see the next page
or call 800-988-0886 or 617-783-7500
or go to www.hbr.org

## Further Reading

**The *Harvard Business Review* Paperback Series**

Here are the landmark ideas—both contemporary and classic—that have established *Harvard Business Review* as required reading for businesspeople around the globe. Each paperback includes eight of the leading articles on a particular business topic. The series includes over thirty titles, including the following best-sellers:

**Harvard Business Review on Brand Management**
Product no. 1445

**Harvard Business Review on Change**
Product no. 8842

**Harvard Business Review on Leadership**
Product no. 8834

**Harvard Business Review on Managing People**
Product no. 9075

**Harvard Business Review on Measuring Corporate Performance**
Product no. 8826

For a complete list of the *Harvard Business Review* paperback series, go to www.hbr.org.

Harvard Business Review
www.hbr.org

U.S. and Canada
800-988-0886
617-783-7500
617-783-7555 fax

HARVARD | BUSINESS | SCHOOL

9-506-019
REV: APRIL 17, 2006

MODULE NOTE

# Market Segmentation, Target Market Selection, and Positioning

As described in the "Note on Marketing Strategy" (HBS No. 598-061), after the marketing analysis phase, the next stage in the marketing process consists of the following three steps:

- Market segmentation
- Target market selection
- Positioning

These steps are the prerequisites for designing a successful marketing strategy. They allow the firm to focus its efforts on the right customers and also provide the organizing force for the marketing-mix elements. Product positioning, in particular, provides the synergy among the four Ps (product, price, place, and promotion) of the marketing plan.

This note elaborates on each of the three steps.

## Market Segmentation

Market segmentation consists of dividing the market into groups of (potential) customers—called market segments—with distinct characteristics, behaviors, or needs. The aim is to cluster customers in groups that clearly differ from one another but show a great deal of homogeneity within the group. As such, compared with a large, heterogeneous market, those segments can be served more efficiently and effectively with products that match their needs.

It is important that the segments are sufficiently different from one another. In addition, it is critical that the segmentation is based on one or more customer characteristics relevant to the firm's marketing effort. A thorough analysis of the customers is essential in that regard. We can distinguish two (related) types of segmentation:

- Segmentation based on benefits sought by customers
- Segmentation based on observable characteristics of customers

In an ideal scenario, marketers will typically want to segment customers based on the benefits they seek from a particular product. That is, they will try to group customers based on their needs. Take the example of nonprescription drugs treating pain, inflammation, and fever. Market research

---

Professor Miklos Sarvary wrote the original version of this note ("Market Segmentation, Target Market Selection, and Product Positioning," HBS No. 501-018). This version was prepared by Professors Miklos Sarvary and Anita Elberse.

has revealed that people evaluate these drugs along two dimensions: effectiveness and gentleness. There are two basic segments, each valuing one of these dimensions more than the other. Thus, there is one segment that prefers an effective drug even if it has side effects, while the other segment prefers a less effective drug provided that it is gentler, that is, without side effects. The two segments represent benefit segments in that they are based on differences in consumers' preferences or needs.

In practice, marketers tend to delineate segments based on some observable characteristics. Most often, marketers use consumer demographics (such as gender, age, and income), consumers' geographic location, their lifestyles, or behavioral characteristics (such as usage occasions) to create segments. The motivation is clear. Segments created in such a way are easy to identify and address with a marketing message. It is important to realize, however, that such segmentation only works to the extent that it is correlated with benefit segments. In the previous example about nonprescription painkillers, it happens to be the case that older people tend to belong to the benefit segment that values the drugs' gentleness, while younger consumers prefer potent drugs even if they have side effects. Age, therefore, is a good variable by which to segment the market in this case. Age groups are easy to target and, in this case, age strongly correlates with distinct consumer preferences.

In summary, segmentation requires the following steps from the marketer:

- Understand the benefits that customers seek.
- Segment the market and develop prototypical customer profiles based on the customer benefits.
- Find the observable variables (such as demographic characteristics) most likely to discriminate among the benefit segments to identify membership in specific segments.

The segmentation process may seem quite straightforward, but in practice it requires quite a bit of experience and creativity. One complication is that there can be multiple acceptable benefit segmentation schemes. In general, a satisfactory, actionable market segmentation typically requires multiple iterations and informed compromises from the marketer.

## Target Market Selection

Target market selection involves evaluating each market segment's attractiveness and selecting one or more of the market segments to enter. It is the next logical step following segmentation. Once the firm understands the structure of consumer demand, it has to decide which segments it wants to serve and how. In addition to a solid understanding of the customer, analyses of the competitive environment and the company are instrumental to the task of target market selection. The objective is to select segments in such a way that the firm maximizes its profit.

In the case of over-the-counter painkillers discussed above, there are two basic types of drugs competing on the market. One is based on aspirin (e.g., Bayer), and the other is based on acetaminophen (e.g., Tylenol). It turns out that aspirin is more effective but has side effects causing minor stomach irritation. Thus, it is natural for firms producing these different drugs to focus on the segments that best fit their products. In this case, target market selection is relatively simple. In other cases, more elaborate analyses may be required to choose the appropriate segments to serve.

The key to target market selection is understanding differentiation. It involves collecting and comparing data on the company and its competitors to evaluate which is most likely to succeed serving each of the identified segments. The process starts by collecting data for each firm in five areas:

- Ability to conceive and design
- Ability to produce (quality and quantity)
- Ability to market
- Ability to finance
- Ability to manage/execute

Each of these five general areas can be divided into more concrete items. For example, in the "ability to conceive and design" category, the marketer may want to evaluate competitors' research and development (R&D) capability (as reflected in the size and experience of the design group as well as the R&D budget), existing patents and copyrights, access to new technologies through third parties, and so on. Similarly, to assess a firm's "ability to produce," competitors' production technology and capacity as well as flexibility may need to be evaluated.

Once the necessary data are collected, they can be synthesized into so-called competitor capability matrices. One matrix is needed for each segment. In each matrix, the detailed items of the evaluation areas are listed in the rows, and the relevant firms—including both the firm itself and its competitors—are listed in the columns. Each entry consists of a rating (say, on a 10-point scale) of the competitor on the item corresponding to the entry. This format allows the marketer to recognize patterns in the competitive environment and identify the segment (or segments) where his or her firm is likely to be the strongest player. If there are too many items in the rows (as is often the case), it is useful to replicate the matrix by listing only those items that represent critical success factors in the product category. This enables a more parsimonious evaluation of the situation.

It is important to recognize that this "differential advantage analysis" facilitates target market selection by pointing out the relative strengths (and weaknesses) of the focal firm, but it does not predict the competitive reactions the firm might face if it indeed decides to target a segment. Anticipating such reactions typically requires a careful analysis of competitors' overall corporate strategies and their reputation or history for competitive behavior.

## Positioning

In the "Note on Marketing Strategy" (HBS No. 598-061), positioning is defined as the marketer's effort to identify a unique selling proposition for the product. It is arranging for a product to occupy a clear, distinctive, and attractive position relative to competing products in the minds of target consumers.

A good positioning statement answers three questions:

- Who are the customers?
- What is the set of needs that the product fulfills?
- Why is the product the best option to satisfy those needs?

In finding a desirable positioning, the firm has to consider, for each potential segment, how it would approach serving that group of customers and how it would want to be perceived by those customers. The answers should be based on a thorough understanding of the customer, the competitive environment, the company itself, and the conditions of the market in which it operates.

### *The Positioning Statement*

It is typically helpful to formalize the considerations in a "positioning statement" that specifies the place the firm wishes to occupy in its target customers' minds. One commonly used form is:

| Our ______________ | is | ______________ |
|---|---|---|
| (product/brand) | | (single most important claim) |
| | among all | ______________ |
| | | (competitive frame) |
| | because | ______________ |
| | | (single most important support) |

The positioning statement is primarily directed to potential customers. It guides the development of the marketing plan—it is often said that "solving" the positioning problem enables a company to solve its marketing-mix problem. For example, if a computer company finds that a market segment with budgetary constraints prefers its products because they are significantly cheaper than competitive offerings, it could aim for a "no frills" product line, closely monitor its price advantage, emphasize the low price in its advertising, and employ a direct-to-consumer channel strategy that limits the markup on its products. Similarly, if a sports apparel firm understands that customers in its desired market segment buy products that make them feel like professional athletes, it could seek such endorsements from top-ranking athletes and use them in its advertising, emphasize innovative top-of-the-line products, primarily use a high-end sports retailing channel, and aim for a higher price point.

A firm's desired positioning thus is the organizing force among the marketing-mix elements to ensure their synergy. It is also important for internal communication within the firm. It identifies the firm. For example, IBM's famous claim "The solution to your problem is IBM" helped change the firm's internal culture by teaching employees to be problem solvers for their customers.

### *Differentiation*

As the above statement indicates, a good positioning reflects a competitive differentiation. That statement should go beyond clearly articulating to customers the benefits that the product fulfills—the product should also be clearly differentiated from competitive offerings. A firm will not want to introduce products targeted at needs already sufficiently served by competitors, as it could lead to an intense price competition and leave no profit to the firm. In this regard, it is useful to consider the two extreme types of differentiation:

- If all buyers agree that product A is better than product B, they are *vertically differentiated*. Consequently, if products A and B are sold at the same price, nobody will buy product B.
- If products A and B differ in ways independent of buyers' overall judgments about their quality levels, they are *horizontally differentiated*. If A and B are sold at the same price, some people will prefer one, some the other.

A positioning strategy based on a horizontal differentiation uses the fact that consumers differ in their tastes. For example, in the category of passenger cars, some consumers like small cars, others like minivans, while still others like SUVs. Each of these groups consists of a relatively homogeneous set of people with similar needs. A firm pursuing a horizontal differentiation strategy should identify the group(s) whose need(s) are not sufficiently served by a competitor.

Vertical differentiation also exploits the fact that consumers are different but takes advantage of consumers' differences in their willingness to pay for quality. In a pure vertically differentiated world, all customers (and potential customers) agree on the relevant dimensions of product quality. In the example of passenger cars, quality can be a combination of speed, comfort, and reliability. In addition, all customers prefer more quality to less. However, they differ in their valuation of quality. Staying with the example of passenger cars, most consumers prefer a BMW to a Ford, but only few can—or would be willing to—pay the price for the BMW. A firm pursuing a vertical differentiation strategy should position products to customers with a specific level of willingness to pay for quality that is not sufficiently served by a competitor.

In practice, in most product categories, marketers have the option to differentiate their products both horizontally and vertically. Creativity and marketing expertise plays an important role. Some skilled marketers may discover or "create" a set of needs among customers not yet served or tap into a market segment previously not regarded as a viable group of customers to serve. Some firms even completely change the paradigm of differentiation in a category, for example by moving the focus from performance to style, as in Swatch's redefinition of the watches category.

Any element of the marketing mix can be the primary instrument of differentiation. *Product* attributes or features are often a key differentiator (think of the importance of packaging for environmentally conscious, or "green," consumers, for example). *Price* can be a useful signal of quality and thus a tool for vertical differentiation. *Place* can bring critical advantages (examples are online distribution, where consumers can shop in the privacy of their own home, or vending machines, where products are available instantaneously and 24 hours a day). *Promotion* is an obvious tool to communicate to consumers to what extent and along what dimensions the product is different from alternatives.

## *The Role of Brands*

Positioning and branding are inextricably linked. Brands can be thought of simply as nouns that marketers have introduced into consumers' language to make product differentiation concrete. At a minimum, they want to assert that their offering is not like those of their competitors. When marketers call a fruit juice "Snapple," for instance, they are asserting that it is worth noting some special distinctions between Snapple and all other fruit juices. Some of these assertions can be viewed as promises or pledges about attributes of the product. Other assertions may have to do with how Snapple users are differentiated from Cola users, or how Snapple-usage occasions are differentiated from other beverage-usage occasions. Most ambitiously, a brand can assert that it is the category. Perhaps the highest goal to which a brand builder can aspire is to have the noun that he or she has imposed on the language displace the natural language word (as in using Kleenex to denote facial tissue, or speaking of Fedexing a package or Xeroxing a document). However, not all brands come to mean what the marketers have intended, and many brands struggle to denote anything that the consumer finds worthy of notice.

The discussion on brand development is continued in the submodule on integrated marketing communications. Differentiation in the context of product policy decisions is explored further in the note "Principles of Product Policy" (HBS No. 506-018).

# Why Capitalism Has an Image Problem

## Charles Murray examines the cloud now hanging over American business—and what today's capitalists can do about it.

By
Charles Murray
Updated July 30, 2012 1:20 a.m. ET

Mitt Romney's résumé at Bain should be a slam dunk. He has been a successful capitalist, and capitalism is the best thing that has ever happened to the material condition of the human race. From the dawn of history until the 18th century, every society in the world was impoverished, with only the thinnest film of wealth on top. Then came capitalism and the Industrial Revolution. Everywhere that capitalism subsequently took hold, national wealth began to increase and poverty began to fall. Everywhere that capitalism didn't take hold, people remained impoverished. Everywhere that capitalism has been rejected since then, poverty has increased.

A butcher *Hulton Archive/Getty Images*

Enlarge Image

Henry Ford with his Model T *Getty Images*

Enlarge Image

*Summary

① Collusive Capitalism which includes Crony Capitalism where the people at the top take care of each other, and the corruption caused by excess gov't regulation.

② Timidity on the part of capitalists who value their own work, but not the system itself. Ironically, this mirrors the very successful who lean left. They tend to believe it was their effort that built their BUZ while their political leaders insist it was NOT.

③ The segregation of capitalism from virtue. This requires that the successful become judgemental, accepting that certain behaviors are more beneficial than others to attain success

Wall Street traders around 1925. *Hulton Archive/Getty Images*

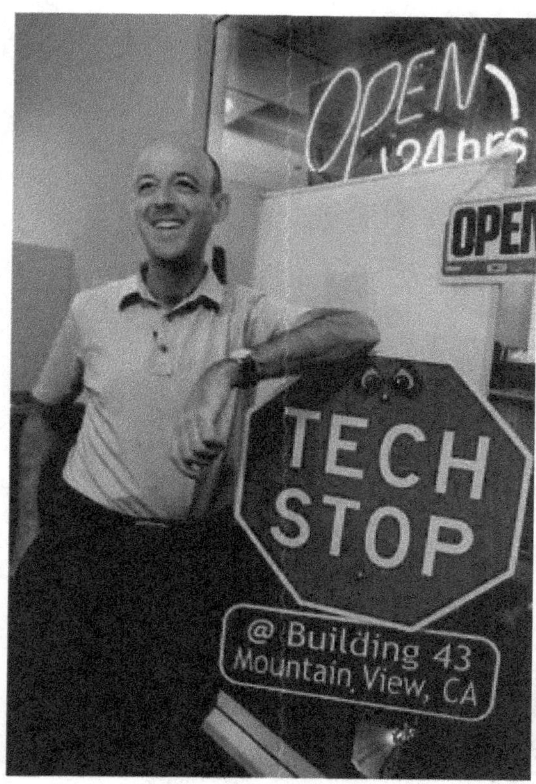


The Google office in 2008 *Associated Press*

Enlarge Image

A dry-cleaning store *Corbis*

Enlarge Image

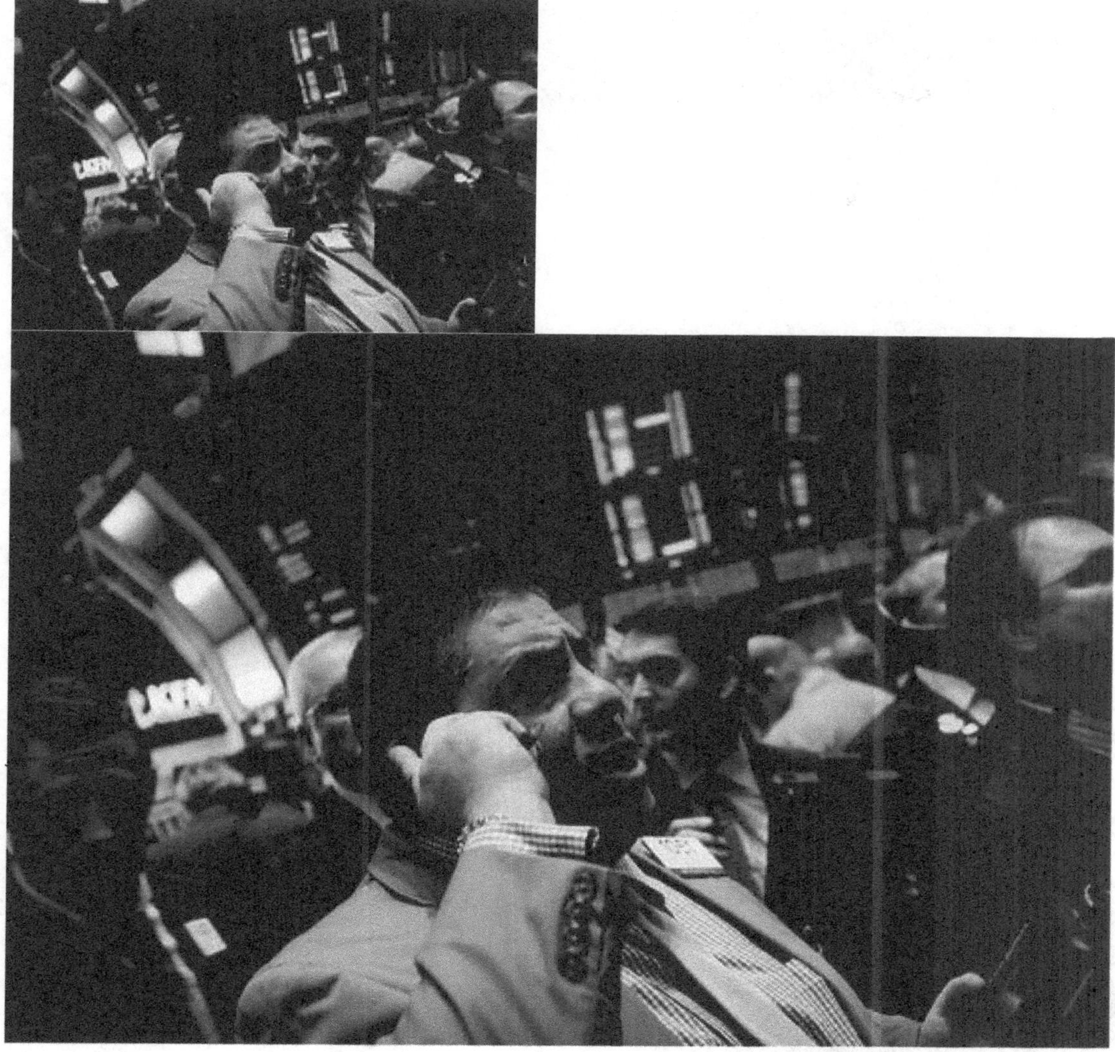

Traders on the NYSE floor in 2011 *Getty Images*

While Ray Kroc (shown) and Mark Zuckerberg have been lauded as innovators, financial moguls attract more suspicion. *Time Life Pictures/Getty images*

Mark Zuckerberg *WireImage/Getty images*

Capitalism has lifted the world out of poverty because it gives people a chance to get rich by creating value and reaping the rewards. Who better to be president of the greatest of all capitalist nations than a man who got rich by being a brilliant capitalist?

Yet it hasn't worked out that way for Mr. Romney. "Capitalist" has become an accusation. The creative destruction that is at the heart of a growing economy is now seen as evil. Americans increasingly appear to accept the mind-set that kept the world in poverty for millennia: If you've gotten rich, it is because you made someone else poorer.

What happened to turn the mood of the country so far from our historic celebration of economic success?

Two important changes in objective conditions have contributed to this change in mood. One is the rise of collusive capitalism. Part of that phenomenon involves crony capitalism, whereby the people on top take care of each other at shareholder expense (search on "golden parachutes").

But the problem of crony capitalism is trivial compared with the collusion engendered by government. In today's world, every business's operations and bottom line are affected by rules set by legislators and bureaucrats. The result has been corruption on a massive scale. Sometimes the corruption is retail, whereby a single corporation creates a competitive advantage through the cooperation of regulators or politicians (search on "earmarks"). Sometimes the corruption is wholesale, creating an industrywide potential for profit that would not exist in the absence of government subsidies or regulations (like ethanol used to fuel cars and low-interest mortgages for people who are unlikely to pay them back). Collusive capitalism has become visible to the public and increasingly defines capitalism in the public mind.

Another change in objective conditions has been the emergence of great fortunes made quickly in the financial markets. It has always been easy for Americans to applaud people who get rich by creating products and services that people want to buy. That is why Thomas Edison and Henry Ford were American heroes a century ago, and Steve Jobs was one when he died last year.

When great wealth is generated instead by making smart buy and sell decisions in the markets, it smacks of inside knowledge, arcane financial instruments, opportunities that aren't accessible to ordinary people, and hocus-pocus. The good that these rich people have done in the process of getting rich is obscure. The benefits of more efficient allocation of capital are huge, but they are really, really hard to explain simply and persuasively. It looks to a large proportion of the public as if we've got some fabulously wealthy people who haven't done anything to deserve their wealth.

The objective changes in capitalism as it is practiced plausibly account for much of the hostility toward capitalism. But they don't account for the unwillingness of capitalists who are getting rich the old-fashioned way—earning it—to defend themselves.

I assign that timidity to two other causes. First, large numbers of today's successful capitalists are people of the political left who may think their own work is legitimate but feel no allegiance to capitalism as a system or kinship with capitalists on the other side of the political fence. Furthermore, these capitalists of the left are concentrated where it counts most. The most visible entrepreneurs of the high-tech industry are predominantly liberal. So are most of the people who run the entertainment and news industries. Even leaders of the financial industry increasingly share the politics of George Soros. Whether measured by fundraising data or by the members of Congress elected from the ZIP Codes where they live, the elite centers with the most clout in the culture are filled with people who are embarrassed to identify themselves as capitalists, and it shows in the cultural effect of their work.

Another factor is the segregation of capitalism from virtue. Historically, the merits of free enterprise and the obligations of success were intertwined in the national catechism. McGuffey's Readers, the books on which generations of American children were raised, have plenty of stories treating initiative, hard work and entrepreneurialism as virtues, but just as many stories praising the virtues of self-restraint, personal integrity and concern for those who depend on you. The freedom to act and a stern moral obligation to act in certain ways were seen as two sides of the same American coin. Little of that has survived.

To accept the concept of virtue requires that you believe some ways of behaving are right and others are wrong always and everywhere. That openly judgmental stand is no longer acceptable in America's schools nor in many American homes. Correspondingly, we have watched the deterioration of the sense of stewardship that once was so widespread among the most successful Americans and the near disappearance of the sense of seemliness that led successful capitalists to be obedient to unenforceable standards of propriety. Many senior figures in the financial world were appalled by what was going on during the run-up to the financial meltdown of 2008. Why were they so silent before and after the catastrophe? Capitalists who behave honorably and with restraint no longer have either the platform or the vocabulary to preach their own standards and to condemn capitalists who behave dishonorably and recklessly.

And so capitalism's reputation has fallen on hard times and the principled case for capitalism must be made anew. That case has been made brilliantly and often in the past, with Milton Friedman's "Capitalism and Freedom" being my own favorite. But in today's political climate, updating the case for capitalism requires a restatement of old truths in ways that Americans from across the political spectrum can accept. Here is my best effort:

The U.S. was created to foster human flourishing. The means to that end was the exercise of liberty in the pursuit of happiness. Capitalism is the economic expression of liberty. The pursuit of happiness, with happiness defined in the classic sense of justified and lasting satisfaction with life as a whole, depends on economic liberty every bit as much as it depends on other kinds of freedom.

"Lasting and justified satisfaction with life as a whole" is produced by a relatively small set of important achievements that we can rightly attribute to our own actions. Arthur Brooks, my colleague at the American Enterprise Institute, has usefully labeled such achievements "earned success." Earned success can arise from a successful marriage, children raised well, a valued place as a member of a community, or devotion to a faith. Earned success also arises from achievement in the economic realm, which is where capitalism comes in.

Earning a living for yourself and your family through your own efforts is the most elemental form of earned success. Successfully starting a business, no matter how small, is an act of creating something out of nothing that carries satisfactions far beyond those of the money it brings in. Finding work that not only pays the bills but that you enjoy is a crucially important resource for earned success.

Making a living, starting a business and finding work that you enjoy all depend on freedom to act in the economic realm. What government can do to help is establish the rule of law so that informed and voluntary trades can take place. More formally, government can vigorously enforce laws against the use of force, fraud and criminal collusion, and use tort law to hold people liable for harm they cause others.

Everything else the government does inherently restricts economic freedom to act in pursuit of earned success. I am a libertarian and think that almost none of those restrictions are justified. But accepting the case for capitalism doesn't require you to be a libertarian. You are free to argue that certain government interventions are justified. You just need to acknowledge this truth: Every intervention that erects barriers to starting a business, makes it expensive to hire or fire employees, restricts entry into vocations, prescribes work conditions and facilities, or confiscates profits interferes with economic liberty and usually makes it more difficult for both employers and employees to earn success. You also don't need to be a libertarian to demand that any new intervention meet this burden of proof: It will accomplish something that tort law and enforcement of basic laws against force, fraud and collusion do not accomplish.

People with a wide range of political views can also acknowledge that these interventions do the most harm to individuals and small enterprises. Huge banks can, albeit at great expense, cope with the Dodd-Frank law's absurd regulatory burdens; many small banks cannot. Huge corporations can cope with the myriad rules issued by the Occupational Safety and Health Administration, the Environmental Protection Agency, the Equal Employment Opportunity Commission and their state-level counterparts. The same rules can crush small businesses and individuals trying to start small businesses.

Finally, people with a wide range of political views can acknowledge that what has happened incrementally over the past half-century has led to a labyrinthine regulatory system, irrational liability law and a corrupt tax code. Sweeping simplifications and rationalizations of all these systems are possible in ways that even moderate Democrats could accept in a less polarized political environment.

To put it another way, it should be possible to revive a national consensus affirming that capitalism embraces the best and most essential things about American life; that freeing capitalism to do what it does best won't just create national wealth and reduce poverty, but expand the ability of Americans to achieve earned success—to pursue happiness.

Reviving that consensus also requires us to return to the vocabulary of virtue when we talk about capitalism. Personal integrity, a sense of seemliness and concern for those who depend on us are not "values" that are no better or worse than other values. Historically, they have been deeply embedded in the American version of capitalism. If it is necessary to remind the middle class and working class that the rich are not their enemies, it is equally necessary to remind the most successful among us that their obligations are not to be measured in terms of their tax bills. Their principled stewardship can nurture and restore our heritage of liberty. Their indifference to that heritage can destroy it.

—Mr. Murray is the author of "Coming Apart: The State of White America, 1960-2010" and the W.H. Brady Scholar at the American Enterprise Institute.

# How to Write a Great Business Plan

by William A. Sahlman

Reprint 97409

*Which information belongs – and which doesn't – may surprise you.*

# How to Write a Great

**by William A. Sahlman**

Few areas of business attract as much attention as new ventures, and few aspects of new-venture creation attract as much attention as the business plan. Countless books and articles in the popular press dissect the topic. A growing number of annual business-plan contests are springing up across the United States and, increasingly, in other countries. Both graduate and undergraduate schools devote entire courses to the subject. Indeed, judging by all the hoopla surrounding business plans, you would think that the only things standing between a would-be entrepreneur and spectacular success are glossy five-color charts, a bundle of meticulous-looking spreadsheets, and a decade of month-by-month financial projections.

*William A. Sahlman is Dimitri V. d'Arbeloff Professor of Business Administration at the Harvard Business School in Boston, Massachusetts. He has been closely connected with more than 50 entrepreneurial ventures as an adviser, investor, or director. He teaches a second-year course at the Harvard Business School called "Entrepreneurial Finance," for which he has developed more than 100 cases and notes.*

Nothing could be further from the truth. In my experience with hundreds of entrepreneurial start-ups, business plans rank no higher than 2 – on a scale from 1 to 10 – as a predictor of a new venture's success. And sometimes, in fact, the more elaborately crafted the document, the more likely the venture is to, well, flop, for lack of a more euphemistic word.

What's wrong with most business plans? The answer is relatively straightforward. Most waste too much ink on numbers and devote too little to the information that really matters to intelligent investors. As every seasoned investor knows, financial projections for a new company – especially detailed, month-by-month projections that stretch out for more than a year – are an act of imagination. An entrepreneurial venture faces far too many unknowns to predict revenues, let alone profits. Moreover, few if any entrepreneurs correctly anticipate how much capital and time will be required to accomplish their objectives. Typically, they are wildly optimistic, padding their projections. Investors know about the padding effect and therefore discount the figures in business plans. These ma-

# Business Plan

neuvers create a vicious circle of inaccuracy that benefits no one.

Don't misunderstand me: business plans should include some numbers. But those numbers should appear mainly in the form of a business model that shows the entrepreneurial team has thought through the key drivers of the venture's success or failure. In manufacturing, such a driver might be the yield on a production process; in magazine publishing, the anticipated renewal rate; or in software, the impact of using various distribution channels. The model should also address the break-even issue: At what level of sales does the business begin to make a profit? And even more important, When does cash flow turn positive? Without a doubt, these questions deserve a few pages in any business plan. Near the back.

What goes at the front? What information does a good business plan contain?

If you want to speak the language of investors – and also make sure you have asked yourself the right questions before setting out on the most daunting journey of a businessperson's career – I recommend basing your business plan on the framework that follows. It does not provide the kind of "winning" formula touted by some current how-to books and software programs for entrepreneurs. Nor is it a guide to brain surgery. Rather, the framework systematically assesses the four interdependent factors critical to every new venture:

**The People.** The men and women starting and running the venture, as well as the outside parties providing key services or important resources for it, such as its lawyers, accountants, and suppliers.

**The Opportunity.** A profile of the business itself – what it will sell and to whom, whether the business can grow and how fast, what its economics are, who and what stand in the way of success.

**The Context.** The big picture – the regulatory environment, interest rates, demographic trends, inflation, and the like – basically, factors that inevitably change but cannot be controlled by the entrepreneur.

**Risk and Reward.** An assessment of everything that can go wrong and right, and a discussion of how the entrepreneurial team can respond.

# BUSINESS PLANS: FOR ENTREPRENEURS ONLY?

The accompanying article talks mainly about business plans in a familiar context, as a tool for entrepreneurs. But quite often, start-ups are launched within established companies. Do those new ventures require business plans? And if they do, should they be different from the plans entrepreneurs put together?

The answer to the first question is an emphatic yes; the answer to the second, an equally emphatic no. All new ventures – whether they are funded by venture capitalists or, as is the case with intrapreneurial businesses, by shareholders – need to pass the same acid tests. After all, the marketplace does not differentiate between products or services based on who is pouring money into them behind the scenes.

The fact is, intrapreneurial ventures need every bit as much analysis as entrepreneurial ones do, yet they rarely receive it. Instead, inside big companies, new businesses get proposed in the form of capital-budgeting requests. These faceless documents are subject to detailed financial scrutiny and a consensus-building process, as the project wends its way through the chain of command, what I call the "neutron bomb" model of project governance. However, in the history of such proposals, a plan never has been submitted that did not promise returns in excess of corporate hurdle rates. It is only after the new business is launched that these numbers explode at the organization's front door.

That problem could be avoided in large part if intrapreneurial ventures followed the guidelines set out in the accompanying article. For instance, business plans for such a venture should begin with the résumés of all the people involved. What has the team done in the past that would suggest it would be successful in the future, and so on? In addition, the new venture's product or service should be fully analyzed in terms of its opportunity and context. Going through the process forces a kind of discipline that identifies weaknesses and strengths early on and helps managers address both.

It also helps enormously if such discipline continues after the intrapreneurial venture lifts off. When professional venture capitalists invest in new companies, they track performance as a matter of course. But in large companies, scrutiny of a new venture is often inconsistent. That shouldn't or needn't be the case. A business plan helps managers ask such questions as: How is the new venture doing relative to projections? What decisions has the team made in response to new information? Have changes in the context made additional funding necessary? How could the team have predicted those changes? Such questions not only keep a new venture running smoothly but also help an organization learn from its mistakes and triumphs.

Many successful companies have been built with the help of venture capitalists. Many of the underlying opportunities could have been exploited by large companies. Why weren't they? Perhaps useful lessons can be learned by studying the world of independent ventures, one lesson being: Write a great business plan.

The assumption behind the framework is that great businesses have attributes that are easy to identify but hard to assemble. They have an experienced, energetic managerial team from the top to the bottom. The team's members have skills and experiences directly relevant to the opportunity they are pursuing. Ideally, they will have worked successfully together in the past. The opportunity has an attractive, sustainable business model; it is possible to create a competitive edge and defend it. Many options exist for expanding the scale and scope of the business, and these options are unique to the enterprise and its team. Value can be extracted from the business in a number of ways either through a positive harvest event – a sale – or by scaling down or liquidating. The context is favorable with respect to both the regulatory and the macroeconomic environments. Risk is understood, and the team has considered ways to mitigate the impact of difficult events. In short, great businesses have the four parts of the framework completely covered. If only reality were so neat.

## The People

When I receive a business plan, I always read the résumé section first. Not because the people part of the new venture is the most important, but because without the right team, none of the other parts really matters.

I read the résumés of the venture's team with a list of questions in mind. (See the insert "Who Are These People, Anyway?") All these questions get at the same three issues about the venture's team members: What do they know? Whom do they know? and How well are they known?

What and whom they know are matters of insight and experience. How familiar are the team members with industry players and dynamics? Investors, not surprisingly, value managers who have been around the block a few times. A business plan should candidly describe each team member's knowledge of the new venture's type of product or service; its production processes; and the market itself, from competitors to customers. It also helps to indicate whether the team members have worked together before. Not played – as in roomed together in college – but *worked*.

Investors also look favorably on a team that is known because the real world often prefers not to deal with start-ups. They're too unpredictable. That changes, however, when the new company is run by people well known to suppliers, customers, and employees. Their enterprise may be brand new, but they aren't. The surprise element of working with a start-up is somewhat ameliorated.

Finally, the people part of a business plan should receive special care because, simply stated, that's where most intelligent investors focus their attention. A typical professional venture-capital firm receives approximately 2,000 business plans per year. These plans are filled with tantalizing ideas for new products and services that will change the world and reap billions in the process – or so they say. But the fact is, most venture capitalists believe that ideas are a dime a dozen: only execution skills count. As Arthur Rock, a venture capital legend associated with the formation of such companies as Apple, Intel, and Teledyne, states, "I invest in people, not ideas." Rock also has said, "If you can find good people, if they're wrong about the product, they'll make a switch, so what good is it to understand the product that they're talking about in the first place?"

Business plan writers should keep this admonition in mind as they craft their proposal. Talk about the people – exhaustively. And if there is nothing solid about their experience and abilities to herald, then the entrepreneurial team should think again about launching the venture.

## Who Are These People, Anyway?

Fourteen "Personal" Questions Every Business Plan Should Answer

- ☐ Where are the founders from?
- ☐ Where have they been educated?
- ☐ Where have they worked – and for whom?
- ☐ What have they accomplished – professionally and personally – in the past?
- ☐ What is their reputation within the business community?
- ☐ What experience do they have that is directly relevant to the opportunity they are pursuing?
- ☐ What skills, abilities, and knowledge do they have?
- ☐ How realistic are they about the venture's chances for success and the tribulations it will face?
- ☐ Who else needs to be on the team?
- ☐ Are they prepared to recruit high-quality people?
- ☐ How will they respond to adversity?
- ☐ Do they have the mettle to make the inevitable hard choices that have to be made?
- ☐ How committed are they to this venture?
- ☐ What are their motivations?

## The Opportunity

When it comes to the opportunity itself, a good business plan begins by focusing on two questions: Is the total market for the venture's product or service large, rapidly growing, or both? Is the industry now, or can it become, structurally attractive? Entrepreneurs and investors look for large or rapidly growing markets mainly because it is often easier to obtain a share of a growing market than to fight with entrenched competitors for a share of a mature or stagnant market. Smart investors, in fact, try hard to identify high-growth-potential markets early in their evolution: that's where the big payoffs are. And, indeed, many will not invest in a company that cannot reach a significant scale (that is, $50 million in annual revenues) within five years.

As for attractiveness, investors are obviously looking for markets that actually allow businesses to make some money. But that's not the no-brainer it seems. In the late 1970s, the computer disk-drive business looked very attractive. The technology was new and exciting. Dozens of companies jumped into the fray, aided by an army of professional investors. Twenty years later, however, the thrill is gone for managers and investors alike. Disk drive companies must design products to meet the perceived needs of original equipment manufacturers (OEMs) and end users. Selling a product to OEMs is complicated. The customers are large relative to most of their suppliers. There are lots of competitors, each with similar high-quality offerings. Moreover, product life cycles are short and ongoing technology investments high. The industry is

## The Opportunity of a Lifetime – or Is It?

Nine Questions About the Business Every Business Plan Should Answer

- ☐ Who is the new venture's customer?
- ☐ How does the customer make decisions about buying this product or service?
- ☐ To what degree is the product or service a compelling purchase for the customer?
- ☐ How will the product or service be priced?
- ☐ How will the venture reach all the identified customer segments?
- ☐ How much does it cost (in time and resources) to acquire a customer?
- ☐ How much does it cost to produce and deliver the product or service?
- ☐ How much does it cost to support a customer?
- ☐ How easy is it to retain a customer?

subject to major shifts in technology and customer needs. Intense rivalry leads to lower prices and, hence, lower margins. In short, the disk drive industry is simply not set up to make people a lot of money; it's a structural disaster area.

The information services industry, by contrast, is paradise. Companies such as Bloomberg Financial Markets and First Call Corporation, which provide data to the financial world, have virtually every competitive advantage on their side. First, they can assemble or create *proprietary* content – content that, by the way, is like life's blood to thousands of money managers and stock analysts around the world. And although it is often expensive to develop the service and to acquire initial customers, once up and running, these companies can deliver content to customers very cheaply. Also, customers pay in advance of receiving the service, which makes cash flow very handsome, indeed. In short, the structure of the information services industry is beyond attractive: it's gorgeous. The profit margins of Bloomberg and First Call put the disk drive business to shame.

> The market is as fickle as it is unpredictable. Who would have guessed that plug-in room deodorizers would sell?

Thus, the first step for entrepreneurs is to make sure they are entering an industry that is large and/or growing, and one that's structurally attractive. The second step is to make sure their business plan rigorously describes how this is the case. And if it isn't the case, their business plan needs to specify how the venture will still manage to make enough of a profit that investors (or potential employees or suppliers, for that matter) will want to participate.

Once it examines the new venture's industry, a business plan must describe in detail how the company will build and launch its product or service into the marketplace. Again, a series of questions should guide the discussion. (See the insert "The Opportunity of a Lifetime–or Is It?")

Often the answers to these questions reveal a fatal flaw in the business. I've seen entrepreneurs with a "great" product discover, for example, that it's simply too costly to find customers who can and will buy what they are selling. Economically viable access to customers is the key to business, yet many entrepreneurs take the *Field of Dreams* approach to this notion: build it, and they will come. That strategy works in the movies but is not very sensible in the real world.

It is not always easy to answer questions about the likely consumer response to new products or services. The market is as fickle as it is unpredictable. (Who would have guessed that plug-in room deodorizers would sell?) One entrepreneur I know proposed to introduce an electronic news-clipping service. He made his pitch to a prospective venture-capital investor who rejected the plan, stating, "I just don't think the dogs will eat the dog food." Later, when the entrepreneur's company went public, he sent the venture capitalist an anonymous package containing an empty can of dog food and a copy of his prospectus. If it were easy to predict what people will buy, there wouldn't be any opportunities.

Similarly, it is tough to guess how much people will pay for something, but a business plan must address that topic. Sometimes, the dogs will eat the dog food, but only at a price less than cost. Investors always look for opportunities for value pricing–that is, markets in which the costs to produce the product are low, but consumers will still pay a lot for it. No one is dying to invest in a company when margins are skinny. Still, there is money to be made in inexpensive products and services–even in commodities. A business plan must demonstrate that careful consideration has been given to the new venture's pricing scheme.

The list of questions about the new venture's opportunity focuses on the direct revenues and the costs of producing and marketing a product. That's fine, as far as it goes. A sensible proposal, however, also involves assessing the business model from a perspective that takes into account the investment required – that is, the balance sheet side of the equation. The following questions should also be addressed so that investors can understand the cash flow implications of pursuing an opportunity:

☐ When does the business have to buy resources, such as supplies, raw materials, and people?
☐ When does the business have to pay for them?
☐ How long does it take to acquire a customer?
☐ How long before the customer sends the business a check?
☐ How much capital equipment is required to support a dollar of sales?

Investors, of course, are looking for businesses in which management can buy low, sell high, collect early, and pay late. The business plan needs to spell out how close to that ideal the new venture is expected to come. Even if the answer is "not very" – and it usually is – at least the truth is out there to discuss.

The opportunity section of a business plan must also bring a few other issues to the surface. First, it must demonstrate and analyze how an opportunity can grow – in other words, how the new venture can expand its range of products or services, customer base, or geographic scope. Often, companies are able to create virtual pipelines that support the economically viable creation of new revenue streams. In the publishing business, for example, *Inc.* magazine has expanded its product line to include seminars, books, and videos about entrepreneurship. Similarly, building on the success of its personal-finance software program Quicken, Intuit now sells software for electronic banking, small-business accounting, and tax preparation, as well as personal-printing supplies and on-line information services – to name just a few of its highly profitable ancillary spin-offs.

Now, lots of business plans runneth over on the subject of the new venture's potential for growth and expansion. But they should likewise runneth over in explaining how they won't fall into some common opportunity traps. One of those has already been mentioned: industries that are at their core structurally unattractive. But there are others. The world of invention, for example, is fraught with danger. Over the past 15 years, I have seen scores of individuals who have devised a better mousetrap – newfangled creations from inflatable pillows for use on airplanes to automated car-parking systems. Few of these idea-driven companies have really taken off, however. I'm not entirely sure why. Sometimes, the inventor refuses to spend the money required by or share the rewards sufficiently with the business side of the company. Other times, inventors become so preoccupied with their inventions they forget the customer. Whatever the reason, better-mousetrap businesses have an uncanny way of malfunctioning.

Another opportunity trap that business plans – and entrepreneurs in general – need to pay attention to is the tricky business of arbitrage. Basically, arbitrage ventures are created to take advantage of some pricing disparity in the marketplace. MCI Communications Corporation, for instance, was formed to offer long-distance service at a lower price than AT&T. Some of the industry consolidations going on today reflect a different kind of arbitrage – the ability to buy small businesses at a wholesale price, roll them up together into a larger package, and take them public at a retail price, all without necessarily adding value in the process.

## Whatever the reason, better-mousetrap businesses have an uncanny way of malfunctioning.

=strange

Taking advantage of arbitrage opportunities is a viable and potentially profitable way to enter a business. In the final analysis, however, all arbitrage opportunities evaporate. It is not a question of whether, only when. The trick in these businesses is to use the arbitrage profits to build a more enduring business model, and business plans must explain how and when that will occur.

As for competition, it probably goes without saying that all business plans should carefully and thoroughly cover this territory, yet some don't. That is a glaring omission. For starters, every business plan should answer the following questions about the competition:

☐ Who are the new venture's current competitors?
☐ What resources do they control? What are their strengths and weaknesses?
☐ How will they respond to the new venture's decision to enter the business?
☐ How can the new venture respond to its competitors' response?

## Visualizing Risk and Reward

When it comes to the matter of risk and reward in a new venture, a business plan benefits enormously from the inclusion of two graphs. Perhaps *graphs* is the wrong word; these are really just schematic pictures that illustrate the most likely relationship between risk and reward, that is, the relationship between the opportunity and its economics. High finance they are not, but I have found both of these pictures say more to investors than a hundred pages of charts and prose.

The first picture depicts the amount of money needed to launch the new venture, time to positive cash flow, and the expected magnitude of the payoff.

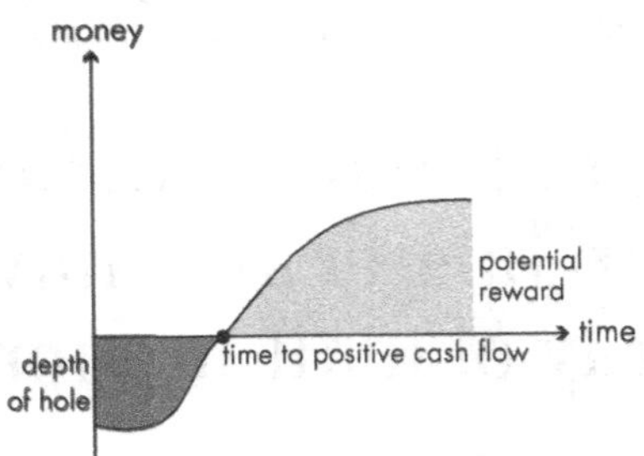


This image helps the investor understand the depth and duration of negative cash flow, as well as the relationship between the investment and the possible return. The ideal, needless to say, is to have cash flow early and often. But most investors are intrigued by the picture even when the cash outflow is high and long–as long as the cash inflow is more so.

Of course, since the world of new ventures is populated by wild-eyed optimists, you might expect the picture to display a shallower hole and a steeper reward slope than it should. It usually does. But to be honest, even that kind of picture belongs in the business plan because it is a fair warning to investors that the new venture's team is completely out of touch with reality and should be avoided at all costs.

The second picture complements the first. It shows investors the range of possible returns and the likelihood of achieving them. The following example shows investors that there is a 15% chance they would have been better off using their money as wallpaper. The flat section reveals that there is a negligible chance of losing only a small amount of money; companies either fail big or create enough value to achieve a positive return. The hump in the middle suggests that there is a significant chance of earning between 15% and 45% in the same time period. And finally, there is a small chance that the initial outlay of cash will spawn a 200% internal rate of return, which might have occurred if you had happened to invest in Microsoft when it was a private company.

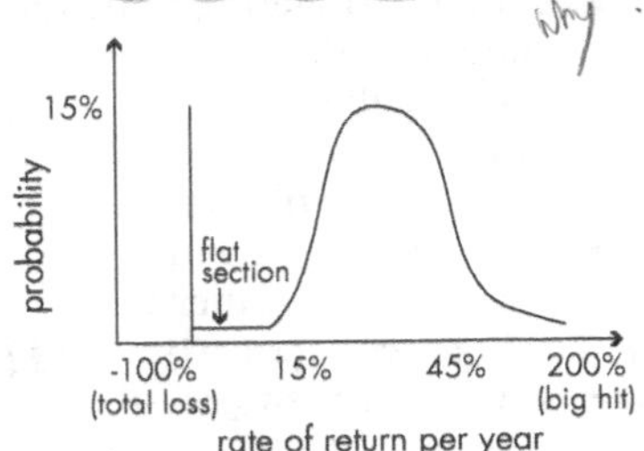


Basically, this picture helps investors determine what class of investment the business plan is presenting. Is the new venture drilling for North Sea oil – highly risky with potentially big payoffs – or is it digging development wells in Texas, which happens to be less of a geological gamble and probably less lucrative, too? This image answers that kind of question. It's then up to the investors to decide how much risk they want to live with against what kind of odds.

Again, the people who write business plans might be inclined to skew the picture to make it look as if the probability of a significant return is downright huge and the possibility of loss is negligible. And, again, I would say therein lies the picture's beauty. What it claims, checked against the investor's sense of reality and experience, should serve as a simple pictorial caveat emptor.

- ☐ Who else might be able to observe and exploit the same opportunity?
- ☐ Are there ways to co-opt potential or actual competitors by forming alliances?

Business is like chess: to be successful, you must anticipate several moves in advance. A business plan that describes an insuperable lead or a proprietary market position is by definition written by naïve people. That goes not just for the competition section of the business plan but for the entire discussion of the opportunity. All opportunities have promise; all have vulnerabilities. A good business plan doesn't whitewash the latter. Rather, it proves that the entrepreneurial team knows the good, the bad, and the ugly that the venture faces ahead.

### The Context

Opportunities exist in a context. At one level is the macroeconomic environment, including the level of economic activity, inflation, exchange rates, and interest rates. At another level are the wide range of government rules and regulations that affect the opportunity and how resources are marshaled to exploit it. Examples extend from tax policy to the rules about raising capital for a private or public company. And at yet another level are factors like technology that define the limits of what a business or its competitors can accomplish.

Context often has a tremendous impact on every aspect of the entrepreneurial process, from identification of opportunity to harvest. In some cases, changes in some contextual factor create opportunity. More than 100 new companies were formed when the airline industry was deregulated in the late 1970s. The context for financing was also favorable, enabling new entrants like People Express to go to the public market for capital even before starting operations.

Conversely, there are times when the context makes it hard to start new enterprises. The recession of the early 1990s combined with a difficult financing environment for new companies: venture capital disbursements were low, as was the amount of capital raised in the public markets. (Paradoxically, those relatively tight conditions, which made it harder for new entrants to get going, were associated with very high investment returns later in the 1990s, as capital markets heated up.)

Sometimes, a shift in context turns an unattractive business into an attractive one, and vice versa. Consider the case of a packaging company some years ago that was performing so poorly it was about to be put on the block. Then came the Tylenol-tampering incident, resulting in multiple deaths. The packaging company happened to have an efficient mechanism for installing tamper-proof seals, and in a matter of weeks its financial performance could have been called spectacular. Conversely, U.S. tax reforms enacted in 1986 created havoc for companies in the real estate business, eliminating almost every positive incentive to invest. Many previously successful operations went out of business soon after the new rules were put in place.

Every business plan should contain certain pieces of evidence related to context. First, the entrepreneurs should show a heightened awareness of the new venture's context and how it helps or hinders their specific proposal. Second, and more important, they should demonstrate that they know the venture's context will inevitably change and describe how those changes might affect the business. Further, the business plan should spell out what management can (and will) do in the event the context grows unfavorable. Finally, the business plan should explain the ways (if any) in which management can affect context in a positive way. For example, management might be able to have an impact on regulations or on industry standards through lobbying efforts.

## Risk and Reward

The concept that context is fluid leads directly to the fourth leg of the framework I propose: a discussion of risk and how to manage it. I've come to think of a good business plan as a snapshot of an event in the future. That's quite a feat to begin with – taking a picture of the unknown. But the best business plans go beyond that; they are like movies of the future. They show the people, the opportunity, and the context from multiple angles. They offer a plausible, coherent story of what lies ahead. They unfold possibilities of action and reaction.

Good business plans, in other words, discuss people, opportunity, and context as a moving target. All three factors (and the relationship among them) are likely to change over time as a company evolves from start-up to ongoing enterprise. Therefore, any business plan worth the time it takes to write or read needs to focus attention on the dynamic aspects of the entrepreneurial process.

Of course, the future is hard to predict. Still, it is possible to give potential investors a sense of the kind and class of risk and reward they are assuming with a new venture. All it takes is a pencil and two simple drawings. (See the insert "Visualizing Risk and Reward.") But even with these drawings, risk is, well, risky. In reality, there are no immutable distributions of outcomes. It is ultimately the responsibility of management to change the distribution, to increase the likelihood and consequences of success, and to decrease the likelihood and implications of problems.

**One of the greatest myths about entrepreneurs is that they are risk seekers. All sane people want to avoid risk.**

One of the great myths about entrepreneurs is that they are risk seekers. All sane people want to avoid risk. As Harvard Business School professor (and venture capitalist) Howard Stevenson says, true entrepreneurs want to capture all the reward

## A Glossary of Business Plan Terms

| What They Say… | and What They Really Mean |
|---|---|
| We conservatively project… | We read a book that said we had to be a $50 million company in five years, and we reverse-engineered the numbers. |
| We took our best guess and divided by 2. | We accidentally divided by 0.5. |
| We project a 10% margin. | We did not modify any of the assumptions in the business plan template that we downloaded from the Internet. |
| The project is 98% complete. | To complete the remaining 2% will take as long as it took to create the initial 98% but will cost twice as much. |
| Our business model is proven… | if you take the evidence from the past week for the best of our 50 locations and extrapolate it for all the others. |
| We have a six-month lead. | We tried not to find out how many other people have a six-month lead. |
| We only need a 10% market share. | So do the other 50 entrants getting funded. |
| Customers are clamoring for our product. | We have not yet asked them to pay for it. Also, all of our current customers are relatives. |
| We are the low-cost producer. | We have not produced anything yet, but we are confident that we will be able to. |
| We have no competition. | Only IBM, Microsoft, Netscape, and Sun have announced plans to enter the business. |
| Our management team has a great deal of experience… | consuming the product or service. |
| A select group of investors is considering the plan. | We mailed a copy of the plan to everyone in Pratt's Guide. |
| We seek a value-added investor. | We are looking for a passive, dumb-as-rocks investor. |
| If you invest on our terms, you will earn a 68% internal rate of return. | If everything that could ever conceivably go right does go right, you might get your money back. |

and give all the risk to others. The best business is a post office box to which people send cashier's checks. Yet risk is unavoidable. So what does that mean for a business plan?

It means that the plan must unflinchingly confront the risks ahead – in terms of people, opportunity, and context. What happens if one of the new venture's leaders leaves? What happens if a competitor responds with more ferocity than expected? What happens if there is a revolution in Namibia, the source of a key raw material? What will management actually *do*?

Those are hard questions for an entrepreneur to pose, especially when seeking capital. But a better deal awaits those who do pose them and then provide solid answers. A new venture, for example, might be highly leveraged and therefore very sensitive to interest rates. Its business plan would benefit enormously by stating that management intends to hedge its exposure through the financial-futures market by purchasing a contract that does well when interest rates go up. That is the equivalent of offering investors insurance. (It also makes sense for the business itself.)

Finally, one important area in the realm of risk/reward management relates to harvesting. Venture capitalists often ask if a company is "IPOable," by which they mean, Can the company be taken public at some point in the future? Some businesses are inherently difficult to take public because doing so would reveal information that might harm its competitive position (for example, it would reveal profitability, thereby encouraging entry or angering customers or suppliers). Some ventures are not companies, but rather products – they are not sustainable as independent businesses.

Therefore, the business plan should talk candidly about the end of the process. How will the investor eventually get money out of the business, assuming it is successful, even if only marginally so? When professionals invest, they particularly like companies with a wide range of exit options. They like companies that work hard to preserve and enhance those options along the way, companies that don't, for example, unthinkingly form alliances with big corporations that could someday actually *buy* them. Investors feel a lot better about risk if the venture's endgame is discussed up front. There is an old saying, "If you don't know where you are going, any road will get you there." In crafting sensible entrepreneurial strategies, just the opposite is true: you had better know where you might end up and have a map for getting there. A business plan should be the place where that map is drawn, for, as every traveler knows, a journey is a lot less risky when you have directions.

## The Deal and Beyond

Once a business plan is written, of course, the goal is to land a deal. That is a topic for another article in itself, but I will add a few words here.

When I talk to young (and old) entrepreneurs looking to finance their ventures, they obsess about the valuation and terms of the deal they will receive. Their explicit goal seems to be to minimize the dilution they will suffer in raising capital. Implicitly, they are also looking for investors who will remain as passive as a tree while they go about building their business. On the food chain of investors, it seems, doctors and dentists are best and venture capitalists are worst because of the degree to which the latter group demands control and a large share of the returns.

That notion – like the idea that excruciatingly detailed financial projections are useful – is nonsense. From whom you raise capital is often more important than the terms. New ventures are inherently risky, as I've noted; what can go wrong will. When that happens, unsophisticated investors panic, get angry, and often refuse to advance the company more money. Sophisticated investors, by contrast, roll up their sleeves and help the company solve its problems. Often, they've had lots of experience saving sinking ships. They are typically process literate. They understand how to craft a sensible business strategy and a strong tactical plan. They know how to recruit, compensate, and motivate team members. They are also familiar with the Byzantine ins and outs of going public – an event most entrepreneurs face but once in a lifetime. This kind of know-how is worth the money needed to buy it.

> **The best business is a post office box to which people send cashier's checks.**

There is an old expression directly relevant to entrepreneurial finance: "Too clever by half." Often, deal makers get very creative, crafting all sorts of payoff and option schemes. That usually backfires. My experience has proven again and again that sensible deals have the following six characteristics:

- ☐ They are simple.
- ☐ They are fair.
- ☐ They emphasize trust rather than legal ties.
- ☐ They do not blow apart if actual differs slightly from plan.
- ☐ They do not provide perverse incentives that will cause one or both parties to behave destructively.
- ☐ They are written on a pile of papers no greater than one-quarter inch thick.

But even these six simple rules miss an important point. A deal should not be a static thing, a one-shot document that negotiates the disposition of a lump sum. Instead, it is incumbent upon entrepreneurs, before they go searching for funding, to think about capital acquisition as a dynamic process – to figure out how much money they will need and when they will need it.

How is that accomplished? The trick is for the entrepreneurial team to treat the new venture as a series of experiments. Before launching the whole show, launch a little piece of it. Convene a focus group to test the product, build a prototype and watch it perform, conduct a regional or local rollout of a service. Such an exercise reveals the true economics of the business and can help enormously in determining how much money the new venture actually requires and in what stages. Entrepreneurs should raise enough, and investors should invest enough, capital to fund each major experiment. Experiments, of course, can feel expensive and risky. But I've seen them prevent disasters and help create successes. I consider it a prerequisite of putting together a winning deal.

## Beware the Albatross

Among the many sins committed by business plan writers is arrogance. In today's economy, few ideas are truly proprietary. Moreover, there has never been a time in recorded history when the supply of capital did not outrace the supply of opportunity. The true half-life of opportunity is decreasing with the passage of time.

A business plan must not be an albatross that hangs around the neck of the entrepreneurial team, dragging it into oblivion. Instead, a business plan must be a call for action, one that recognizes management's responsibility to fix what is broken proactively and in real time. Risk is inevitable, avoiding risk impossible. Risk management is the key, always tilting the venture in favor of reward and away from risk.

A plan must demonstrate mastery of the entire entrepreneurial process, from identification of opportunity to harvest. It is not a way to separate unsuspecting investors from their money by hiding the fatal flaw. For in the final analysis, the only one being fooled is the entrepreneur.

We live today in the golden age of entrepreneurship. Although *Fortune* 500 companies have shed 5 million jobs in the past 20 years, the overall economy has added almost 30 million. Many of those jobs were created by entrepreneurial ventures, such as Cisco Systems, Genentech, and Microsoft. Each of those companies started with a business plan. Is that why they succeeded? There is no knowing for sure. But there is little doubt that crafting a business plan so that it thoroughly and candidly addresses the ingredients of success–people, opportunity, context, and the risk/reward picture–is vitally important. In the absence of a crystal ball, in fact, a business plan built of the *right* information and analysis can only be called indispensable.

Reprint 97409 

OPINION

# CLASS WAR? AMERICANS DISLIKE INEQUALITY, BUT THEY DON'T ALL BLAME THE RICH *by* Nina Easton

AFTER THE 1987 stock market crash, the *New York Times* offered up a page-one obituary for a "gilded, impudent age," quoting great minds who predicted the demise of unbridled self-interest in America. Three short years later, when a recession marked the official end of the '80s, commentators (including in this magazine) predicted a "brewing revolt against the rich" and the coming of a "post-affluent society."

It's instructive in 2012—when words like "tinderbox" and "explosive" dot so many descriptions of class relations in the U.S.—to revisit those cloudy crystal balls of yore. As it turned out, there was no class revolt against the '80s, the "decade of greed." In the 1990s, McMansions sprouted like kudzu across the land, the rich got filthy rich, and all that supposed nascent populist anger was lost in a swirl of mortgage-financed consumer gluttony (behavior shared by the affluent and middle class alike).

Maybe this time is different. Maybe comparisons to the outpourings in the streets of Europe are apt. Certainly today's unemployment rate dwarfs that of the 1990s, and long-term joblessness is stuck at historic highs. So is anxiety about personal economic futures. With an economy that seems paralyzed, these are scary times; the '90s weren't. But predictions of impending class warfare miss the fundamental nature of the American psyche. There is a tendency within the chattering classes to overstate the American public's disdain for affluence—and to understate people's passion for pursuing their own wealth.

The Occupy Wall Street protests that played out last fall drew comparisons to the Arab Spring (a movement that actually toppled governments) and Europe's anti-austerity eruptions (protests that actually overshadowed OWS's biggest days here). In mid-May, OWS jumped back on the media radar screen with a "financial crimes walking tour" and Times Square rally against the big banks.

While OWS deserves credit for injecting discussion of economic inequality into the country's political bloodstream—no small feat, it should be noted—its calls for a "revolution" against a system that "impoverishes the 99%" hasn't exactly translated into a mass movement. And it remains unlikely to.

Historically Americans haven't shown much appetite for class strife. As professors Benjamin Page and Lawrence Jacobs noted in their 2009 book *Class War?*: "While Americans are alert to inequality and support measures to reduce it ... they remain conservative by instinct ... Responsibility for an individual's economic position and life conditions rests chiefly with him- or herself." So why all the talk of revolution? "Us-vs.-them-ism" is an especially tempting theme for a media desperately looking for ways to grab our short attention spans. Therefore, much was made of a recent Pew Research poll purporting to show a sharp rise in conflicts between rich and poor.

In fact, the poll showed that public attitudes toward the wealthy remain largely unchanged—with a near-even split between those who think the rich were born into money or connections and those who think people are rich "mainly because of their own hard work, ambition, or education." There hasn't been an increase in people's own grievances against the rich; rather, there was a 19-point increase in people saying they believe there are very strong or strong conflicts between rich and poor—not a surprise given all the media attention to the OWS protests.

Indeed, the headline Pew produced for its research reads "For the Public, It's Not About Class Warfare, but Fairness." Pew's conclusion? While Americans are hearing more about class conflict, "there is no sense that the American people are on the verge of class conflict; they just want a better chance of achieving success themselves."

That's worth remembering as the media and politicians fuel divisions along the income scale this election year. In the 1800s, French political thinker Alexis de Tocqueville was famously impressed by Americans' dedication to the idea of equality. But he was also struck by another character trait: "The love of wealth ... is at the bottom of all Americans do." On that score, times haven't changed all that much. ■



COMMENTS: *nina_easton@fortunemail.com*

# Don't blame the 1% for America's pay gap

April 24, 2012: 5:00 AM ET

**It's time to end the myth that the nation's wealthy are getting rich off the backs of the poor. Instead let's figure out what they're doing right.**

By Nina Easton, senior editor-at-large

ILLUSTRATION: GETTY IMAGES/STOCK ILLUSTRATION SOURCE

FORTUNE -- What if I told you that there was a group of hard-driving workaholics who tend to have advanced degrees and bring a level of talent and skill to their jobs that attracts premium pay in the global economy? Scholars have found that this group is more likely than much of the population to raise their children in two-parent homes.

You might think this was a group people would admire, even emulate, right? Not so. For this is the much-maligned 1%, whose media infamy via the Occupy Wall Street protests, followed by President Obama's **populist reelection message**, is now firmly embedded in the American psyche.

The 1% club stands accused, accurately, of more than doubling its share of the nation's income since 1980. By 2007 it controlled nearly 24% of total income, the second highest in history, after 1929. (In 2009 its share dropped to 17%, suggesting that recessions aren't necessarily kind to the rich.)

Railing about the 1% club has become shorthand for expressing outrage not only over growing income disparity but also about the state of the nation's working class. Wages of men without college diplomas, for example, have dropped by a whopping third over the past three decades.

That's deeply troubling. Socially and politically, there are plenty of reasons to worry about the growing income gap. But rage against the 1% is misplaced. Income is not a zero-sum game: The rich aren't getting wealthier at the expense of the poor. Harvard's Lawrence Katz has calculated that even if all the gains of the top 1% were redistributed to the 99%, household incomes would go up by less than half of what they would if everyone had a college degree. In other words, **the financial rewards of higher education** are a big contributor to the income gap.

**More: Five tax breaks Washington has given the rich**

Indeed, researchers say the reasons for the rich getter richer are complex and nuanced. One-percenters are a large and varied lot, consisting of 1.38 million households, with total household incomes starting at $344,000 in 2009. (Nearly all scholars rely on income figures because of the difficulty in obtaining reliable net-worth data.) Yes, **finance is well-represented** in the 1% club, but there is also an especially high portion of the self-employed, along with a variety of other professions. And while CEO incomes rose astronomically through the 1990s, their incomes have actually declined over the past decade, according to University of Chicago's Steven N. Kaplan.

So what is behind the income gains of the 1%? Let's start with the global and technological changes that pump up the salaries of superstars in a range of professions: Call it the Yo-Yo Ma effect. In 1600 a famous cellist would have reached his career peak by playing for the king. Now Ma can stage concerts all over the world, with commensurate earnings. Apply that same concept to the in-demand skills of star lawyers or bankers or doctors in the 1% club, or of hungry entrepreneurs plying new markets.

Women in high-paying professions are another factor. Researchers from Indiana University and the Treasury Department studied the top 1% of households and found that by 2005 the number of taxpayers (largely men) with working spouses rose to almost 40%, up from 25% in 1979. That spouse tends to be a wealthy professional as well.

Scholars are also taking note of social issues underlying America's income divide. In his new book, *Coming Apart*, conservative social scientist Charles Murray documents far higher divorce rates and more children living with one parent in working-class communities. That's a trend that has also caught the attention of liberals like Harvard's Robert Putnam, who describes "gaps that didn't exist decades ago but are widening at an alarming rate today" and are reinforced as wealthy parents spend far more time with their children.

It's entertaining to wail about **fat cats and the greedy rich**. But if we're serious about addressing widening inequality, we should figure out what the 1% is doing right -- and apply some of those ideas to closing the gap.

*Nina Easton is currently a fellow at the Harvard Kennedy School's Shorenstein Center.*

*This story is from the April 30, 2012 issue of* Fortune.

Posted in: **1%**, **99%**, **Macro**, **Middle class**, **Nina Easton**, **pay divide**, **the rich**, **wealth gap**

# 5 Steps to a Performance Evaluation System

*Keep your staff productive and motivated by conducting regular performance evaluations.*

Judy Capko

*Fam Pract Manag.* 2003 Mar;10(3):43-48.

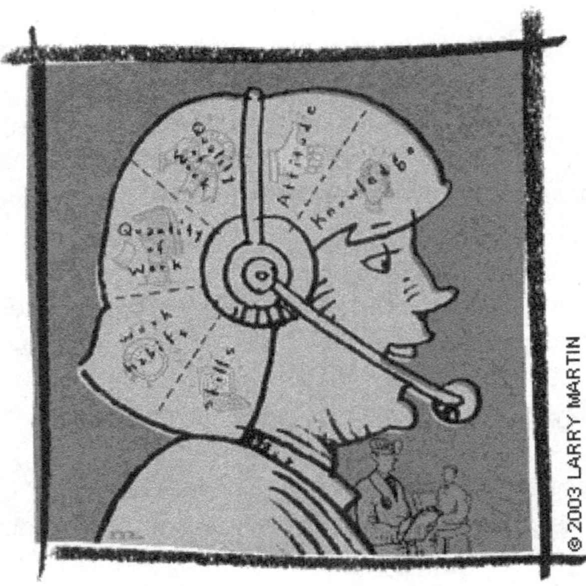

© 2003 LARRY MARTIN

Performance evaluations, which provide employers with an opportunity to assess their employees' contributions to the organization, are essential to developing a powerful work team. Yet in some practices, physicians and practice managers put performance evaluations on the back burner, often because of the time involved and the difficulties of critiquing employees with whom they work closely. The benefits of performance evaluations outweigh these challenges, though. When done as part of a performance evaluation system that includes a standard evaluation form, standard performance measures, guidelines for delivering feedback, and disciplinary procedures, performance evaluations can enforce the acceptable boundaries of performance, promote staff recognition and effective communication and motivate individuals to do their best for themselves and the practice.

The primary goals of a performance evaluation system are to provide an equitable measurement of an employee's contribution to the workforce, produce accurate appraisal documentation to protect both the employee and employer, and obtain a high level of quality and quantity in the work produced. To create a performance evaluation system in your practice, follow these five steps:

1. Develop an evaluation form.
2. Identify performance measures.
3. Set guidelines for feedback.
4. Create disciplinary and termination procedures.
5. Set an evaluation schedule.

It is also advisable to run the finished system by your attorney to identify any potential legal problems that should be fixed.

**KEY POINTS**

- A performance evaluation system can motivate staff to do their best for themselves and the practice by promoting staff recognition and improving communication.
- Evaluations should be conducted fairly, consistently and objectively to protect your employees and your practice.
- An effective performance evaluation system has standardized evaluation forms, performance measures, feedback guidelines and disciplinary procedures.

**1. Develop an evaluation form.**

Performance evaluations should be conducted fairly, consistently and objectively to protect your employees' interests and to protect your practice from legal liability. One way to ensure consistency is to use a standard evaluation form for each evaluation. The form you use should focus only on the essential job performance areas. Limiting these areas of focus makes the assessment more meaningful and relevant and allows you and the employee to address the issues that matter most. You don't need to cover every detail of an employee's performance in an evaluation.

For most staff positions, the job performance areas that should be included on a performance evaluation form are job knowledge and skills, quality of work, quantity of work, work habits and attitude. In each area, the appraiser should have a range of descriptors to choose from (e.g., far below requirements, below requirements, meets requirements, exceeds requirements, far exceeds requirements). Depending on how specific the descriptors are, it's often important that the appraiser also have space on the form to provide the reasoning behind his or her rating. (Click below for a one-page evaluation form that covers these essential performance areas without overwhelming the employee or the appraiser.)

Performance evaluations for those in management positions should assess more than just the essential job performance areas mentioned above. They should also assess the employee's people skills, ability to motivate and provide direction, overall communication skills and ability to build teams and solve problems. You should have either a separate evaluation form for managers or a special managerial section added to your standard evaluation form. (Click below for an example of a performance evaluation form that covers all the areas essential to rating the performance of management staff.)

**2. Identify performance measures.**

Standard performance measures, which allow you to evaluate an employee's job performance objectively, can cut down on the amount of time and stress involved in filling out the evaluation form. Although developing these measures can be one of the more time-consuming parts of creating a performance evaluation system, it's also one of the most powerful.

If you have current job descriptions for each position in your practice, you've already taken the first step toward creating standard performance measures, which are essentially specific quantity and quality goals attached to the tasks listed in a job description. A job description alone can serve as a measurement tool during an evaluation if, for example, you're assessing whether an employee's skills match the requirements of the position. But standard performance measures take the job description one step further. For example, one task listed in a receptionist's job description might be entering new and updated patient registrations into the computer. The standard performance measure for that task might be to enter 6 to 12 registrations per day (quantity) with an error rate of less than 2 percent (quality). (See the box on page 44 for some other standard performance measures that were created for a receptionist in a two-physician primary care practice.)

**STANDARD PERFORMANCE MEASURES: RECEPTIONIST**

Standard performance measures can even objectively measure some of the more subjective job performance areas, such as work habits. For example, you can establish an objective measure for attendance by defining the acceptable number of times an employee can be tardy or absent during a specific time frame.

However, standard performance measures don't always work for other subjective areas, such as attitude. In these cases, it's still important to be as objective as possible in your evaluation. Don't attempt to describe attitude, for instance; instead, describe the employee's behavior, which is what conveys the attitude, and the consequences of that behavior for the practice. For example: "This employee has failed to support her co-workers. When another member of her department is absent, she refuses to take on the additional tasks required to process patients in a timely manner. This behavior causes patient backlog, places a burden on staff and compromises effective teamwork."

To begin developing standard performance measures in your practice, review the job descriptions for each position and select the key components of the job that can be specifically measured. Then, work with the employees in each position to gather quantitative data, examine historical patterns of volume and determine qualitative measurements that reflect the practice's mission and goals. Depending on how large your practice is and how many positions need standard performance measures, you may want to select a committee to develop them. Then, with help from the employees in each position, the supervisors should maintain them. It's important to keep job descriptions and standard performance measures as current as possible. Otherwise, when an employee doesn't measure up to the standards you've set, you can't be sure whether he or she has a performance problem or whether your expectations of the position have become unrealistic based on increased volume or a change in circumstances.

### REWARDING PERFORMANCE WITH PAY

If your practice's pay increases are based on merit, it may be appropriate and efficient to review an employee's salary at the time of the performance evaluation. Such a direct link between performance and pay could make you and your employees take the performance evaluations even more seriously than you might have otherwise. However, if your pay increases are based only partially on merit and partially on annual changes in the Consumer Price Index, it may not be quite as easy to review and change individual salaries at various times during the year.

Whether you plan to include a review of the employee's salary during each performance evaluation should be communicated to all employees verbally and in writing when they are hired. It is important that employees understand this so that their expectations are realistic and they are not disappointed.

### 3. Set guidelines for feedback.

Feedback is what performance evaluations are all about. So before you implement your performance evaluation system, make sure that everyone who will be conducting evaluations knows what kind of feedback to give, how to give it and how to get it from the employee in return.

**Give balanced feedback.** Don't make the common error of glossing over an employee's deficiencies and focusing only on his or her strengths. It is by understanding their weaknesses that employees can take ownership of their performance and role in the practice. And when given the support they need to make improvements in these areas, employees learn to take pride in their work and are willing to take on new challenges with confidence. [For more information about giving feedback, see "Serving Up the Feedback Sandwich," *FPM*, November/December 2002, page 43.]

**Outline expectations for improvement.** When you address areas where improvement is needed, outline your expectations for improvement and how you intend to help the employee meet them. For example, if an employee is speaking harshly with other employees and does not seem tolerant with patients, give the employee some examples of his or her behavior and offer some suggestions to resolve the problem, such as role-playing sessions or a communication skills/customer-service workshop or seminar. Define the boundaries by letting the employee know what is acceptable and what will not be tolerated, and then establish a plan for monitoring performance and re-evaluating the employee.

**Encourage feedback from the employee.** After you've discussed the results of the evaluation with the employee, encourage him or her to give you some nondefensive feedback. Ask the employee whether he or she agrees with your assessment, and/or invite suggestions for improvement. For example: "You seem to become impatient and short with patients when the physician is running late. Since there are times when running late cannot be avoided, how do you suggest we handle this to avoid such a reaction?" This should lead to an open exchange of information that will allow you and the employee to better understand each other's perspective.

**4. Create disciplinary and termination procedures.**

In some cases, even after a thorough performance evaluation and a discussion of expected improvements, an employee will continue to perform poorly. You need to be prepared to handle such a situation by having well-defined, written disciplinary and termination procedures in place. These procedures should outline the actions that will be taken when performance deteriorates – a verbal warning, a written warning if there is no improvement or a recurrence, and termination if the situation is not ultimately resolved.

**Verbal warning.** This should be given in private, with the behavior or reason for the discipline clearly stated. For example: "I observed you talking disrespectfully to another employee at the front desk. You said she was brain-dead and tossed a chart at her. We will not tolerate disrespect in the workplace. Furthermore, this outburst could be overheard from the reception room. If this occurs again, a report will be written up and placed in your file. Do you understand the importance of this?" After the verbal warning is given, allow the employee to respond, but keep the exchange brief.

**Written warning.** How you handle the written warning plays a critical role in the success of your disciplinary and termination procedures. This is the time to make it clear to the employee just how serious his or her performance problem is. Unfortunately, many practices fail to do this and/or to follow through with termination if necessary. Once the written warning is mishandled in this way, it no longer has any merit. A standard, written, warning form should include the following:

- A description of the behavior or problem that includes objective findings,
- The measurable actions and changes expected of the employee,
- The support the employer will provide for improvement,
- A description of what will occur (e.g., unpaid time off or termination) and when (e.g., after one more occurrence or two) if the warning is not heeded,
- The signature of the employee and appraiser and the date of the warning.

**Termination.** Explain the reason for the termination but do so briefly and objectively to avoid getting into an elaborate discussion that puts you in a defensive position. Validate the employee as a person, perhaps by giving a positive slant to the employee's potential in the job market. For example, although an employee might have been a poor file clerk for you because he or she didn't pay attention to detail, the employee may have a friendly personality that would make him or her a good telephone operator. Also, let the employee know what will become of any accrued vacation or sick leave, pension benefits, etc. Know your state's laws on these issues. Finally, ask if the employee has any further questions and then assist the employee in retrieving all of his or her belongings and leaving with as much dignity as possible. If you handle termination well, you are less likely to have an employee who wants to "get even" by badmouthing you in the community or seeking legal revenge.

**5. Set an evaluation schedule.**

Once you've built your performance evaluation system – the evaluation form, the performance measures, the feedback guidelines and the disciplinary procedures – you just need to decide when to conduct the performance evaluations. Some practices do all employee evaluations at the same time of year, while others conduct them within 30 days of each employee's anniversary of employment (the latter may work better since it spreads the work of the evaluations out for employer and employee). However you decide to schedule the evaluations, ensure that each appraiser consistently meets the deadline. Ignoring employees' overdue evaluations will make them feel devalued and may hurt morale and performance.

## The last analysis

A performance evaluation system should be a key component of your practice structure. When implemented effectively, it ensures fairness and accountability, promotes growth and development and encourages a sense of pride in your employees' contributions to the practice.

---

*Judy Capko is a senior consultant with The Sage Group Inc., a national health care firm based in Newbury Park, Calif., that specializes in strategic planning, restructuring, practice management and marketing. She is also the director of practice management for the Professional Association of Health Care Office Management and the marketing chairperson for the Society of Medical Dental Management Consultants.*

Harvard Business Review
www.hbrreprints.org

*And what you should expect in return.*

# What Your Leader Expects of You

by Larry Bossidy

Included with this full-text *Harvard Business Review* article:



Reprint R0704C

# What Your Leader Expects of You

## The Idea in Brief

Relationships between bosses and their subordinates figure strongly in any team's success. When those bonds are working as they should, they drive performance and growth over the long haul. Yet while the leadership literature specifies actions bosses should take, it says little about the actions leaders should expect from their followers.

How to promote effective leader-follower relationships in *your* team? Former Allied-Signal CEO Bossidy advises forging a **boss-subordinate compact** that defines a mutual set of crystal-clear expectations.

For example, as a *direct report*, you're expected to offer your creative ideas. Your boss wants to hear them, because even seemingly crazy ideas can spark spectacular successes. As the boss, you're expected to tell your people where the business is going, why, and how they'll benefit if they accomplish key goals. This clarity helps people see how their jobs contribute to the enterprise overall.

When each side fulfills its part of the boss-subordinate compact, your team *and* company benefit.

## The Idea in Practice

The boss-subordinate compact spells out additional expectations for both parties:

**AS A SUBORDINATE...**

- **Get involved.** If you're a manager, step in the moment someone falls behind with his commitments, when an interpersonal conflict crops up, and when a crisis erupts. And deliver bad news to your boss yourself.
- **Collaborate.** Overcome differences between you and others so you work together effectively—even if you don't like each other.
- **Lead initiatives.** Don't be reluctant to associate yourself with unproven ideas, especially those that cross functional or unit boundaries. Raise your hand, and you'll climb the ladder faster than those who don't.
- **Develop your own people.** Take as active an interest in your employees' development as you do in your own—if not more. Go out of your way to criticize and praise your people when they need it. And get directly involved in performance reviews, supplying people with specific, candid, and useful feedback.
- **Stay current.** Regularly read and watch the news. What happens in the world affects what happens with your team, your marketplace, and your competition. Also know what's going on with your customers—how they're changing, how their competition is changing, and how technology and world events are affecting their strategies. Your customer relationships are key assets: bring them to the table.
- **Drive your own growth.** Seek perpetual education and development—not necessarily by going to school but by finding exposure to new people and ideas. Seek feedback from your boss, and accept demanding assignments.
- **Be a player for all seasons.** Demonstrate positive behaviors even during hard times. You'll sustain your ability to motivate and inspire your own people no matter what's going on around you.

**AS A LEADER...**

- **Define specific goals for your people.** Specify the achievements you expect from your employees as a team and as individuals, as well as what they are going to be measured on over a given period. You'll help them decide where to invest their energy and time.
- **Be available.** If you expect your people to stay up to date and keep you informed about what's going on, be accessible when they need to see you. And don't come down on them if they bring you bad news.
- **Compensate employees fairly.** Ensure that people understand how the compensation system works, and that they're rewarded for specific contributions to goals you've laid out.

*And what you should expect in return.*

# What Your Leader Expects of You

by Larry Bossidy

It's well understood that the relationships between a boss and his or her direct reports are important ones and figure strongly in the success of a team. Yet while much has been written about character traits and issues of openness and trust, the leadership literature has had strikingly little to say about what a leader should be able to expect from his people. Over the years, I've observed that certain behaviors, on the part of both the subordinate and the boss, are conducive to productive and rewarding relationships. Indeed, I'll favor someone who exhibits the behaviors I expect over someone who doesn't, even if the latter's numbers are slightly better, because I know the former has the potential to contribute more to the organization over time.

In sharing the lists below—what I've come to think of as the CEO compact, a set of expectations both from and for a leader—I hope that I can help other leaders and teams improve their relationships and, as a consequence, their performance.

## What I Expect from My Direct Reports

The following behaviors are powerful individually, but taken together they drive performance and growth in a way that has a significant effect on long-term results.

**Get involved.** Good executives know how to delegate. But more important, they know when a situation calls for their immediate involvement, whether it's in redirecting resources to a product that's suddenly taking off in the market, helping to resolve a breakdown in quality, or visiting a plant to discover why its productivity has faltered. There's no excuse for not taking responsibility when you see a problem growing. I count on my reports to take the blame for things that go wrong and give credit for positive developments to their employees. And I expect them to have the courage to deliver bad news. If you've got to close a plant, go to the plant and tell those employees yourself.

While there are no hard-and-fast rules about when your involvement will have the most im-

**Larry Bossidy** was the chairman and CEO of AlliedSignal from 1991 through 1999 and the chairman and CEO of Honeywell from 2001 to 2002. He has also served as the COO of General Electric Credit Corporation (now GE Capital) and as the vice chairman of General Electric.

pact on the business (that's a judgment call), I've found that good managers generally step in under three types of circumstances: when somebody is falling behind in her commitments; when important personnel matters arise, particularly if there is conflict; and in a crisis. Just because you're an executive vice president doesn't mean you don't have to work anymore.

**Generate ideas.** A common frustration in corporate America is a lack of ideas. A person who is innovative and creative is a pearl to be treasured. Unfortunately, idea people are not generally applauded in organizations. They're frequently at the periphery, because people think they're off the wall. But I want to hear what they have to say; it's my job to sift through ideas and decide which ones have merit. Often the best ideas sound crazy at first. For instance, when I got to AlliedSignal, people were very dispirited by the company's lagging performance, and I was looking for a way to raise morale. Somebody suggested that we hire a band, put out hamburgers and hot dogs at midday, and make lots of noise, so the employees would feel there was a reason for optimism. A lot of people said it was corny and wouldn't work—but it did, and it became an annual event. Another example: When sales of a particular liquid we offered declined, one manager proposed we paint the canisters bright colors instead of the industrial gray we had been using. The idea was met with derision, but we tried it, and it made a difference. Sales recovered.

As for more mainstream executives, they can come up with good ideas too, but often they are reluctant to speak out. I'm willing to give them a little push. If I'm in a meeting and people aren't volunteering anything on a controversial subject, I tell them we're going to be there for a while. The subsequent silence gets uncomfortable—eventually enough so that people start to talk. In one case, I came to a meeting to discuss a management problem we'd noticed in a customer organization. I listed three or four reasons why it was important for me to speak with the customer's CEO about it. People resisted, but they weren't offering any alternatives. We waited for quite a while, and finally somebody spoke up. After some dialogue we decided that a person lower in our organization would speak to a person lower in the customer organization, rather than risk the flap that would come out of elevating the issue to the highest level.

**Be willing to collaborate.** It's surprising how many people still resist collaboration or sharing credit, even though we know how much more we can achieve when we bring everyone to the table at once. There can be very practical reasons for this—for example, it may not be in someone's financial interest to cooperate. But I expect people to trust that I will notice when they take an action that, say, costs their unit $2 million in the short run but will benefit the company overall in the long run.

This is something I take very seriously. Some years ago I was running a big business that was functionally structured. The person who ran manufacturing and the one who ran marketing and sales did not get along well; they just wouldn't communicate. And because they didn't work together well, neither did their organizations. As a consequence, our inventories were always out of balance. The three of us met, and I told them that it didn't matter whether they liked each other or not, but the way they worked together had to change. They left the meeting with instructions to overcome their differences, but three months later, nothing had changed. I called them back into my office and gave them both separation packages on the spot, telling them that although I thought they were good performers individually, their failure to collaborate was hurting the enterprise. An imposing guard was waiting at the door to take their badges and escort them from the plant.

At about 3:00 that afternoon the telephone rang. It was the two of them, asking to gain entrance to the plant. The first thing they said upon arrival was "We get it." They came back to work, and I don't know that they ever learned to like each other, but they learned to work well together—and more important, so did their organizations. Our overall performance improved considerably.

**Be willing to lead initiatives.** There's no way of knowing how a challenging new project will turn out, so people are often reluctant to be associated with an untested idea, particularly if it crosses functional or unit boundaries. They duck under the radar screen rather than risk going up in flames. But I want people to raise their hands. When we started with Six Sigma at AlliedSignal, some people didn't like it or weren't sure about it, but I'll never forget the people who took a chance, who assumed leadership roles even though they didn't know much about the program. That's an attribute I prize in my employees. The ones who led the Six Sigma efforts were told that their careers would be accelerated if they succeeded, and those who made a contribution beyond unit boundaries did in fact climb the ladder faster than those who didn't.

**Develop leaders as you develop.** Too many people are selfish about their development. I want my direct reports to take as much interest in their subordinates' development as they do in their own—if not more. Early in my career, when I was at GE, I had a boss, a midlevel manager, who was a good performer but knew that he had gone as far as he was going to go. He called me in one day and said he felt I had a chance to be a lot better than he was and that he was going to do everything he could to help me reach my potential. From that moment on, he was more interested in my development than in his own. He went out of his way to criticize or praise me when I needed it. I'll never forget him; he played a very meaningful role in my career.

A strong signal that executives are committed to developing their direct reports is involvement in performance appraisals. I expect my people to be personally involved in reviews—not to hand them off to someone in Human Resources—and to supply their employees with specific and useful feedback. When I was at GE and Allied, I regularly reviewed the goals my direct reports were setting for their subordinates. If they were vague, I asked them to keep working until they'd achieved an appropriate level of specificity. For instance, someone might list "improve interpersonal skills" when what he really meant was "be more willing to collaborate." The goals have to be specific enough that people know how to approach the issue and whether or not they've made progress. "Improve interpersonal skills" doesn't tell an employee what to do.

**Stay current.** There's nothing more depressing than sitting in a business meeting with people who don't know what's going on in the world. I expect people to read, to watch the news—not just because it makes them more interesting but because what happens in the world affects what happens to us, to our marketplace, and to our competition. We make decisions in the context of world events, so people need to pay attention to them.

I also expect people to know what's going on with customers—how they're changing, how their competition is changing, how technology and world events are affecting their strategies. Customer relationships are an asset; people should bring them to the table.

**Anticipate.** One consequence of failing to stay current is that you risk a setback you ought to have anticipated—and you either recover more slowly than you should or never recover at all. Political events often trigger strategic threats. I'm a board member at Merck. With the Democrats in control of Congress, Merck is thinking about how to address that party's longtime platform on pharmaceutical pricing. It would be foolish to wait for new regulations; far better to get ready now.

A talented executive who once worked for me was perpetually caught off guard by adverse events—a new competitor, a negative regulatory development, an unforeseen customer problem. He worked very hard and he was smart, but he was frenetic and reactive, and never looked up to see the iceberg ahead of him. He even brought in a consultant to help him think through where the business would be in a couple of years, which culminated in a nice book that went up on the shelf while he went right back to his in-box. Eventually I began to spend the first 20 minutes of every meeting with him asking what he thought was about to happen. We went over competitors, customers, the regulatory environment—anything that might have an impact on the business. He improved, and he went on to become a CEO at another company, but anticipating change remained a struggle for him. The fact is, if it isn't in your DNA to anticipate, you don't. You can move the bar a little and find ways to compensate, but you can't change your nature. The people who are constantly looking around corners are best suited to leadership positions.

**Drive your own growth.** I expect people to seek perpetual education and development—not necessarily by going back to school but by exposing themselves to new people and ideas. Ask your boss for feedback, and if he or she isn't willing to give it, then turn to peers and subordinates, or find a mentor. Accept demanding assignments; you learn much more from them than you do from cushy projects.

*I expect people to read, to watch the news—not just because it makes them more interesting but because what happens in the world affects what happens to us, to our marketplace, and to our competition.*

This takes some courage, because the outcome may not be as good, but it demonstrates that you're interested in your own development. It also prepares you for difficult challenges in the future. I'll promote somebody who has stretched his limits in tough assignments with sometimes disappointing results over somebody who met his targets by taking less taxing roles.

**Be a player for all seasons.** It's one thing to sustain the behaviors I've described in good times. It's easy to collaborate, to stick up your hand, to offer ideas, when sales and earnings are growing by 20% a year. But how do you behave when they're in decline? I expect positive behaviors no matter what, and people who can live up to that stand out in my eyes. I can think of several people who were leading businesses, beating their forecasts, able to attract quality people—as long as the market was good. In a downturn they'd lose their ability to motivate and inspire people, their self-confidence would begin to wane, and I'd have to take them off the job.

On the flip side, some people are well suited to containing costs and keeping a business afloat when opportunities for growth are minimal, but are so perpetually paranoid that they can't take advantage of an upswing. I always look for someone who can thrive in either circumstance, and I'm amazed at the number of people who can't.

*If it isn't in your DNA to anticipate, you don't. You can find ways to compensate, but you can't change your nature.*

## What My Direct Reports Can Expect from Me

The CEO compact has two sides, of course, and I know my subordinates will do their jobs most effectively if they can expect a few things of me as well.

**Provide clarity of direction.** If I'm the leader, it's my job to communicate clearly where the business is going, why, and what the benefits will be if we accomplish what we set out to achieve. Every quarter the boss should get up in front of her team and explain the financial results and the progress of any operational or strategic initiative. This provides a crucial context for the work. If I simply tell someone, for instance, that he needs to improve cash flow, that's not terribly motivating. If I show him the actual numbers, he has some perspective on why and to what degree cash flow is an issue, and a better sense of how his job contributes to the enterprise as a whole.

**Set goals and objectives.** An executive may assume he's doing a good job, but he can't know for sure that his boss would agree if he has no specific goals and objectives to strive for. In addition to team goals, each person should know exactly what individual goals he or she is going to be measured on over a given period and where to invest precious time.

When goals and objectives are clear, promotion and bonus decisions can be based on merit. Morale suffers if people think there's some mystery to the process, some behind-the-scenes explanation. They're much happier and more comfortable when they know they're working in a meritocracy. As a CEO, I never felt uncomfortable when somebody came to ask me why I had put one person into a role rather than another. If I couldn't explain my decision, then shame on me.

**Give frequent, specific, and immediate feedback.** When I give feedback, I'm signaling to people that I'm interested in their growth and that I see a path for their future. Employees shouldn't have to wait for an annual review to learn how they are doing, and if the feedback is going to help drive their growth, then it needs to be as specific as possible. I hate it when a boss says simply, "Great job, Joe." Joe may have done a great job, but possibly he could have done even better, and if I point out how, maybe he will do better next time. If Joe gives a presentation, I owe him feedback right on the spot. I might say, "You came prepared, you seem to know your stuff, but I heard five 'um's in the first two minutes, and that distracts your audience." If he did particularly well, it's helpful to point out why, so he can repeat the behavior: "Great job, Joe, because you did your homework and made your point clearly in less than five minutes."

When the annual review comes, it should be simple. Forget HR jargon that attempts to disguise reality. An effective performance review tells the employee what he does well, what he could do better, and how he and his boss can work together to fill any gaps—no complicated forms or ambiguous language. (See the exhibit "A Simple Assessment.")

**Be decisive and timely.** Decisiveness isn't useful if it isn't timely. People should expect me to make decisions as soon as I have the information I need, and not to be careless or impetuous but to give clear, unambiguous answers. When a big contract is on the line,

## A Simple Assessment

I consult to a number of companies, and the first thing I look at is performance appraisals. Often I'll find three pages of the vaguest, most uncommunicative language imaginable. People write and write and write—and say nothing. Appraisals ought to be half a page that says what your boss likes, what you can improve, and what the two of you are going to do about it—simple and to the point, like the form shown here.

**PERFORMANCE EVALUATION**

**Name:** Joe Swift **Date:** 6/09/07

| What I Like | What Can Improve |
|---|---|
| Ambitious | Inconsistent communicator |
| Team player | Impetuous |
| Volunteers to lead initiatives | Often fails to anticipate |
| Innovative | Vague in appraising performance of others |
| Meets commitments | |
| Interested in the development of others | |
| Stays current | |
| Quashes bureaucracy | |

**Comments**

Joe, it's great to have you and your talents, but we need to decide how to progress on your development. Let's meet on Tuesday, after you've had a chance to consider an action plan.

*As a CEO, I never felt uncomfortable when somebody came to ask me why I had put one person into a role rather than another. If I couldn't explain my decision, then shame on me.*

the time for the boss to pitch in is not the last minute, it's a month earlier. At Allied, a salesperson who was working on a deal with Boeing, say, might ask me to place a phone call—not because I could sell the job any better but because I represented the organization. I shouldn't be making the call at the eleventh hour; I should make it well before the deal is set to close, when I can have more impact.

The problem is, people are often reluctant to get the boss involved for fear that asking for help will be perceived as a sign of weakness. They end up asking just when they think they're going to lose the deal. I consider asking for help a sign not of weakness but of self-confidence.

**Be accessible.** If I expect people to keep me informed about what's going on, then I need to be available when they need to see me. It's certainly in my interest. Frequently a boss doesn't learn that someone is leaving the company until he's about to walk out the door. If she'd known the employee was contemplating a move a month earlier, she could have taken him to lunch, talked to him about opportunities within the company, and maybe changed his mind.

And people should know that I'm not going to come down on them if they bring me bad news. In fact, I'm quite aware that if they're coming to me, more often than not the news is bad. Most people can handle good news on their own; they turn to the boss when they need some help.

**Demonstrate honesty and candor.** People spend far too much time figuring out how to tell others something unpleasant—how to deliver the news in a diplomatic way. This is common in performance appraisals. When I visit companies that I consult to, the first thing I ask leaders for is copies of their appraisals of subordinates, and I am continually amazed at the avoidance in their language. Look at the difference between vague and specific characterizations:

**Vague / Specific**
Hard worker / Results oriented
Attentive / Anticipatory
Detail oriented / Analytic problem solver
Good listener / Great communicator
Watches over his people / Holds people accountable
Amiable / Team player

The language on the left means nothing. Masking the truth doesn't help people develop. If I can say something sensitively and diplomatically, so much the better. But if I can't, I owe it to my employee to say it anyway.

**Offer an equitable compensation plan.** People want to be compensated fairly, in a way that reflects their contributions, and they want to understand how the compensation plan works. Employees should be able to estimate the size of their bonuses at the end of the year, because if the boss has also set clear goals and objectives, they know whether they have lived up to them, and they have a good idea of how the company did overall. The process shouldn't be shrouded in mystery or overly complicated.

• • •

Much of what I've described here has to do with keeping bureaucracy at bay. Bureaucracy is self-perpetuating, and cutting through it is a constant battle; because it's a fact of organizations, you can never truly get rid of it. You can tell it's creeping in when decision making slows to a crawl, or when the battery of forms needed for performance reviews begins to obscure meaningful feedback. Maintaining these behaviors helps to show when red tape is encroaching on productivity—and helps to minimize the effect.

Of course, it's much easier to live up to the first of the lists I've outlined if you have a boss who lives up to the second. But you won't always be blessed with such a boss. If you aren't, the best thing to do is create a CEO compact with your own subordinates, and demonstrate by example. These behaviors will make you a better employee and may help you get promoted. They will certainly serve you well should you leave for another job. The purpose, after all, is to improve team and company performance, which should accelerate your own growth.

Reprint R0704C
To order, see the next page
or call 800-988-0886 or 617-783-7500
or go to www.hbrreprints.org

# What Your Leader Expects of You

## Further Reading

ARTICLES

**Why Should Anyone Be Led by You?**
by Rob Goffee and Gareth Jones
*Harvard Business Review*
January 2001
Product no. 5890

This article focuses on the boss side of the boss-subordinate equation. The authors identify four behaviors that, when demonstrated by leaders, will cause people to want to follow them: 1) Reveal nonfatal flaws to underscore your approachability and build solidarity with followers. 2) Hone your ability to collect and interpret subtle interpersonal cues, then validate your perceptions with a trusted advisor. 3) Openly and directly explain the reasoning behind painful decisions. 4) Differentiate yourself from followers just enough to signal your status as a leader but not enough to lose contact with followers.

Harvard Business Review

**To Order**

For *Harvard Business Review* reprints and subscriptions, call 800-988-0886 or 617-783-7500. Go to www.hbrreprints.org

For customized and quantity orders of *Harvard Business Review* article reprints, call 617-783-7626, or e-mail customizations@hbsp.harvard.edu

# Ankerman

PRESENTATIONS BY NICK MORGAN

# Opening Options: How to Grab Your Audience's Attention

## *Six great ways to begin a presentation*

THE BEGINNING MOMENTS of a presentation are the most difficult moments both to create and to deliver. Audiences tend to make up their minds about speakers within the first minute or two—so the pressure is very definitely on. You need to start with something clever enough to catch everyone's attention, but you're at your most nervous, and thus it's hard to shine like you want to.

So how do you get started?

The traditional advice—still followed by many business speakers—is to begin with a joke. As we have told our readers many times in these pages, for everyone except the professional comedian, this is bad counsel indeed. You're at your worst in terms of nerves. Don't compound the problem by setting for yourself one of the most difficult public speaking chores of all right off the bat: Delivering a punch line with brilliant comic timing. It's extremely difficult to do under the best of circumstances—even for seasoned professionals.

Instead, you might want to take the advice of James Wagstaffe, a successful trial attorney, in his book on public speaking, *Romancing the Room: How to Engage Your Audience, Court Your Crowd, and Speak Successfully in Public* (Three Rivers Press, 2002). In it, Wagstaffe offers no fewer than eight ways to get started—and none of them involves telling a joke.

What are the other options? Try the "Grabber." That's where you say something surprising or do something shocking to grab everyone's attention right at the outset.

Wagstaffe says, "I knew of a criminal defense lawyer who employed the Grabber technique at the beginning of his summation to the jury. He started by handing out airsickness bags to each member of the jury. He announced, 'I know you'll need these after what you have just heard from the prosecution!' The jury certainly wanted to know what came next."

Or try the "Curiosity Arousal." If you start with an unusual thought or image, one that piques the curiosity of the audience, you'll have them from the start.

Wagstaffe offers this example: "A student in my class started off her speech the following way: 'Lines. There are lines all around us. As the wall meets the ceiling, that forms a line. As the door meets its edge, that forms a line. And there are lines in your hand.' The speaker then went on with a fascinating description of the meaning of lines in the hand and how one reads palms."

**Pique your audience's interest by offering a hint of what's to come.**

Here are Wagstaffe's half-dozen other ways to begin a presentation:

### The problem to solve

The idea here is to present the audience with a problem that you then solve together. You have to convince the audience that the problem is sufficiently intriguing or important such that it is worth solving.

For example, instead of merely announcing to your internal sales force that numbers are down for the year, and then exhorting them to go out and work harder, ask them right from the start to help you solve the problem. Get their suggestions and creative input first, before you exhort them to go out and work harder.

### The "Hey, yeah"

The "Hey, yeah" opening means telling audiences something they haven't thought of before but that they recognize as the truth once it's pointed out to them.

This one is easier to create than it might first seem. There is a deluge of bad news in the media—bad news sells—so look for something good. A trend, perhaps, that others haven't spotted. Or a development that we all take for granted. There's lots of good news out there—find a bit of it, and tell your audience.

### The "Whoa" introduction

This opening looks to catch the audience off-guard with a surprising bit of information that causes them to sit up and take notice.

For instance, think of people from the World War II generation, born in the early part of the last century. They may well have gone from living with gaslight and candles to the VCR and computer. That puts any kind of change we've experienced in the past decade or two into perspective. We think that the Internet is a huge change—but going from candles to voice-activated electric lights?

### Presuming audience involvement

Here, the speaker starts right in the middle of a story and lets the audience do the work of filling in the beginning from the clues that you give them as the speech goes on. Audiences put in this situation work hard to fill in the picture, and that work means that they stay involved in your presentation.

*Grabbing the Audience's Attention*, continued

Think of a movie that begins with the hero in a mysterious situation where the rules aren't clear. You are much more likely to sit on the edge of your seat trying to get oriented in the story. I once heard a speaker enthrall his university audience with the following opening: "Flames were shooting out of my hands as I walked down the pathway to my afternoon class." Don't you want to know more?

### The room reference

The goal with the room reference is to personalize your talk in a real, authentic way by relating your topic to something that is directly relevant to the audience in front of you. Do you know some members of the audience personally? Do you know something about the history of the space you're in or the company you're talking to? Do you know something about the professions of the people in the audience? All efforts at personalization richly pay off in audience interest.

### The movie preview

Finally, you can pique your audience's interest in what's to come by promising them something that they will get out of the talk—a bit later on. Will they learn how to do something valuable? Will you give them some insight that will help them run their businesses better? Will they know how to see the world in a new way once you're done? If you have something exciting to share, don't share it fully at the beginning. Rather, tease the audience with a hint at what's to come.

If you lose your audience at the top of your speech, it's very hard to get them back. So use one of these openers to engage your listeners from the start and keep them with you till the end. ❑

**Nick Morgan** *can be reached at nmorgan@hmcl.harvard.edu*

HARVARD MANAGEMENT COMMUNICATION LETTER

A NEWSLETTER FROM HARVARD BUSINESS SCHOOL PUBLISHING | TOOLS, TECHNIQUES, AND IDEAS FOR THE ARTICULATE EXECUTIVE

Article Reprint No. C0111E

# Lessons in Public Speaking from Recent Presidents

by Nick Morgan

# HARVARD MANAGEMENT COMMUNICATION LETTER

A NEWSLETTER FROM HARVARD BUSINESS SCHOOL PUBLISHING | TOOLS, TECHNIQUES, AND IDEAS FOR THE ARTICULATE EXECUTIVE

***Harvard Management Communication Letter*** **Subscriptions**

*Harvard Management Communication Letter*
Subscription Service Center
P.O. Box 257
Shrub Oak, NY 10588-0257

Phone: U.S. and Canada (800) 668-6705
Outside U.S. and Canada (617) 783-7474
Fax: (914) 962-1338
Web: www.hbsp.harvard.edu/hmcl

American Express, MasterCard, Visa accepted.
Billing available.

***Harvard Management Communication Letter*** **Custom Reprints**

Please inquire about our custom service and quantity discounts. We will print your company's logo on the cover of reprints or collections in black and white or two-color. The process is easy, cost effective, and quick.

Phone: (617) 783-7626 or Fax: (617) 783-7658

**Permissions**

For permission to copy or republish please write or call:

Permissions Department
Harvard Business School Publishing
60 Harvard Way
Boston, MA 02163

Phone: (617) 783-7587

**For a print or electronic catalog of our publications, please contact us:**

Harvard Business School Publishing
Customer Service
60 Harvard Way
Boston, MA 02163

Phone: U.S. and Canada (800) 668-6705
Outside U.S. and Canada (617) 783-7474
Fax: (617) 783-7555
Web: www.hbsp.harvard.edu/hmcl

# Lessons in Public Speaking from Recent Presidents

***Business leaders can learn from the communication strengths and weaknesses of the last four chief executives.***

REGARDLESS OF their politics, Americans have consistently rated Reagan and Clinton as better than average, and the two Bushes, father and son, as below average in their presentation skills. While the current president's first formal speech to Congress in response to the September 11th tragedy received high marks around the country and indeed around the world, it is too early to tell whether that rhetorical triumph will mark an enduring shift in President Bush's ability to connect with the public, or merely a high water mark.

But nonetheless each of these presidents has an important lesson to teach us about successful oratory. If you can combine these attributes in your presentations, you don't need to worry about having Clintonian charisma or Reaganesque affability. You can deliver your speech secure in the knowledge that you'll be benefiting from the rhetorical examples of four historic public speakers. Let's begin with the most recent.

**1 Good listening is more important than partisan passion.** We live in an era of passionate, partisan speaking. Turn on any TV talk show, and you're liable to watch the often less-than-edifying spectacle of public figures interrupting each other to sling distortions, half-truths, and outright lies at one another. The nature of the medium, indeed, calls for hot tempers and simple messages. If you can't get the idea out in a 12-second sound bite, then TV audiences aren't interested. And it had better be emotional, or it won't hold anyone's attention.

The result is the oft-noted "dumbing down" of American public rhetoric. So anxious are public figures to get their 15 minutes of attention that they would prefer to spend the time shouting rather than actually entering into a dialogue that might move the debate forward.

Thus, important political issues are reduced to simple "either-or" positions, greatly diminishing the chances of any useful debate. You're either pro-life or pro-choice, when in fact most (non-shouting) Americans are somewhere in between. You're either for prayer in public schools or anti-religion. You're either pro-defense or "soft" on our enemies. And on and on, down the list. Important public issues that call out for reasoned discussion are reduced to two extreme alternatives that few adults with any depth of understanding would care to hold.

Into this deplorable state of public affairs comes President George W. Bush with a rhetorically elegant, thoughtful speech in August 2001 on stem cell research.

Stem cell research is an issue that the pro-life hardliners have tried to polarize into a simple either-or debate. By arguing the logical fallacy of the "slippery slope," which holds that one small step will necessarily lead to a host of evils, the hardliners have tried to make stem cell research stand for baby-killing.

What slippery slope arguments ignore is humankind's ability to make moral distinctions. We hold murder to be a crime, for example, but judge Hitler to be a worse villain than the garden-variety thug who shoots someone during a robbery. Both are villains, and both should be punished, but one is worse than the other.

President Bush faced a challenging assignment: make a decision either to allow stem cell research to go forward with federal support or to stop federal spending in this area. Either way, he risked alienating voters.

Bush reached back to ancient Greek tradition and used the "residues method" of dealing with a controversial topic. It's a strategy that anyone faced with divided opinion on a hot topic can use effectively.

What you do is first lay out the question under debate, as neutrally as possible. Then, one by one, you address the possible answers that have already been put forward. Once again, the idea is to present the opposing viewpoints as fairly as possible. Without this step, the various partisans will not feel that they have been heard.

As you describe each answer, you raise the problems with that answer, as Bush did. He described the position of those who favor stem cell research for its potential ability to cure some of our most deadly and intractable diseases. Then he raised the problem with that position—it involves working with cells from discarded human embryos.

Bush also took up the position of those who favor no research at all, and looked at the objections to that position, including the need not to fetter research, and for America not to fall behind globally in the bio-tech race, as well as the argument that the embryos in question were by and large already discarded anyway.

Finally, Bush announced his own, Solomon-like decision: to allow work with already harvested stem cells, but not to publicly fund any research from cells harvested after the day of the speech. The rhetorical technique is called the residues method because the position adopted by the speaker is the last one in the speech—the "residue" when all the other positions have been investigated and critiqued.

*Lessons in Public Speaking*, continued

While extremists on either side of the issue were not delighted with the solution Bush proposed, there was surprisingly widespread support for a position that had not been articulated widely before. Because Bush carefully worked through the possible answers to the difficult question of public funding for stem cell research, the public and the various partisans were able to feel that at least Bush had listened carefully to many voices on the subject and had thoughtfully developed his own answer.

In an era of shouted, polarized opinion, Bush showed us what the ancient Greeks knew: there will always be a respected place accorded to those who take the trouble to listen rather than to shout their passions, even if we finally don't agree precisely with where the argument ends.

**❷ Audience focus is more important than rhetorical brilliance.** President Clinton is a rare bright spot in American public rhetoric of the last 20 years. Articulate, deeply conversant in both politics and policy, and able to speak off the cuff better than most politicians with extensive preparation, Clinton commanded the podium, the pulpit, and the Oval Office with an ability to reach his audience that few possess.

But sometimes that connection with the audience faltered. When Clinton tried to split rhetorical hairs, he could be correct, and even brilliant, but still fail in the basic job of an orator: to reach his audience.

The most glaring example of this lapse came during the Monica Lewinsky scandal. Most Americans recall the President's rhetorical evasions ("it depends on what the meaning of 'is' is") and attempts to answer questions with the letter of full disclosure without, in fact, the spirit.

But few Americans know that during the height of the grand jury revelations, Clinton prepared a speech admitting his relationship with Ms. Lewinsky that he never gave. Instead, he substituted a far less contrite and forthcoming speech, one which was rhetorically shrewd and yet failed to convince anyone that he was indeed remorseful.

Here's what he originally planned to say:

*I have fallen short of what you should expect from a president. I have failed my own religious faith and values. I have let too many people down. I take full responsibility for my actions—for hurting my wife and daughter, for hurting Monica Lewinsky and her family, for hurting friends and staff, and for hurting the country I love. None of this ever should have happened.*

*I never should have had any sexual contact with Monica Lewinsky, but I did.... What I did was wrong—and there is no excuse for it.*

And here's what he actually said:

*As you know, in a deposition in January, I was asked questions about my relationship with Monica Lewinsky. While my answers were legally accurate, I did not volunteer information. Indeed, I did have a relationship with Ms. Lewinsky that was not appropriate. In fact, it was wrong. It constituted a critical lapse in judgment and a personal failure on my part for which I am solely and completely responsible.*

The first speech would have come a lot closer to satisfying the audience because it is about remorse for wrong action. The second speech leaves out the remorse and instead substitutes a description of the inaccuracy of earlier announcements.

Had Clinton given the first speech, would his avowal of remorse have defused the political situation and enabled the President to avoid impeachment? We'll never know, but it is clear that the speech Clinton gave failed to achieve the closure he sought.

**❸ Dignity is more important than accuracy.** When the first President Bush announced the Gulf War, most Americans had little difficulty switching their view of Iraqi leader Saddam Hussein from American ally to archenemy—largely because they had paid no attention to the country or its leader before January 16, 1991.

The President had an opportunity to create virtually a first impression of Iraq and declare war on it in one speech. Such a combination of rhetorical tasks demands care. If for no other reason than that the country might eventually become our ally once the war was over, the President needed to separate the dictator from his people in the American mind and create a clear rationale for removing the former while avoiding demonizing the latter.

He did too good a job. The speech is highly partisan, full of intemperate rhetoric, and belittles "Saddam" at every turn of phrase.

*While the world waited, Saddam Hussein systematically raped, pillaged, and plundered a tiny nation, no threat to his own. He subjected the people of Kuwait to unspeakable atrocities—and among those maimed and murdered innocent children.*

*While the world waited, Saddam sought to add to the chemical arsenal he now possesses an infinitely more dangerous weapon of mass destruction—a nuclear weapon....*

*While the world waited, while Saddam stalled, more damage was being done to the fragile economies of the Third World, emerging democracies of Eastern Europe, to the entire world, including to our own economy....*

Bush's rhetoric, while accurate enough, is unnecessarily shrill in tone. It sounds neither presidential nor appropriate coming from the most powerful nation on earth. It is merely strident where it should be strong, overly magnifying the threat that this little country represents to the U.S. We lurch from "unspeakable" atrocities (which are immediately named) to the "damage" being done "the entire world" by "Saddam's" inaction. Which is he, active or inactive?

*Lessons in Public Speaking,* continued

The result is a kind of rhetorical hysteria that ultimately weakens the case for war because the text is so confused. The honor due sovereign nations in times of great historical import—such as war and peace—is lacking. The leader of a foreign nation doesn't even get the dignity of a last name, so eager is Bush to make him into a complete villain. It would have been better to talk of Hussein in more restrained terms—better for both the picture of America the speech creates and the picture of Iraq. Here, the whole world was watching.

Ultimately, Bush's rhetoric limited his options. By demonizing "Saddam," Bush made it more difficult to negotiate a peace with him (how can you negotiate with a demon?). But because the President didn't pursue complete victory, negotiation was his only real option. The outcome? The stalemate we still suffer from today.

❹ **Simple optimism is more important than a clever solution.** When candidate Ronald Reagan accepted the Republican nomination for president in July 1980, the country was in the throes of horrendous inflation, an energy crisis, a hostage crisis, and a sense that we had lost the ability to control events on the world stage or at home. To solve these problems, Reagan, in one of the half-dozen best speeches of his career, offered the following solutions in the form of pledges to the American people:

*The American people deserve better (than mediocre leadership)...and we stand united in our resolve to do something about it....*

*We need a rebirth of the American tradition of leadership....*

*The first task of national leadership is to set realistic and honest priorities...and I pledge that my administration will do that....*

*We have to move ahead, but we're not going to leave anyone behind....*

*It's time to put America back to work..., to make America great again....*

What's striking about this rhetoric is its vagueness. Just what exactly is Mr. Reagan promising? In contrast with President Carter, who often went into painful detail about the specifics of his policies, Reagan merely offered us hope and platitudes. And something more important: he showed the American people that he understood the emotional depth of their problems.

Where Carter scolded Americans for feeling "malaise," Reagan validated our feelings. He acknowledged our helplessness and offered to make us feel better. Most Americans loved him for it. ❑

—***Nick Morgan*** *can be reached at nmorgan@hbsp.harvard.edu*

Module

# Planning, Writing, and Revising

4

## LEARNING OBJECTIVES

Module 4 shows the value of using a multistep approach to create the best documents. After completing the module, you should be able to

- LO 4-1 **Apply processes for writing quality improvement.**
- LO 4-2 **Manage time for writing projects.**
- LO 4-3 **Plan writing and speaking projects for increased success.**
- LO 4-4 **Apply strategies for revision.**
- LO 4-5 **Support writing with grammar and spell-checkers.**
- LO 4-6 **Apply strategies for feedback and revision with it.**
- LO 4-7 **Apply strategies for form letter use.**
- LO 4-8 **Apply strategies for writer's block and procrastination solutions.**

Skilled performances look easy and effortless. In reality, as every dancer, musician, or athlete knows, they're the product of hard work, hours of practice, attention to detail, and intense concentration. Like all skilled performances, writing rests on a base of work.

The pace at which writers compose has increased. While memos and letters are still standard business documents, e-mail messages are commonplace, and increasingly, people use social media at work. The pressure may be to dash off messages as quickly as possible, but a better strategy is to send messages as quickly as *necessary,* with the appropriate amount of planning, writing, and revising. Practicing the techniques in this module until they become second nature will help you compose messages efficiently and successfully.

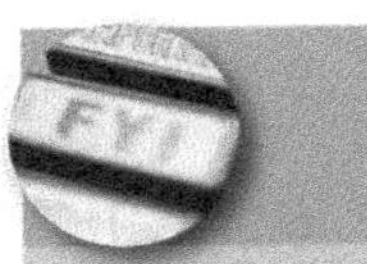


What constitutes revision—and when it's acceptable—depends on many factors, including audience expectations. For instance, Broadway producers found themselves facing criticism when revising the George Gershwin classic *Porgy and Bess*, which was "reimagined" for contemporary audiences. Revising history texts can elicit similar results, and even the term can create arguments as some people argue it's really about being more inclusive. Said author Kenneth C. Davis, "In school, we focus on the 'important people' and Founding Fathers, but what that 'great man version' of history does is really leave out an awful lot of people who have tremendous impact."

*Sources:* Anthony Tommasini, "Adapting, Revising, Provoking," *The New York Times*, March 9, 2012, http://www.nytimes.com/2012/03/11/arts/music/some-ground-rules-for-revising-operas-and-musicals.html?pagewanted=all; and Ashley Strickland, "Revising History to Show America's 'Secret Heroes,'" *CNN*, April 17, 2012, http://www.cnn.com/2012/04/17/living/secret-american-heroes/index.html.

Planning, writing, and revising include the following activities:

### Planning

- Analyzing the problem, defining your purposes, and analyzing the audience; thinking of information, benefits, and objections; choosing a pattern of organization or making an outline; and so on.
- Gathering the information you need—from the message you're answering, a person, a book, or the web.

### Writing

- Putting words on paper or on a screen. Writing can be lists, fragmentary notes, stream-of-consciousness writing, or a formal draft.

### Revising

- Evaluating your work and measuring it against your goals and the requirements of the situation and audience. The best evaluation results from *re-seeing* your draft as if someone else had written it. Will your audience understand it? Is it complete? Convincing? Friendly?
- Getting feedback from someone else. Is your pattern of organization appropriate? Does a revision solve an earlier problem? Are there any typos in the final copy?
- Adding, deleting, substituting, or rearranging. Revision can be changes in single words or in large sections of a document.
- Editing the draft to see that it satisfies the requirements of standard English. Here you'd correct spelling and mechanical errors and check word choice and format. Unlike revision, which can produce major changes in meaning, editing focuses on the surface of writing.
- Proofreading the final copy to see that it's free from typographical errors.

Note the following points about these activities:

- **The activities do not have to come in this order.** Some people may gather information *after* writing a draft when they see that they need more specifics to achieve their purposes.
- **You do not have to finish one activity to start another.** Some writers plan a short section and write it, plan the next short section and write it, and so on throughout the document. Evaluating what is already written may cause a writer to do more planning or to change the original plan.
- **You may do an activity several times, not just once.** For an important document, you might get feedback, revise, get more feedback, revise yet again, and so on.
- **Most writers do not use all activities for all the documents they write.** You'll use more activities when you write a new kind of document, about a new subject, or to a new audience.

## Does it matter what process I use? LO 4-1

▶ *Using expert processes will improve your writing.*

Just as athletes can improve their game by studying videotapes and working on just how they kick a ball or spin during a jump, so writers can improve their writing by studying their own processes. No single writing process works for all writers all of the time. However, expert writers seem to use different processes than novice writers.[1] Expert writers are more likely to

Proofread carefully to communicate a clear message and to protect your credibility.

A 15-year-old in Japan sold 110,000 paper copies of the three-volume novel, *Wolf Boy x Natural Girl*, she composed on her cell phone. *Keitai*, the name for the genre, allows writers to publish manuscript pages on a website as soon as they are finished. Popular novels are later printed and sold, in this case grossing more than $611,000.

***Source:*** Yuriko Nagano, "For Japan's Cell Phone Novelists, Proof of Success is in the Print," *The LosAngeles Times*, February 9, 2010,http://www.latimes.com/news/nation-and-world/la-fg-japanphone-novel9-2010feb 09,0,116266, story?track = rss.

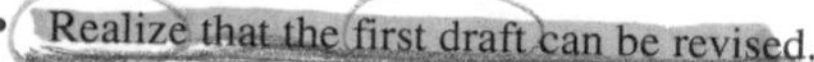

- Realize that the first draft can be revised.
- Write regularly.
- Break big jobs into small chunks.
- Have clear goals focusing on purpose and audience.
- Have several different strategies to choose from.
- Use rules flexibly.
- Wait to edit until after the draft is complete.

Research shows that experts differ from novices in identifying and analyzing the initial problem more effectively, understanding the task more broadly and deeply, drawing from a wider repertoire of strategies, and seeing patterns more clearly. Experts actually composed more slowly than novices, perhaps because they rarely settled for work that was just "OK." Finally, experts were better at evaluating their own work.[2]

Thinking about the writing process and consciously adopting "expert" processes will help you become a better writer.

**Site to See**

**Go to**

**www.ucc.vt.edu/stdysk/tminteractive.html**

Use this calculator from Virginia Polytechnic Institute and State University to see how much time you have for schoolwork weekly. Then see how much of that time you can spend planning, writing, and revising.

## I don't have much time. How should I use it? LO 4-2

*Save two-thirds of your time for planning and revising.*

To get the best results from the time you have, spend only a third of your time actually "writing." Spend at least one-third of your time analyzing the situation and your audience, gathering information, and organizing what you have to say. Spend another third evaluating what you've said, revising the draft(s) to meet your purposes and the needs of the audience and the organization, editing a late draft to remove any errors in grammar and mechanics, and proofreading the final typed copy.

When you first get an assignment, think about all the steps you'll need to go through so you can plan your time for that project. Certainly two writers might need different amounts of time to produce the same quality document. Figure 4.1 shows how a writer might use six hours needed to plan, write, and revise a memo.

The habits of professional writers are as diverse as the prose they create. When composing *Interview with the Vampire,* Anne Rice revised each typed page before she wrote the next. Michael Ondaatje, whose *The English Patient* won the Booker Prize, literally cuts and pastes handwritten passages. While drafting *Lowboy,* John Wray rode subways with a laptop, sometimes six hours a day.

*Source:* Alexandra Alter, "How to Write a Great Novel," *The Wall Street Journal,* November 13, 2009, W4.

**Figure 4.1 Allocating Time in Writing a Memo** — Total time: 6 hours

| | |
|---|---|
| Planning<br>Understand the policy.<br>Answer the PAIBOC questions (◄◄ Module 1).<br>Think about document design (►► Module 5).<br>Organize the message. | 1.5 hours |
| Writing<br>Create a draft. | 1.5 hours |
| Revising<br>Reread draft.<br>Measure draft against PAIBOC questions and against principles of business communication.<br>Revise draft.<br>Ask for feedback.<br>Revise draft based on feedback.<br>Edit to catch grammatical errors.<br>Run spell-check.<br>Proof by eye.<br>Initial memo.<br>Duplicate and distribute document. | 3.0 hours |

Creative planning can lead to creative solutions. Mortgage Resolution Partners offers a plan in California that has local government use eminent domain to condemn a distressed home, pay fair market value for it to the mortgage owner, and then help to refinance the home through the company, lowering mortgage payments in hopes of keeping people in their homes. While the plan irks some banks and financial experts, others see it as potentially useful, even if they have their doubts. The University of Missouri's Randall Wray, for instance, notes that because foreclosures are hampering America's economic recovery, "Anything that will stop that I think is worth looking at."

*Source:* Illyce R. Glink, "Could Seizing a Home Save a Homeowner?" July 17, 2012, http://realestate.yahoo.com/news/could-seizing-a-home-save-a-homeowner-.html.

## What planning should I do before I begin writing or speaking? LO 4-3

► *As much as you can!*

Spend at least one-third of your time planning and organizing before you begin to write. The better your ideas are when you start, the fewer drafts you'll need to produce a good document. Start by using the analysis questions from Module 1 to identify purpose and audience. Use the strategies described in Module 2 to analyze audience and in Module 8 to develop reader benefits. Gather information you can use for your document.

If ideas won't come, try the following techniques.

- **Brainstorm.** Think of all the ideas you can, without judging them. Consciously try to get at least a dozen different ideas before you stop. The first idea you have may not be the best.
- **Freewrite.**[3] Make yourself write, without stopping, for 10 minutes or so, even if you must write "I will think of something soon." At the end of 10 minutes, read what you've written and identify the best point in the draft. Get a clean paper or screen and write for another 10 uninterrupted minutes. Read this draft, marking anything that's good and should be kept, and then write again for another 10 minutes. By the third session, you will probably produce several sections that are worth keeping—maybe even a complete draft that's ready to be revised.
- **Cluster.**[4] Write your topic in the middle of the page and circle it. Write down the ideas the topic suggests, circling them, too. (The circles are designed to tap into the nonlinear half of your brain.) When you've filled the page, look for patterns or repeated ideas. Use different colored pens to group related ideas. Then use these ideas to develop reader benefits in a memo, questions for a survey, or content for the body of a report. Figure 4.2 presents the clusters that one writer created about business communication in the United States and France.
- **Talk to your audiences.** As Rachel Spilka's research shows, talking to internal and external audiences helped writers involve readers in the planning process,

**Figure 4.2** Clustering Helps Generate Ideas

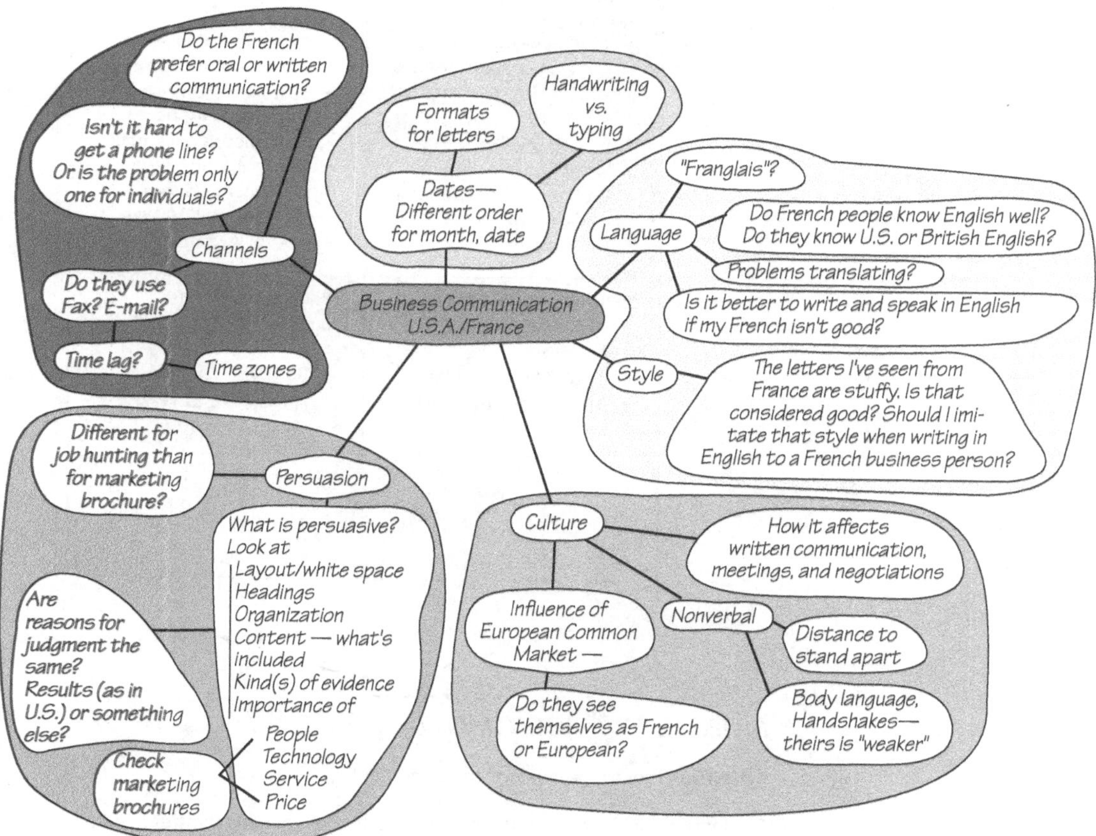


understand the social and political relationships among readers, and negotiate conflicts orally rather than depending solely on the document. These writers were then able to think about content as well as about organization and style, appeal to common grounds (such as reducing waste or increasing productivity) that several readers shared, and reduce the number of revisions needed before documents were approved.[5]

Thinking about the content, layout, or structure of your document can also give you ideas. For long documents, write out the headings you'll use. For anything that's under five pages, less formal notes will probably work. You may want to jot down ideas you can use as the basis for a draft. For an oral presentation, a meeting, or a document with lots of visuals, try creating a **storyboard**, with a rectangle representing each page or unit. Draw a box with a visual for each main point. Below the box, write a short caption or label.

Letters and memos will go faster if you choose a basic organizational pattern before you start. Modules 10, 11, and 12 give detailed patterns of organization for the most common kinds of letters and memos. You may want to customize those patterns with a **planning guide**[6] to help you keep the "big picture" in mind as you write. Figure 4.3 shows planning guides developed for specific kinds of documents.

**How Experts Write**

Expert writers

- Realize that the first draft can be revised.
- Write regularly.
- Break big jobs into small chunks.
- Have clear goals focusing on purpose and audience.
- Have several different strategies to choose from.
- Use rules flexibly.
- Wait to edit until after the draft is complete.

**Figure 4.3** Customized Planning Guides for Specific Documents

*Source:* E-mail and proposal guides based on Fred Reynolds, "What Adult Work-World Writers Have Taught Me About Adult Work-World Writing," *Professional Writing in Context: Lessons from Teaching and Consulting in Worlds of Work* (Hillsdale, NJ: Lawrence Erlbaum Associates, 1995), 18, 20.

| **Planning guide for a trip report** | **Planning guide for a proposal** |
|---|---|
| • The Big Picture from the Company's Point of View: We Can Go Forward on the Project<br>• Criteria/Goals<br>• What We Did<br>• Why We Know Enough to Go Forward<br>• Next Steps | • Customer's Concern #1 Our Proposal/Answer<br>• Customer's Concern #2 Our Proposal/Answer<br>• Customer's Concern #3 Our Proposal/Answer<br>• Customer's Concern #4 Our Proposal/Answer<br>• Ask for Action |
| **Planning guide for an e-mail message**<br>• My Purpose<br>• Points I Want to Make<br>• Document(s) to Attach<br>• Next Steps | **Planning guide for a credit rejection**<br>• Reason<br>• Refusal<br>• Alternative (Layaway/ Co-signer/Provide more information)<br>• Goodwill Ending |

## What is revision? How do I do it? LO 4-4

► *Revision means "re-seeing" the document.*

Good writers make their drafts better by judicious revising, editing, and proofreading.

- **Revising** means making changes that will better satisfy your purposes and your audience.
- **Editing** means making surface-level changes that make the document grammatically correct.
- **Proofreading** means checking to be sure the document is free from typographical errors.

Site to See

**Go to www.gcflearnfree.org/word2010**

for tips on using Microsoft Word when writing and revising.

When you're writing to a new audience or have to solve a particularly difficult problem, plan to revise the draft at least three times. The first time, look for content and clarity. The second time, check the organization and layout. Finally, check style and tone, using the information in Modules 15 and 16. Figure 4.4 summarizes the questions you should ask.

Often you'll get the best revision by setting aside your draft, getting a blank page or screen, and redrafting. This strategy takes advantage of the thinking you did on your first draft without locking you into the sentences in it.

As you revise, be sure to read the document through from start to finish. This is particularly important if you've composed in several sittings or if you've used text from other documents. Researchers have found that such documents tend to be well organized but don't flow well.[7] You may need to add transitions, cut repetitive parts, or change words to create a uniform level of formality throughout the document.

If you're really in a time bind, do a light revision (see Figure 4.5). The quality of the final document may not be as high as with a thorough revision, but even a light revision is better than skipping revision.

**Checklist for** Thorough Revision

**Content and Clarity**

- ☐ Does your document meet the needs of the organization and of the reader—and make you look good?
- ☐ Have you given readers all the information they need to understand and act on your message?
- ☐ Is all the information accurate?
- ☐ Is each sentence clear? Is the message free from apparently contradictory statements?
- ☐ Are generalizations and benefits backed up with adequate supporting detail?

**Organization and Layout**

- ☐ Is the pattern of organization appropriate for your purposes, audience, and situation?
- ☐ Are transitions between ideas smooth? Do ideas within paragraphs flow smoothly?
- ☐ Does the design of the document make it easy for readers to find the information they need? Is the document visually inviting?
- ☐ Are the points emphasized by layout ones that deserve emphasis?
- ☐ Are the first and last paragraphs effective?

**Style and Tone**

- ☐ Is the message easy to read?
- ☐ Is the message friendly and free from biased language?
- ☐ Does the message build goodwill?

**Figure 4.4** Thorough Revision Checklist

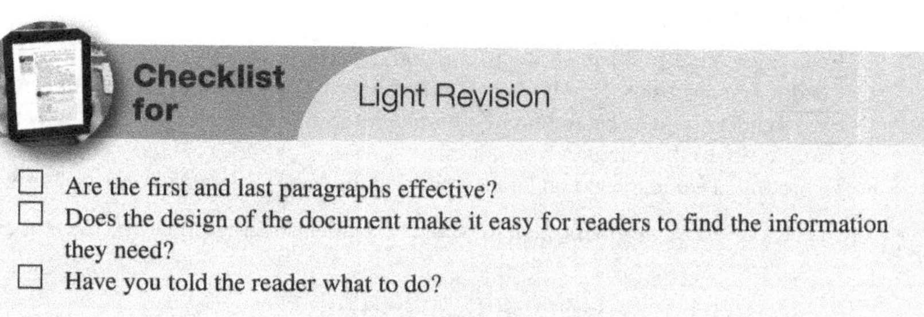

**Checklist for** Light Revision

- ☐ Are the first and last paragraphs effective?
- ☐ Does the design of the document make it easy for readers to find the information they need?
- ☐ Have you told the reader what to do?

**Figure 4.5** Light Revision Checklist

## Can a grammar checker do my editing for me? LO 4-5

► *No. You have to decide whether to make each change.*

Grammar checkers are good at finding missing halves. For example, if you open a parenthesis and never close it, a grammar checker will note that a second one is needed. Of course, you have to decide where it goes. In terms of other errors, all a grammar checker can do is ask you about what you have done. A grammar checker can tell you that you've used a passive verb, and ask if you want to change it. But you have to decide whether the passive is justified. If it finds the word *well*, the grammar checker can tell

**Revising, Editing, and Proofreading**

**Revising** means making changes that will better satisfy your purposes and your audience.

**Editing** means making surface-level changes that make the document grammatically correct.

**Proofreading** means checking to be sure the document is free from typographical errors.

you that *good* and *well* are sometimes confused. But you have to decide which word fits your meaning (▶▶ Module 15). You still need to know the rules so that you can decide which changes to make.

Check to be sure that the following are accurate:

- Sentence structure
- Subject–verb and noun–pronoun agreement
- Punctuation
- Word usage
- Spelling—including spelling of names
- Numbers

You need to know the rules of grammar and punctuation to edit. Module 14 reviews grammar and punctuation. Module 15 reviews words that are often confused. Most writers make a small number of errors over and over. If you know that you have trouble with dangling modifiers or subject–verb agreement, for example, specifically look for them in your draft. Also look for any errors that especially bother your boss and correct them.

Editing should always *follow* revision. There's no point in taking time to fix a grammatical error in a sentence that may be cut when you clarify your meaning or tighten your style. Some writers edit more accurately when they print out a copy of a document and edit the hard copy. But beware: Laser printing makes a page look good but does nothing to correct errors.

## I spell-check. Do I still need to proofread? LO 4-5

▶ *Yes.*

**How to Revise**

When you're writing to a new audience or have to solve a particularly difficult problem, plan to revise the draft at least three times. The first time, look for content and clarity. The second time, check the organization and layout. Finally, check style and tone. Do all this **before** you edit and proofread.

Proofread every document both with a spell-checker and by eye to catch the errors a spell-checker can't find.

Proofreading is hard because writers tend to see what they know should be there rather than what really is there. Because it's always easier to proof something you haven't written, you may want to swap papers with a proofing buddy. (Be sure the person looks for typos, not for content.)

To proofread,

- Read once quickly for meaning to see that nothing has been left out.
- Read a second time, slowly. When you find an error, correct it and then *reread that line.* Readers tend to become less attentive after they find one error and may miss other errors close to the one they've spotted.
- To proofread a document you know well, read the lines backward or the pages out of order.

Always triple-check numbers, headings, the first and last paragraphs, and the reader's name.

## How can I get better feedback? LO 4-6

▶ *Ask for the kind of feedback you need.*

**Go to**

**www.wisc.edu/writing/Handbook/Proofreading.html**

The University of Wisconsin Writing Center offers tips on proofreading.

The process of drafting, getting feedback, revising, and getting more feedback is called **cycling**. Dianna Booher reports that documents in her clients' firms cycled an average of 4.2 times before reaching the intended audience.[8] Susan Kleimann studied a 10-page document whose 20 drafts made a total of 31 stops on the desks of nine reviewers on four different levels.[9] Being asked to revise a document is a fact of life in businesses, government agencies, and nonprofit organizations.

To improve the quality of the feedback you get, tell people which aspects you'd especially like comments about. For example, when you give a reader the outline or planning draft,[10] you might want to know whether the general approach is appropriate. After your second draft, you might want to know whether reader benefits are well developed.

**Checklist for** Questions to Ask Readers

**Outline or Planning Draft**

- ☐ Does the plan seem "on the right track"?
- ☐ What topics should be added? Should any be cut?
- ☐ Do you have any other general suggestions?

**Revising Draft**

- ☐ Does the message satisfy all its purposes?
- ☐ Is the message adapted to the audience(s)?
- ☐ Is the organization effective?
- ☐ What parts aren't clear?
- ☐ What ideas need further development?
- ☐ Do you have any other suggestions?

**Polishing Draft**

- ☐ Are there any problems with word choice or sentence structure?
- ☐ Did you find any inconsistencies?
- ☐ Did you find any typos?
- ☐ Is the document's design effective?

**Figure 4.6** Questions to Ask Readers

When you reach the polishing draft, you'll be ready for feedback on style and grammar. Figure 4.6 lists questions to ask.

It's easy to feel defensive when someone criticizes your work. If the feedback stings, put it aside until you can read it without feeling defensive. Even if you think the reader has misunderstood what you were trying to say, the fact that the reader complained means the section could be improved. If the reader says "This isn't true" and you know that the statement is true, several kinds of revision might make the truth clear to the reader: rephrasing the statement, giving more information or examples, or documenting the source.

Before sending out any message—paper or electronic—address it correctly and proof it carefully. Employees at Aviva Investors thought they were being dismissed after receiving an e-mail message, a blow made plausible because the company had announced it would trim its workforce. It turns out the message was meant for only one employee who was leaving the company, but the language wishing the reader "all the best for the future" was chilling to workers already worried about job security. Needless to say, such actions may produce less-than-positive feedback from the remaining employees.

*Source:* Fox Van Allen, "E-mail Accident Leads an Entire Company to Think It's Being Fired," April 23, 2012, http://news.yahoo.com/blogs/technology-blog/email-accident-leads-entire-company-think-being-fired-165511639.html.

## Can I use form letters? LO 4-7

*Yes. But make sure they're good.*

A **form letter** is a prewritten fill-in-the-blank letter designed for routine situations. Some form letters have different paragraphs that can be inserted, depending on the situation. For example, a form letter admitting students to college might have additional paragraphs to be added for students who were going to receive financial aid.

**Boilerplate** is language—sentences, paragraphs, even pages—from a previous document that a writer includes in a new document. In academic papers, material written by others must be quoted and documented. However, because businesses own the documents their employees write, old text may be included without attribution.

In some cases, boilerplate may have been written years ago. For example, many legal documents, including apartment leases and sales contracts, are almost completely boilerplated. In other cases, writers may use boilerplate they themselves have written. For example, a section from a proposal describing the background of the problem could also be used in the final report after the proposed work was completed. A section from a progress report describing what the writer had done could be used with only a few changes in the Methods section of the final report.

Building a Critical Skill

## Revising after Feedback LO 4-6

When you get feedback that you understand and agree with, make the change.

If you get feedback you don't understand, ask for clarification.

- Paraphrase: "So you're asking me to give more information?"
- Ask for more information: "Can you suggest a way to do that?"
- Test your inference: "Would it help if I did such and such?"

Sometimes you may get feedback you don't agree with.

- If it's an issue of grammatical correctness, check this book. (Sometimes even smart people get things wrong.)
- If it's a matter of content, recognize that *something* about the draft isn't as good as it could be: something is leading the reader to respond negatively.
- If the reader thinks a fact is wrong (and you know it's right), show where the fact came from. "According to. . . ."
- If the reader suggests a change in wording you don't like, try another option.
- If the reader seems to have misunderstood or misread the text, think about ways to make the meaning clearer.

Your supervisor's comments on a draft can help you improve that document, help you write better drafts the next time, and teach you about the culture of your organization. Look for patterns in the feedback you receive. Are you asked to use more formal language or to make the document more conversational? Does your boss want to see an overview before details? Does your company prefer information presented in bulleted lists rather than in paragraphs? Are your photos or artwork bias free?

Feedback is sometimes painful, but focus on the point of the feedback rather than feelings. Ford Motor Company CEO Alan Mulally raised eyebrows when he publicly criticized the looks of the 2008 Taurus. Derrick Kuzak, head of global development, went on to compare the car to TV's Homer Simpson, and the two stressed that a more attractive successor would be in the works. "That's only delivered when the engineering team does not dumb down the design because of engineering and manufacturing feasibility concerns," Kuzak added. While the comments may have rankled some insiders, analysts welcomed the company's willingness to fix problems.

If honest, sharp criticism or even a rebuke can be beneficial. Pay close attention to what is at the heart of a comment rather than how the comment is delivered. Remember, though, what it feels like to be on the receiving end when *you* give feedback. Temper your words, and let your example encourage others to be more gracious.

*Source:* "Taurus and Homer Simpson—Separated at Birth?" January 29, 2008, downloaded at www.cnn.com/2008/LIVING/wayoflife/01/29/ford.homer.simpson.ap/index.html.

Writers use form letters and boilerplate to save time and energy and to use language that has already been approved by the organization's legal staff. However, as Glenn Broadhead and Richard Freed point out, reusing old text creates two problems.[11]

- Using unrevised boilerplate can create a document with incompatible styles and tones.
- Form letters and boilerplate can encourage writers to see situations and audiences as identical when in fact they differ.

Before you use a form letter, make sure it is well written and that it applies to the situation in which you are thinking of using it.

Before you incorporate old language in a new document,

- Check to see that the old section is well written.
- Consciously look for differences between the two situations, audiences, or purposes that may require different content, organization, or wording.
- Read through the whole document at a single sitting to be sure that style, tone, and level of detail are consistent in the old and new sections.

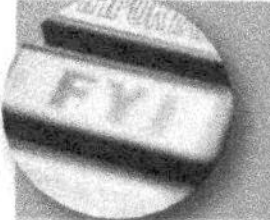


Proofreading is especially important when reusing language. For 2009, a mint produced Chilean 50-pesos coins, each worth about a U.S. dime, with the name of the country spelled "CHIIE." Chile's Central Bank did not learn of the engraver's error until a year later, when the newspaper *El Mercurio* reported the story. About 1.5 million of the errant coins were in circulation by then.

*Source:* Eva Vergara, "Is It 'Chiie' or 'Chile'? Mint Issues Bad Coins," *The Boston Globe,* February 12, 2010, http://www.boston.com/news/world/latinamerica/articles/2010/02/12/is_it_chiie_or_chile_mint_issues_bad_coins/.

## How can I overcome writer's block and procrastination? LO 4-8

► *Talk, participate, and practice. Reward yourself for activities that lead to writing.*

According to psychologist Robert Boice, a combination of five actions works best to overcome writer's block:[12]

- **Participate actively in the organization and the community.** The more you talk to people, the more you interact with some of your audiences, the more you learn about the company, its culture, and its context, the easier it will be to write—and the better your writing will be.
- **Practice writing regularly and in moderation.**
- **Learn as many strategies as you can.** Good writers have a "bag of tricks" to draw on; they don't have to "reinvent the wheel" in each new situation. This book suggests many strategies and patterns. Try them; memorize them; make them your own.
- **Talk positively to yourself:** "I can do this." "If I keep working, ideas will come." "It doesn't have to be wonderful; I can always make it better later."
- **Talk about writing to other people.** Value the feedback you get from your boss. Talk to your boss about writing. Ask him or her to share particularly good examples—from anyone in the organization. Find colleagues at your own level and talk about the writing you do. Do different bosses value different qualities? What aspects of your own boss's preferences are individual and which are part of the discourse community of the organization? Talking to other people expands your repertoire of strategies and helps you understand the discourse community in which you write.

Dealing with procrastination can be challenging, but Kevin Purdy recommends several strategies. Among them are getting rid of clutter, acknowledging that you're actually procrastinating, and dealing with the more difficult tasks early. Believe in yourself, too. Says Rory Vaden, author of *Take the Stairs: 7 Steps to Achieving True Success,* "The number one reason we procrastinate is we don't believe we have what it takes to pull it off."

*Source:* Kevin Purdy, "Get to Work by Meeting Procrastination Head-On," *Fast Company,* April 10, 2012, http://www.fastcompany.com/1830018/get-work-meetingprocrastination-head.

To avoid procrastination, modify your behavior by rewarding yourself for activities that *lead* to writing:

- **Set a regular time to write.** Sit down and stay there for the time you've planned, even if you write nothing usable.
- **Develop a ritual for writing.** Choose tools—paper, pen, computer, chair— that you find comfortable. Use the same tools in the same place every time you write.
- **Try freewriting.** Write for 10 minutes without stopping.
- **Write down the thoughts and fears you have as you write.** If the ideas are negative, try to substitute more positive statements: "I can do this." "I'll keep going and postpone judging." "If I keep working, I'll produce something that's OK."
- **Identify the problem that keeps you from writing.** Deal with that problem; then turn back to writing.
- **Set modest goals** (a paragraph, not the whole document) **and reward yourself for reaching them.**

## Summary of Learning Objectives

- Processes that help writers write well include expecting to revise the first draft, writing regularly, modifying the initial task if it's too hard or too easy, having clear goals, knowing many different strategies, using rules as guidelines rather than as absolutes, and waiting to edit until after the draft is complete. **(LO 4-1)**
- Spend a third of your time planning, a third writing, and a third revising. **(LO 4-2)**
- To think of ideas, try brainstorming, **freewriting** (writing without stopping for 10 minutes or so), and **clustering** (brainstorming with circled words on a page). **(LO 4-3)**
- Planning, writing, and revising can include analyzing, gathering, writing, evaluating, getting feedback, revising, editing, and proofreading. **Revising** means changing the document to make it better satisfy the writer's purposes and the audience. **Editing** means making surface-level changes that make the document grammatically correct. **Proofreading** means checking to be sure the document is free from typographical errors. **(LO 4-4)**
- If the writing situation is new or difficult, plan to revise the draft at least three times. The first time, look for content and clarity. The second time, check the organization and layout. Finally, check style and tone. **(LO 4-4)**
- Grammar checkers and spell-checkers only catch some errors. Be sure to also check documents manually. **(LO 4-5)**
- You can improve the quality of the feedback you get by telling people which aspects of a draft you'd like comments about. If a reader criticizes something, fix the problem. If you think the reader misunderstood you, try to figure out what caused the misunderstanding and revise the draft so that the reader can see what you meant. **(LO 4-6)**
- If you get feedback you don't understand, paraphrase, ask for more information, or test your inference. **(LO 4-6)**
- If you get feedback you don't agree with, check against a grammar book for grammar issues, consider something could be improved if the comment is about content, show the reader where any disputed facts came from, try another option if the suggestion is about wording, or make information more clear if readers are confused. **(LO 4-6)**
- **Boilerplate** is language from a previous document that a writer includes in a new document. Using form letters and boilerplate can encourage writers to see as identical situations and audiences that in fact differ. Putting boilerplate into a new document can create incompatible styles and tones. **(LO 4-7)**
- To overcome writer's block, **(LO 4-8)**
  1. Participate actively in the organization and the community.
  2. Follow a regimen. Practice writing regularly and in moderation.
  3. Learn as many strategies as you can.
  4. Talk positively to yourself.
  5. Talk about writing to other people.
- To overcome the tendency to procrastinate, modify your behavior to reward yourself for the activities that lead to writing. **(LO 4-8)**

## Assignments for Module 4

### Questions for Comprehension

**4.1** What processes do expert writers use? **(LO 4-1)**

**4.2** How is revision different from editing? From proofreading? **(LO 4-4)**

**4.3** What are good strategies for overcoming writer's block? Procrastination? **(LO 4-8)**

### Questions for Critical Thinking

**4.4** Which processes that expert writers use do you already use? How could you modify your process to incorporate at least one more on the list? **(LO 4-1)**

**4.5** Of the people who have seen your writing, which one(s) have given you the most useful feedback? What makes it useful? **(LO 4-6)**

**4.6** In which areas are you best at giving feedback to other people? How could you make your feedback even better? **(LO 4-6)**

**4.7** Think about the form letters you have received. How do they make you feel? If they have flaws, how could they be improved? **(LO 4-7)**

### Exercises and Problems

**4.8 Interviewing Writers about Their Composing Processes (LO 4-1)**

Interview someone about the composing process(es) he or she uses for on-the-job writing. Questions you could ask include the following:

- What kind of planning do you do before you write? Do you make lists? Formal or informal outlines?
- When you need more information, where do you get it?
- How do you compose your drafts? Do you dictate? Draft with pen and paper? Compose on screen? How do you find uninterrupted time to compose?
- When you want advice about style, grammar, and spelling, what source(s) do you consult?
- Does your superior ever read your drafts and make suggestions?

- Do you ever work with other writers to produce a single document? Describe the process you use.
- Describe the process of creating a document where you felt the final document reflected your best work.
- Describe the process of creating a document that you found difficult or frustrating. What sorts of things make writing easier or harder for you?

*As Your Instructor Directs,*

a. Share your results orally with a small group of students.
b. Present your results in an oral presentation to the class.
c. Present your results in a memo to your instructor.
d. Post an e-mail message to the class discussing your results.
e. Share your results with a small group of students and write a joint memo reporting the similarities and differences you found.

**4.9 Analyzing Your Own Writing Processes (LO 4-1)**

Save your notes and drafts from several assignments so that you can answer the following questions.

- Which of the activities discussed in Module 4 do you use?
- How much time do you spend on each activity?
- What kinds of revisions do you make most often?
- Do you use different processes for different documents, or do you have one process that you use most of the time?
- Which practices of good writers do you follow?
- What parts of your process seem most successful? Are there any places in the process that could be improved? How?
- What relation do you see between the process(es) you use and the quality of the final document?

*As Your Instructor Directs,*

a. Discuss your process with a small group of other students.
b. Write a memo to your instructor analyzing in detail your process for composing one of the papers for this class.
c. Write a memo to your instructor analyzing your process during the term. What parts of your process(es) have stayed the same throughout the term? What parts have changed?

**4.10 Checking Spell and Grammar Checkers (LO 4-5)**

Each of the following paragraphs contains errors in grammar, spelling, and punctuation. Which errors does your spelling or grammar checker catch? Which errors does it miss? Does it flag as errors any words that are correct?

1. Answer to an Inquiry

   Think yoo fur your rescind request about are "Bitter Burger" campaign. We initiated thee champagne after hiring from customers who said they wonted a moor nutritious berger from our companion. Sew, we towed hour chiefs to devise something. And they. Did. To kelp you enjoin your "Better Booger" even mare, here hour to coupons for a free drank wit any purchase off a sandwitch and frie.

2. Performance Appraisal

   This quarterly perform appraise is. Four lisa. She have a good quart, witch ending with a 22 percent in crease in here sales for the three month. In fax Lissa outperform aviary one in her compartment. Lisa is a good employment, often straying late or working threw the weekends. Her dedication is great? Won of her peers, said "She is a la mode salesperson and a goon coat working."

3. Brochure

   Thin Lost Vegans is lonely a place to gambling! Thank again? There is mooch to do do in Las Vega for families to, such as them parks, magic shoes, and sporting. Events. Ewe cane also experience fin dining and tours of the surrendering desert with it's bootyful florid and fawna. The warm colors of the dessert well stay with your four many years two come. Visited Las Vegetables for a vacate of a. Lifeboat. Time.

4. Presentation Slides

   How **to Crate a Web résumé**

   - Omit home addressee and phone numb
   - Use other links only if the help a employer evaluate ewe.

   A. be Professionally!
   B. Carelessly craft and proof read the phrase on the index pager.

   **Cow to Create a Scanable Resume**

   - Crate a "plane vanilla' document.
   - Use include a Keywords" section. Include personality trades as will as accomplishments.
   - Be specific aunt Quantifiable.

**4.11 Giving and Evaluating Feedback (LO 4-6)**

In a group with other students, use the Checklist for Thorough Revision in Figure 4.4 to provide feedback on drafts of letters or memos for this course.

As you give feedback, answer the following questions:

- When you give feedback, do you normally start by looking for places to add, delete, substitute, or change? Or do you normally start by looking for grammatical errors and typos?
- On which aspects is it easiest for you to comment? Which aspects require more thought? Why?
- How many times do you have to read the draft to answer all of the questions in the Checklist?
- Do you tend to suggest mostly big changes, mostly small ones, or a mix?
- How do you tend to word your comments? Are they mostly positive or mostly negative? Do you tend to

describe your reaction as a reader, identify why a change is needed, name the change needed, make the change for the writer, or what?

When you read feedback from others, answer the following questions:

- Which comments were new information to you? Which told you something about your draft that you already knew or suspected?
- Did you have any questions that comments did not address?
- What kinds of feedback were most helpful to you? Why?
- Were any comments unclear? Talk to the commenter, and try to figure out what wording would have been clearer to you.
- Did any comments annoy or offend you? Why? Could the commenter have made the same point in a better way?

*As Your Instructor Directs,*

a. Share your answers with other students in your group. Discuss ways that each of you can make your future feedback even more useful.
b. Organize your answers in a memo to your instructor.

## Polishing Your Prose

### Using Spell and Grammar Checkers

Most word-processing programs come with spell and grammar checkers. While these computer tools can be useful, remember that they have limitations.

Spellcheckers identify words that don't match their dictionary. If the word is a real word, the spellchecker can't tell if it's the right word for the context (e.g., "their" versus "there," as in "We will review the report when we get their.").

Grammar checkers only suggest possible errors and solutions; you must make the final decision. That is, a grammar checker may tell you that you've used passive voice, but the checker can't tell you whether the passive is appropriate in that particular sentence.

Therefore, use spell and grammar checkers as one of several tools to make your writing better. In addition, keep a dictionary, thesaurus, and stylebook handy. Work to improve your command of spelling and grammar; take a class or work with a college writing center for help.

**Exercises**

Type the following into your word processor. Are all the words or constructions that show up as errors really wrong? Are there any errors that don't show up?

1. There report notes fore markets wear increased prophets are passable.
2. Even if ewe posses the rite skulls, lending the job you wont cane be trickily.
3. Ill chick with the mangers to fine out if they're employs fell hoppy with there compensated.
4. Quit a phew organisms have a bored of directors that overseas howl the organism operates.
5. Tree investors axed if wee mite consider celling are products inline.
6. Sharon tolled us that thee purchase requests should bee reviewed at lest too thymes before making then.
7. Mike twitted a massage abut the sails kickoff planed for the fiftieth of Augusta.
8. Whale sum people thank a lack of compliants is the same thing as doing will, a true sine of succession is grater market shore.
9. Hour facts machine heartily gets used any moor, butt its steel an imported peace of offense equipment.
10. Win Jenny decided too weight four confirmation from the prediction staph, she maid a whys incision—ant saved this busyness money!

**Check your answers to the odd-numbered exercises at the back of the book.**

# Freel

Reading 1-1

# Value Shift

Lynn Sharp Paine

Business has changed dramatically in the past few decades. Advances in technology, increasing globalization, heightened competition, shifting demographics—these have all been documented and written about extensively. Far less notice has been given to another, more subtle, change—one that is just as remarkable as these more visible developments. What I have in mind is the attention being paid to values in many companies today.

When I began doing research and teaching about business ethics in the early 1980s, skepticism about this subject was pervasive. Many people, in business and in academia, saw it as either trivial or altogether irrelevant. Some saw it as a joke. A few were even hostile. The whole enterprise, said critics, was misguided and based on a naïve view of the business world. Indeed, many had learned in their college economics courses that the market is amoral.

Back then, accepted wisdom held that "business ethics" was a contradiction in terms. People joked that an MBA course on this topic would be the shortest course in the curriculum. At that time, bookstores offered up volumes with titles like *The Complete Book of Wall Street Ethics* consisting entirely of blank pages. The most generous view was that business ethics had something to do with corporate philanthropy, a topic that might interest executives *after* their companies became financially successful. But even then, it was only a frill—an indulgence for the wealthy or eccentric.

Today, attitudes are different. Though far from universally embraced—witness the scandals of 2001 and 2002—ethics is increasingly viewed as an important corporate concern. What is our purpose? What do we believe in? What principles should guide our behavior? What do we owe one another and the people we deal with—our employees, our customers, our investors, our communities? Such classic questions of ethics are being taken seriously in many companies around the world, and not just by older executives in large, established firms. Managers of recently privatized firms in transitional economies, and even some far-sighted high-technology entrepreneurs, are also asking these questions.

Ethics, or what has sometimes been called "moral science," has been defined in many ways—"the science of values," "the study of norms," "the science of right conduct," "the science of obligation," "the general inquiry into what is good." In all these guises, the subject matter of ethics has made its way onto management's agenda. In fact, a succession of definitions have come to the forefront as a narrow focus on norms of right and wrong has evolved into a much broader interest in organizational values and culture. Increasingly, we hear that values, far from being irrelevant, are a critical success factor in today's business world.

The growing interest in values has manifested itself in a variety of ways. In recent years, many managers have launched ethics programs, values initiatives, and cultural change programs in their companies. Some have created corporate ethics offices or board-level ethics committees. Some have set up special task forces to address issues such as conflicts of interest, corruption, or electronic data privacy. Others have introduced educational programs to heighten ethical awareness and help employees integrate ethical considerations into their decision processes. Many have devoted time to defining or revising their company's business principles, corporate values, or codes of conduct. Still others have carried out systematic surveys to profile their company's values and chart their evolution over time.

A survey of U.S. employees conducted in late 1999 and early 2000 found that ethics guidelines and training were widespread. About 79 percent of the respondents said their company had a set of written ethics guidelines, and 55 percent said their company offered some type of ethics training, up from 33 percent in 1994. Among those employed by organizations with more than 500 members, the proportion was 68 percent.

Another study—this one of 124 companies in 22 countries—found that corporate boards were becoming more active in setting their companies' ethical standards. More than three-quarters (78 percent) were involved in 1999, compared to 41 percent in 1991 and 21 percent in 1987. Yet another study found that more than 80 percent of the *Forbes* 500 companies that had adopted values statements, codes of conduct, or corporate credos had created or revised these documents in the 1990s.

During this period, membership in the Ethics Officer Association, the professional organization of corporate ethics officers, grew dramatically. At the beginning of 2002, this group had 780 members, up from 12 at its founding 10 years earlier. In 2002, the association's roster included ethics officers from more than half the *Fortune* 100.

More companies have also undertaken efforts to strengthen their reputations or become more responsive to the needs and interests of their various constituencies. The list of initiatives seems endless. Among the most prominent have been initiatives on diversity, quality, customer service, health and safety, the environment, legal compliance, professionalism, corporate culture, stakeholder engagement, reputation management, corporate identity, cross-cultural management, work–family balance, sexual harassment, privacy, spirituality, corporate citizenship, cause-related marketing, supplier conduct, community involvement, and human rights. A few companies have even begun to track and report publicly on their performance in some of these areas. For a sampling of these initiatives, see Reading figure 1.1.

To aid in these efforts, many companies have turned to consultants and advisors, whose numbers have increased accordingly. A few years ago, *BusinessWeek* reported that ethics consulting had become a billion-dollar business. Though perhaps somewhat exaggerated, the estimate covered only a few segments of the industry, mainly misconduct prevention and investigation, and did not include corporate culture and values consulting or consulting focused in areas such as diversity, the environment, or reputation management. Nor did it include the public relations and crisis management consultants who are increasingly called on to help companies handle values-revealing crises and controversies such as product recalls, scandals, labor disputes, and environmental disasters. Thirty or 40 years ago, such consultants were a rare breed, and many of these consulting areas did not exist at all. Today, dozens of firms—perhaps hundreds, if we count law firms and the numerous consultants specializing in specific issue areas—offer companies expertise in handling these matters. Guidance from nonprofits is also widely available.

## What's Going On?

A thoughtful observer might well ask "What's going on?" Why the upsurge of interest in ethics and values? Why have companies become more attentive to their stakeholders and more concerned about the norms that guide their own behavior? In the course of my teaching, research, and consulting over the past two decades, I have interacted with executives and managers from many parts of the world. In discussing these questions with them, I have learned that their motivating concerns are varied:

- An Argentine executive sees ethics as integral to transforming his company into a "world-class organization."
- A group of Thai executives wants to protect their company's reputation for integrity and social responsibility from erosion in the face of intensified competition.
- A U.S. executive believes that high ethical standards are correlated with better financial performance.
- An Indian software company executive sees his company's ethical stance as important for building customer trust and also for attracting and retaining the best employees and software professionals.
- A Chinese executive believes that establishing the right value system and serving society are key components in building a global brand.
- The executives of a U.S. company see their efforts as essential to building a decentralized organization and entrepreneurial culture around the world.
- Two Nigerian entrepreneurs want their company to become a "role model" for Nigerian society.
- A Swiss executive believes the market will increasingly demand "social compatibility."
- An Italian executive wants to make sure his company stays clear of the scandals that have embroiled others.

**READING FIGURE 1.1 Values in Transition**

| CORPORATE INITIATIVES—A SAMPLER | | |
|---|---|---|
| COMPREHENSIVE (APPLYING TO ALL ACTIVITIES AND FUNCTIONS) | *Internally Oriented:* | Ethics programs<br>Compliance programs<br>Mission and values initiatives<br>Business principles initiatives<br>Business practices initiatives<br>Culture-building initiatives<br>Cross-cultural management programs<br>Crisis prevention and readiness |
| | *Externally Oriented:* | Reputation management programs<br>Corporate identity initiatives<br>Corporate brand-building initiatives<br>Stakeholder engagement activities<br>Societal alignment initiatives<br>Nonfinancial-performance reporting initiatives |
| FOCUSED (APPLYING TO PARTICULAR ISSUES OR CONSTITUENCIES) | *Employee Oriented:* | Diversity initiatives<br>Sexual harassment programs<br>Work–family initiatives<br>Workplace environment initiatives |
| | *Customer Oriented:* | Product and service quality initiatives<br>Customer service initiatives<br>Product safety initiatives<br>Cause-related marketing |
| | *Supplier Oriented:* | Supplier conduct initiatives |
| | *Investor Oriented:* | Corporate governance initiatives |
| | *Community Oriented:* | Environmental initiatives<br>Corporate citizenship initiatives<br>Community involvement initiatives<br>Strategic philanthropy |
| | *Issue Oriented:* | Electronic privacy<br>Human rights initiatives<br>Anticorruption programes<br>Biotechnology issues |

- A U.S. executive believes that a focus on ethics and values is necessary to allow his company to decentralize responsibility while pursuing aggressive financial goals.
- A U.S. executive answers succinctly and pragmatically, "*60 Minutes*."

These responses suggest that the turn to values is not a simple phenomenon. Individual executives have their own particular reasons for tackling this difficult and sprawling subject. Even within a single company, the reasons often differ and tend to change over time. A company may launch an ethics initiative in the aftermath of a scandal for purposes of damage control or as part of a legal settlement. Later on, when the initiative is no longer necessary for these reasons, a new rationale may emerge.

This was the pattern at defense contractor Martin Marietta (now Lockheed Martin), which in the mid-1980s became one of the first U.S. companies to establish what would later come to be called an "ethics program." At the time, the entire defense industry was facing harsh criticism for practices collectively referred to as "fraud, waste, and abuse," and Congress was considering new legislation to curb these excesses. The immediate catalyst for Martin Marietta's program, however, was the threat of being barred from government contracting because of improper billing practices in one of its subsidiaries.

According to Tom Young, the company president in 1992, the ethics program began as damage control. "When we went into this program," he explained, "we didn't anticipate the changes it would bring about. . . . Back then, people would have said, 'Do you really need an ethics program to be ethical?' Ethics was something personal, and you either had it or you didn't. Now that's all changed. People recognize the value." By 1992, the ethics effort was no longer legally required, but the program was continued nonetheless. However, by then it had ceased to be a damage control measure and was justified in terms of its business benefits: problem avoidance, cost containment, improved constituency relationships, enhanced work life, and increased competitiveness.

A similar evolution in thinking is reported by Chumpol NaLamlieng, CEO of Thailand's Siam Cement Group. Although Siam Cement's emphasis on ethics originated in a business philosophy rather than as a program of damage control, Chumpol recalls the feeling he had as an MBA student—that "ethics was something to avoid lawsuits and trouble with the public, not something you considered a way of business and self-conduct." Today, he says, "We understand corporate culture and environment and see that good ethics leads to a better company."

Siam Cement, one of the first Thai companies to publish a code of conduct, put its core values into writing in 1987 so they "would be more than just words in the air," as one executive explains. In 1994, shortly after the company was named Asia's "most ethical" in a survey conducted by *Asian Business* magazine, Chumpol called for a thorough review of the published code. The newly appointed CEO wanted to make sure that the document remained an accurate statement of the company's philosophy and also to better understand whether the espoused values were a help or hindrance in the more competitive environment of the 1990s. In 1995, the company reissued the code in a more elaborate form but with its core principles intact. The review had revealed that while adhering to the code did in some cases put the company at a competitive disadvantage, it was on balance a plus. For example, it helped attract strong partners and employees and also positioned the company, whose largest shareholder was the Thai monarchy's investment arm, as a leader in the country.

A very different evolution in thinking is reported by Azim Premji, chairman of Wipro Ltd., one of India's leading exporters of software services and, at the height of the software boom in 2000, the country's largest company in terms of market capitalization. Wipro's reputation for high ethical standards reflects a legacy that began with Premji's father, M.H. Hasham Premji, who founded the company in 1945 to make vegetable oil. The elder Premji's value system was based on little more than personal conviction—his sense of the right way to do things. Certainly it did not come from a careful calculation of business costs and benefits. In fact, his son noted, "It made no commercial sense at the time."

When his father died in 1966, Azim Premji left Stanford University where he was an undergraduate to assume responsibility for the then-family-owned enterprise. As he sought to expand into new lines of business, Premji found himself repeatedly having to explain why the company was so insistent on honesty when it was patently contrary to financial interest. Over time, however, he began to realize that the core values emphasized by his father actually made for good business policy. They imposed a useful discipline on the company's activities while also helping it attract quality employees, minimize transaction costs, and build a good reputation in the marketplace. In 1998, as part of an effort to position Wipro as a leading supplier of software services to global corporations, the company undertook an intensive self-examination and market research exercise. The result was a reaffirmation and rearticulation of the core values and an effort to link them more closely with the company's identity in the marketplace.

Managers' reasons for turning to values often reflect their company's stage of development. Executives of large, well-established companies typically talk about *protecting* their company's reputation or its brand, whereas entrepreneurs are understandably more likely to talk about *building* a reputation or *establishing* a brand. For skeptics who wonder whether a struggling start-up can afford to worry about values, Scott Cook, the founder of software maker Intuit, has a compelling answer. In his view, seeding a company's culture with the right values is "the most powerful thing you can do." "Ultimately," says Cook, "[the culture] will become more important to the success or failure of your company than you are. The culture you establish will guide and teach all your people in all their decisions."

In addition to company size and developmental stage, societal factors have also played a role in some managers' turn to values. For example, executives in the United States are more likely than those who operate principally in emerging markets to cite reasons related to the law or the media. This is not surprising, considering the strength of these two institutions in American society and their relative weakness in many emerging-markets countries. Since many ethical standards are upheld and reinforced through the legal system, the linkage between ethics and law is a natural one for U.S. executives. In other cases, executives offer reasons that mirror high-profile issues facing their industries or countries at a given time—issues such as labor shortages, demographic change, corruption, environmental problems, and unemployment. Antonio Mosquera, for example, launched a values initiative at Merck Sharp & Dohme Argentina as part of a general improvement program he set in motion after being named managing director in 1995. Mosquera emphasized, however, that promoting corporate ethics was a particular priority for him because corruption was a significant issue in the broader society.

Despite the many ways executives explain their interest in values, we can see in their comments several recurring themes. Seen broadly, their rationales tend to cluster into four main areas:

- Reasons relating to *risk management*
- Reasons relating to *organizational functioning*
- Reasons relating to *market positioning*
- Reasons relating to *civic positioning*

A fifth theme, somewhat less salient but nevertheless quite important for reasons we will come back to later, has to do with the idea simply of "a better way." For some, the rationale lies not in some further benefit or consequence they are seeking to bring about but rather in the inherent worth of the behavior they are trying to encourage. In other words, the value of the behavior resides principally in the behavior itself. For these executives, it is just *better*—full stop—for companies to be honest, trustworthy, innovative, fair, responsible, or good citizens. No further explanation is necessary any more than further explanation is required to justify the pursuit of self-interest or why more money is better than less.



the popular of social media and transparency.

CHAPTER 2

# What the Best Business Leaders Do Best

Anthony J. Rucci

Who's the most effective business leader you can think of in the 20th century? Is it Alfred Sloan of General Motors, John D. Rockefeller of Standard Oil, Henry Ford of Ford Motor Co., Thomas Watson of IBM, Jack Welch of General Electric, or maybe Bill Gates of Microsoft?

Over the past 50 years, the topic of leadership has been a focus among I/O psychologists (Yukl & Van Fleet, 1992). It is easily among the most studied and written-about areas in organizational research. And it's not just psychologists who have focused on the leadership issue. Popular culture, more than ever, seems to be obsessed with the personality and charisma of leaders, whether in business, government, religion, philanthropy, or even sports. The fascination with leaders has been evident in the annals of written history—the heroic, visionary individual who inspires others to achieve more than they conceived themselves capable of achieving, as in Homer's *Iliad* and *Odyssey*, *The Song of Beowulf*, the Bible!

The discussion to follow is about what it takes to be an effective executive in a for-profit enterprise. Do we also expect business executives to be leaders? I suppose we do. It's certainly safe to say that the most effective business executives will typically display many of the traits that would be necessary to be a leader in other contexts. But that may be too simplistic a notion. Consider the diagram in Figure 2.1. With a few moments of thought, it's actually

**Figure 2.1. The Hybrid Model of the Effective Business Leader.**

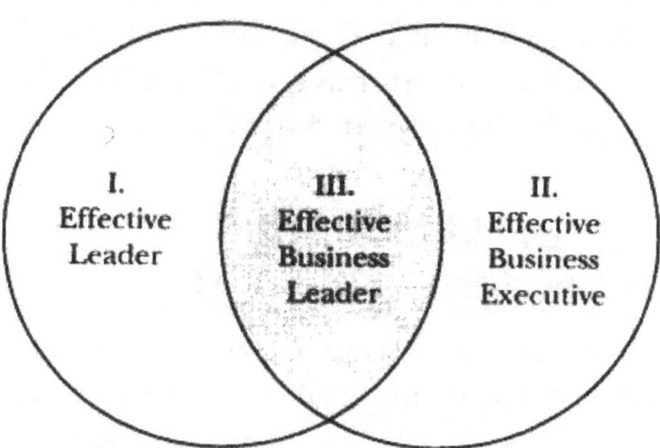


quite easy to think of examples of individuals who might fit the definition of an effective business executive, but not necessarily an effective leader. And there are certainly just as many examples of effective leaders who would be poor business executives. Lastly, there are those individuals who meet both definitions.

Take Group I, the Effective Leader Group. Few would debate that 20th-century leaders like Mother Teresa, Martin Luther King Jr., Lec Walesa, Caesar Chavez, Michael Jordan, or Jack Welch have demonstrated profound personal leadership influence. Would each of these leaders also have been effective business executives? We know Welch is, and we probably don't question Jordan's ability to do practically anything. But as for the others, you could probably generate a serious debate.

How about Group II, the Effective Business Executive who may not be an effective leader? Any list of effective business executives in the 20th century would have to include the names of successful entrepreneurs, venture capitalists, investment bankers, and inventors. That is, of the people who have created enormous economic value for themselves and others, but who would be leadership disasters in large, for-profit enterprises.

So who are the best business executives? For purposes of this discussion, they're the Group III individuals in Figure 2.1, the Business Leaders. These individuals cannot only achieve success as business executives but also meet the criteria for effective leadership. They cannot only create and sustain *economically* viable enterprises and generate acceptable economic returns for the owners of the enterprise, they can also create and sustain *socially* viable enterprises and cause others to voluntarily choose to follow their vision. In that sense, effective business leadership is a special category or subset of effective leadership. That's the group to be treated through the remainder of this discussion.

## Who Decides What a Good Business Leader Looks Like?

Given that the leadership and executive effectiveness literature is so rich and robust, it might seem simple to define the criteria for being a good business leader. Just review the research literature, maybe perform some meta-analytic exercises, and you've got the answer. That approach is expressly avoided through the remainder of this discussion. No longitudinal studies will be cited and no prominent authors or researchers on the topic will be quoted. Instead, this largely (and admittedly) anecdotal discussion relies on a blend of research literature, personal experience, and simple observation of business executives.

A fundamental assumption being made is that setting the criteria for defining an effective business leader is largely an exercise in *emergent* leadership. When the board of directors appoints someone to a leadership role, that doesn't necessarily mean that the individual is a business leader, or at least an effective executive. When a business magazine puts someone on the cover, it doesn't mean that the person is a business leader. In fact, the best operational definition of a good business leader invariably comes from people in individual contributor roles in an organization. If you want to know who the best business leaders in your organization are, go ask your employees. They know. And they also know who your weakest business leaders are, even when your board of directors may not know. Too often, we fail to ask the people who know best what and who an effective leader is.

A business leader—whether chief executive officer, chief operating officer, chief financial officer, or executive vice president—is defined here as an individual whose peers and subordinates would *choose* to follow and support even if they weren't required to do so. It's the business executive who inspires commitment from others. The one who causes others in the organization to want to be part of the event, and makes them want to contribute their discretionary energy and ideas to the business leader and the enterprise. It's the business leader who evokes support for the vision based on three things:

- *Who* they are
- The *traits* they possess
- The *practices* they establish

Our focus here is the best-of-the-best. Many business executives perform adequately. The intent here is to isolate those things that seem to distinguish the outstanding business leader from the average business executive. What do the best business leaders do best?

## Who They Are

Exceptional business leaders seem to have three things in common . . . the Three P's: passion, performance, and principle. Figure 2.2 reflects a brief description of these Three P's. These factors seem to characterize the best business leaders today—the ones who inspire commitment from those around them.

### *Passion*

Exceptional business leaders have a passion for what they do every day. When the alarm goes off at 5:30 A.M., their waking thought is to want to be there as soon as they can, to make something happen. It's the passion you routinely sense in a true entrepreneur—someone who does for a living what they'd do for free if they had to. And the passion is palpable and contagious to others. Ask exceptional business leaders what they do for a living and you can visibly see their affect level change. Their energy level rises as they talk; you can feel their enthusiasm.

The passion is there whether they're the chief executive officer, the corporate treasurer, or the senior human resource executive in the organization. The chief executive officer's passion may be channeled into building the most competitive enterprise in the

**Figure 2.2. Exceptional Business Leaders: Who They Are.**

| The Three P's | Exceptional Business Leaders . . . |
|---|---|
| Passion | • Have a personal passion for what they do. They'd continue to do it if they were independently wealthy. They'd also continue to do it if they were compensated very little. |
| Performance | • They hate to lose. They keep score, and they set high standards. As much as they enjoy winning, they hate losing even more. |
| Principle | • Cheating to win doesn't count. When faced with a decision that puts profit ahead of principle, principle will always win. |

industry. The human resource executive's passion may be channeled into creating the highest level of commitment possible from the workforce. The treasurer's passion may be to execute a creative, elegant debt issuance of corporate bonds. The point here is that each has a personal interest and belief in the value of what they do every day. Too often, in large enterprises, we have "professional managers"—executives who go through the motions every day, adequately executing their assigned roles but lacking a fundamental belief or excitement in the intrinsic nature of their jobs. You rarely see an entrepreneur just going through the motions. The minute that begins to happen to entrepreneurs, they're on to the next big idea or venture.

It might appear that it takes a noble cause or ideology to evoke passion. That's really not the case. Believe it or not, there are business executives who are genuinely passionate about earning more profit, higher EBITDA, or 20-basis-point reductions in expenses. No matter how anyone else may view that individual, it's their passion. No value judgment need apply. It's whatever the individual relates to at a personal level, whatever gets the person's achievement motivation and self-esteem engaged. It can be profits, core ideology, or professional excellence. All the best business leaders have passion, and others can recognize it.

### *Performance*

Exceptional business leaders hate to lose. Coming in even second is distasteful to them. They keep score in obvious and not-so-obvious ways. They enjoy winning, but they hate losing even more. After all, losing not only reflects poorly on them, it makes them feel they've let their people down, too.

Being performance driven at a personal level manifests itself in a number of important ways. First, good business leaders set goals for themselves and others, and the goals are not easy. In fact, good business leaders typically will set goals for themselves that are far more challenging than either their manager or the organization would impose. And they write the goals down and measure progress against them. Second, good business leaders display a sense of urgency about results. Once a course of action is determined, they become immediately impatient to execute the decision and see the outcome. And third, good business leaders do not allow ineffective or even mediocre employees to remain with the organization. Other than personal breaches of ethics or trust, the quickest way for a business executive to lose credibility is to not confront poor performers. Poor performers are conspicuous to everyone else in the organization. Exceptional business executives are as demanding of others' performance as they are of their own. They are tough-minded in assessing poor performance, but compassionate in managing the individual.

### *Principle*

Generally speaking, popular culture and the media portray senior business executives as mercenary and overly concerned about shareholders. National surveys also show a substantial level of public distrust toward business executives, as well. Unfortunately, there are some highly publicized cases that reinforce that stereotype. Executive compensation packages, which have reached incomprehensible levels, haven't helped much either. The fact is, senior business executives as a group are no different from any other slice of the population one could identify. Some business executives are not highly principled people. Some will look the other way when confronted with a convenient ethical shortcut.

But the best business leaders *never* put profits ahead of principle. The best business leaders will always defer to their principles when faced with a business issue. *Business ethics* is not an oxymoron to good business leaders. This arena of principled behavior, or principled leadership, is probably the most critical way a business executive has of gaining or losing the commitment of people in the organization. When business executives take ethical shortcuts, even once, it calls into question their trustworthiness. People in an organization see it and immediately wonder what would happen if it ever became convenient for that executive to make an expedient decision at others' expense. It's an insidious thing that can destroy the level of trust throughout an organization.

The best business leaders hold themselves and others to high standards of professional and personal behavior. They help articulate and enforce the core values of the enterprise. And they have zero tolerance for out-of-bounds behavior when it comes to matters of integrity and ethics. The very best business leaders not only establish ethical boundaries for themselves, they also possess a keen sense of the moral obligation they have toward the people they employ. They have a felt need to create a sustainable economic enterprise that allows employees and their families to experience satisfying lives and rewarding careers.

## Why Do Some Executives Fail?

Before moving on to describe the traits that effective business leaders possess, it's important to ask a simple question: Why do some executives fail? It may seem out of sequence to be posing that question before completing a discussion of the traits and behaviors exhibited by good business leaders. The answer might seem obvious: executives fail when they don't possess the personal traits or practice the behaviors of effective business leaders (the ones to be described later). Unfortunately, it's usually not that simple.

Senior business executives who fail are rarely terminated for performance or skill set deficiencies. Think about it. Business executives who become chief executive officer, president, chief financial officer, or chief information officer of a major economic enterprise have usually demonstrated a consistent, sustained track record of achievement throughout their careers. Typically they've done quite well academically throughout their school years, including college and postgraduate work. (Yes, there are stunning exceptions to this assumption—Bill Gates of Microsoft or Larry Ellison of Oracle.) They've gone on to be effective at producing successful outcomes over a sustained period of time. They've established a reputation for being successful, dependable, and achievement-oriented. They've been promoted. Not just once, but six, eight, a dozen times in their careers before reaching the senior executive level in a major business enterprise. Could it possibly be that those promotions were all a mistake? That this person was really incompetent all along, and nobody recognized it? Highly unlikely.

Executives fail for one of three reasons, as shown in Figure 2.3. The overpromoted executive, typically promoted from within the firm, was a good or even excellent performer in prior assignments but simply does not possess the skills or traits necessary to perform at the senior executive level. As well-intentioned as the promotion decision was, the organization either failed to identify the criteria necessary for executive success or ignored them. Why would anyone ignore their own criteria? Typically out of a sense of obligation for prior contributions or as a reward for loyalty to the firm. This is a regrettable failure, since both the firm and the individual lose. The firm loses an otherwise competent contributor; the individual loses the fulfilling, rewarding career he or she enjoyed earlier.

The second type of failure results from an executive's inability to change. This individual has performed well in an executive-level assignment for some period of time, but fails to adapt to changing demands and conditions. Oftentimes this failure occurs after a merger or takeover by another firm. The executive fails to adapt to the new ownership's expectations, often seeming to regress to tried-and-true methods of success and overrelying on those behaviors even when it becomes obvious they aren't effective. Worse still, for the organization's sake, this failure also occurs when a successful executive begins to play it safe and defend his or her business position in the marketplace. The organization pays a significant price for this type of defensive behavior. It loses its competitiveness in the marketplace and begins a spiral of decline before the cause is identified. This is probably the single most nondiagnosed failure among business executives today.

**Figure 2.3. Why Some Business Executives Fail.**

| Cause | Description |
|---|---|
| A. Overpromoted | These individuals fail because the organization promoted them inappropriately. Their performance in prior jobs was good or excellent, but they simply didn't possess the new skill sets necessary to move to the executive level. This failure typically occurs when executives are promoted from within their current company out of a sense of obligation for past contributions or as a reward for loyalty. |
| B. Inability to Change | These are individuals who have performed well for some period of time in an executive level assignment, but who fail to adapt to change. They rely on their traditional skill set and behaviors when new ideas and behaviors are required. |
| C. Cultural Misfit | These are individuals who have all the required skills and management practices to be successful at the executive level, but there is simply a lack of fit between the individual and the culture or values of the organization. They are often executives recruited in from outside the organization. |

The third and perhaps most common reason business executives fail is a cultural misfit between the individual and the organization. It's the otherwise competent, successful executive who simply doesn't hold the same values as the rest of the executive management team. The individual who always seems just a little oblique to the tempo, rhythm, and conversation going on. Very often, this is an executive who is recruited from outside the organization with an otherwise exceptional résumé and track record. But all the interview and reference checks in the world will rarely allow for a reliable assessment of cultural fit with the organization's core values.

What is noteworthy about all three of the executive failure types described is that they rarely occur because of lapses in performance or competence. These heretofore successful individuals typically fail for intangible, subtle reasons. That's why traditional skills testing and psychological testing are not completely adequate to account for these qualitative factors.

## The Traits of Good Business Leaders

You could find hundreds of studies of traits necessary for executive success. In addition, every company has its own set of criteria, written down or not, and the research literature in I/O psychology is replete with studies on the subject (Bray, Campbell, & Grant, 1974; Bennis & Nanus, 1985; Bass, 1990). How important is intellectual ability to success as a business executive? Consideration and initiating structure were the big two factors to come out of the early I/O research on leadership effectiveness (Fleishman, 1953). And popular business publications are guaranteed to have at least one article in every issue describing "the critical characteristics" of an effective leader or executive.

Figure 2.4 lists the seven key traits the best business leaders seem to possess. This list is an attempt to capture the relevant research literature on the topic, as well as summarize the popular business literature. Most specifically, this list comes from observation of good business leaders over the years.

### *Business Acumen*

Business, like any profession, has components of science and art associated with it. The science of business is what one learns in college, and certainly in an MBA curriculum. The science is also learned by practicing the operational responsibilities of being a business manager.

In most professions, although understanding the science is a fundamental ingredient for success, it is those individuals who practice the art of the trade who typically excel. This is no less true in business. The term *business acumen* here refers to the art of being

**Figure 2.4. Seven Traits of Effective Business Leaders.**

1. *Business Acumen*
   Assesses the financial implications of decisions and actions. Understands how strategies and tactics work in the marketplace. Balances data analysis with good judgment and common sense.
2. *Customer Orientation*
   Understands who the customers are, how they are motivated, and the current and future business challenges they face. Demonstrates a strong bias toward service, quality, and customer satisfaction.
3. *Results Orientation*
   Stays the course from start to finish. Does not confuse effort with results. Separates what is important from what is not. Demonstrates a persistent bias for action. Is tough-minded in assessing performance.
4. *Strategic Thinking*
   Anticipates future trends and directional shifts in the relevant marketplace, industry, and environment. Able to construct meaningful competitive strategies for addressing the knowns and unknowns of future business scenarios.
5. *Innovation and Risk Taking*
   Willing to explore new possibilities and approach issues differently. Focuses on a desire to achieve a goal rather than a fear of failure. Views honest mistakes as an investment in better outcomes.
6. *Integrity*
   Has an uncomplicated and uncompromising understanding of right from wrong, both publicly and privately. Values a fair playing field for everyone, and demonstrates courage of conviction for personal belief.
7. *Interpersonal Maturity*
   Is other-oriented rather than focused on self. Listens effectively and communicates ideas and opinions clearly. Is assertive while showing respect and positive regard for others. Considers the consequences of personal actions and decisions. Takes a collaborative approach that brings out the best thinking, attitude, and performance in others.

a business executive. Business acumen does not mean the ability to read a profit-and-loss statement or to calculate return ratios from a balance sheet, although those skills are necessary. The best executives have business acumen as a result of having an in-depth understanding of three critical questions about the enterprise:

- Who is the enterprise's core customer?
- Who is the competition?
- What is a realistic assessment of the enterprise's competitive strengths and weaknesses?

Understanding one's core customer is a fundamental but often misunderstood ingredient of success. Many firms assume they know the answer. Good business leaders never assume they know for very long. They're constantly asking about the demographic profile and purchasing trends of their core customer, and they talk to customers frequently. Next, good business leaders are obsessed with their competition. They know how customers assess their competitors, and they attempt to anticipate each competitor's next move. Very often, good business leaders get to know the personality of their competitors at a personal level. They include an assessment of a competitor's personality when making key decisions. Finally, good business leaders are brutally objective about their own firm's strengths and weaknesses. They view their enterprise as it really is, not as they'd like it to be.

It should be noted that business acumen is a common trait of all good business leaders, not just chief executive officers. The best chief financial officers know the answers to the three questions, as do the best senior human resource executives and the best heads of quality affairs. No matter what functional role one holds as an executive, business acumen—understanding the art of business—is a key trait to be among the best business leaders.

### *Customer Orientation*

Customer orientation is another critical trait for good business leaders. Once they understand who the core customer is, they talk to those customers. They listen to what they say—both about their own company and also about the competition. They measure the customer's satisfaction with both product and service quality, and they take action.

At a personal level, good business leaders have a high sense of urgency about being responsive to customers. And they have a personal bias toward service. They'll pick up a phone if it's ringing. They'll get someone pointed in the right direction, and they'll interrupt what they're doing in favor of a customer's need.

### *Results Orientation*

People who finish what they start are results-oriented. They stay focused on the desired outcome, and they do not get diverted from the goal. Good business leaders possess this trait. They are personally action-oriented, and display a high sense of urgency about results. Most important, they do not confuse effort or activity with results. Results-oriented people get to the point when they are communicating, and they emphasize the outcomes of a situation: "We won the championship"—"I graduated with a 3.8 GPA"—"We increased earnings that year by 20 percent."

Good business leaders measure things and track their organization's progress. They hold themselves accountable for results, and they intervene when progress is delayed. They also hold others accountable for their performance, and they are tough-minded in assessing the performance of others.

### *Strategic Thinking*

As important as results are, good business leaders recognize the need to think about where the organization needs to be next month, next year, and next decade. Strategic thinking is much more than intellectual ability, although good intellectual ability in an executive never hurts. Strategic thinking has to do with abstract cognitive processes like pattern recognition, cognitive complexity, and tolerance for uncertainty. It is the ability to anticipate where markets are headed, and what the competition will do next.

Is strategic thinking the same as strategic planning? No. In fact, strategic planning processes in many organizations can actually constrain strategic thinking by forcing regimented approaches and disciplines to problem solving. Strategic thinking is an abstract reasoning process that is usually *not* linear or sequential. The most effective strategic thinkers are those who are intuitive as well as logical and fact-based.

### *Innovation and Risk Taking*

Good business leaders take risks. They perform excellent due diligence, they are detail-oriented on facts and figures, and they demand precision. But after all those prudent activities, they do not hesitate to make the leap of faith that no set of facts can ever solidify. They recognize the power of being first to market with an idea or product.

Good business leaders not only tolerate change well, they initiate change. They're actually afraid of the status quo, and are constantly pushing themselves and their organizations for the next new idea or product. Most important, good business leaders do not view mistakes born of prudent analysis as failures. Quite the contrary, mistakes are viewed as an investment in a better ultimate outcome. And, of course, risk taking requires a high tolerance for ambiguity.

### *Integrity*

Good business leaders meet all the traditional standards of integrity. They are honest and truthful. They are ethical, and they do not compromise themselves or their organizations. They don't cheat on travel expense vouchers. They don't use company resources for personal activities, and they don't ask secretaries to balance their checkbooks, pick up their laundry, or make family vacation travel arrangements.

In addition to these obvious indices of personal integrity, good business leaders ensure a fair playing field for others in the organization. They view their role as doing what's necessary to make others successful, not to catch others making mistakes. And last, good business leaders demonstrate courage of conviction for their ideas and behaviors. They state their opinions when they disagree, and they do not remain silent about issues in the organization. When something they've done or some idea they've had is not successful, they assume responsibility and do not look to place blame elsewhere.

### *Interpersonal Maturity*

Good business leaders have a healthy self-esteem and are assertive but not egocentric. They are other-oriented, and they listen to people. They show a genuine respect and regard for others, and they do not abuse the power their position authority could provide. They are as respectful and considerate of an hourly employee as they are of a board member or the chief executive officer.

Good business leaders take a collaborative approach with others. They do not feel the need to do all the talking and they resist imposing a solution on others. What does it take to be a good business leader of people? It boils down to the fundamentals. You say "good morning" when you come in each day. You say "thank you" when someone has done something on your behalf. You look at people when they are talking to you to ensure they know you're listening. This is hardly rocket science, but good business leaders recognize the power in caring about employees as people.

## The Practices of Good Business Leaders

Thus far, we've discussed who good business leaders are and what traits they possess. And while those elements must be present, they are not sufficient to create a good business leader. No matter how strong the personal traits, an executive who cannot introduce and sustain good practices will not be a good business leader.

So what practices exemplify good business leaders? Figure 2.5 shows the VOICE model. These five practices were identified by examining nearly 50 high-performance business enterprises (Rucci, Ulrich, & Gavino, 2000). The definition of "high performance" included criteria like superior five-year total shareholder return, high customer satisfaction ratings, and recognition as a superior place for people to work. The sample included organizations such as Cisco Systems, 3M, Southwest Airlines, Dell Computers, Harley Davidson, and the Mayo Clinic.

Business leaders in these high-performance organizations have introduced practices and organizational systems related to the VOICE components model. It's because of good business leaders that these processes and systems are sustained and improved. These practices have been shown to affect employee attitudes that are directly predictive of improved customer satisfaction, better profits, and superior total shareholder return (Rucci, Kirn, & Quinn, 1998; Schlesinger, 1994).

**Figure 2.5. Key Practices of Good Business Leaders: VOICE.**

| | | |
|---|---|---|
| V | Vision | Have a purpose and create a clear line of sight. |
| O | Opportunity | Evaluate and develop people obsessively. |
| I | Incentives | Reward results and let employees share the financial success. |
| C | Communication | Share information widely and listen. |
| E | Entrepreneurship | Promote innovation and risk taking. |

### *Vision*

Good business leaders identify and communicate the purpose for their enterprise. Purpose is not strategy. It is a much more fundamental reason why an enterprise is allowed to exist by its customers (Collins & Porras, 1996). Disney's purpose is not to operate theme parks, it is to make people happy. Merck's purpose is not to make pharmaceuticals, it is to preserve and improve human life. Good business leaders articulate their company's core purpose, and it becomes a clear, elevating goal for people to be proud of (LaFasto & Larson, 1989).

In addition, good business leaders clearly articulate the core values of an enterprise. Core values are the guiding principles of an organization. These are beliefs that would not change over time, even if the company's strategy changed. The beliefs are held for their *intrinsic* value, not because they help produce profits. Truly "core" values would be maintained even if they became a competitive disadvantage for a firm. And core values need not be the Boy Scout oath. Making a profit can be a core value, if it meets the test of intrinsic value.

Good business leaders proactively communicate the enterprise's purpose and core values. They talk about these things. Most important, they attempt to create a clear line of sight from each employee's job to the enterprise's purpose. Whether you're a fork lift operator or the chief executive officer, you should be able to come to work each day at 8 A.M. seeing the connection between what you do for eight hours and the purpose, goals, and values of your organization.

This vision practice was clearly the most common characteristic among the high-performance companies. One other key practice related to vision is critical. Good business leaders hold people accountable for both their results and their compliance with the core values. The best business leaders eliminate from the organization those employees who don't share the core values, even if they are competent performers.

### *Opportunity*

Good business leaders put systems in place to hire and develop the best people. And once they've hired good people, they give them meaningful work and decision-making authority, and they help them achieve balance between their work and personal lives.

Most important, good business leaders know the hiring template for success in their organizations. They develop criteria for executive success, and they use those criteria in disciplined selection and human resource planning systems. They are constantly assessing both performance and long-range potential, and they provide developmental opportunities for their employees. The very best business leaders spend as much of their time reviewing people as they do reviewing the financials of the company.

Good business leaders give people meaningful decision-making authority and they allow employees to act on their ideas. They give people managerial and profit-and-loss responsibility very early in their careers. And they allow people to balance work requirements with their personal lives and families.

### *Incentives*

Good business leaders understand that even though people don't work exclusively for compensation, effective incentive systems are still a key part of an organization's success. Incentive systems need to be simple and they must pass the clear-line-of-sight test proposed earlier. They must also be consistent with the culture and values of the enterprise.

Generally speaking, good business leaders establish incentive systems with the following features:

- Rewards are performance-based.
- Rewards are tied to goals that support the strategy.
- Both financial and nonfinancial results are rewarded.
- Financial rewards are shared broadly throughout the organization.
- Individual and team-based rewards are balanced.
- Nonfinancial rewards are used liberally.

To be performance-based, incentives must be contingent upon the organization achieving certain performance goals. Those performance thresholds should be tied directly to creating value for the owners of the enterprise. Meanwhile, key contributors in an enterprise should be owners, receiving a portion of their compensation in some form of equity in the firm.

Increasingly, good business leaders establish incentive systems that reward nonfinancial outcomes as well as financial results. For example, customer satisfaction, product quality, and employee attitudes are increasingly viewed as *leading indicators* or predictors of future financial performance of an enterprise. Incentive systems should reward people for improving these leading indicators, just as they reward profit performance.

Broadly sharing the success of an enterprise is a key consideration. Good business leaders push equity participation well down into an organization. Stock options and discount stock purchase plans are two valuable ways of doing so. Profit-sharing plans and gain-sharing techniques are also excellent ways to include a broad segment of people in the performance-based incentive.

The critical component in any incentive system is the clear-line-of-sight test. Individual and team goals should be established, and those goals should relate directly and simply to the organization's strategic objectives. An employee at any level in an organization should be able to see a clear connection between individual effort, organization goal achievement, and incentive rewards. Good business leaders create incentive systems that cause employees to see how their job and effort ultimately creates positive rewards for themselves and the owners of the enterprise.

### *Communication*

Perhaps the most overused word in management practices, *communication* is a hallmark of effective business leaders. First, good business leaders share and disseminate information broadly. Rather than hoard important information about financial performance and customers, they give people information to allow them to improve and do their jobs better. They do this through formal channels like newsletters and financial reports, but they are equally focused on informal channels like town hall meetings, staff meetings, or even hallway conversation. More than ever, people need information to do their jobs well. It's the executives in an organization who have access to the broadest amount of information. Good business leaders share information, and do it frequently and routinely.

The most overlooked and underutilized skill among business executives today is listening. Good business leaders listen to people at all levels in the organization. In fact, the best business leaders know that it takes conscious effort not to lose touch with people in large, complex organizations. They also know that politics and human dynamics cause others to be less than candid when talking to a senior executive. So good business leaders devise both formal and informal ways of staying in touch. They use employee surveys, but they also use the lunchroom to get a sense of the mood and concerns of employees. Employees at all levels in an organization know what their company does well and not so well. They also know when a company is in trouble. If business executives simply took the time to ask their own employees for impressions and ideas, they would learn a tremendous amount.

Though good business leaders communicate frequently, they recognize the importance and benefit of a simple, repeated message. In today's large, complex organizations, simplicity of key messages is a prerequisite to creating a clear line of sight for employees.

### *Entrepreneurship*

Good business leaders possess the personal traits of innovation and risk taking, but they also establish processes to promote those behaviors in others. Most directly, they involve people at all levels in creating strategy for the enterprise. That is, they actively engage in formal strategic planning efforts, but they also informally ask for ideas and suggestions. Good business leaders not only allow mistakes, they actually encourage mistakes.

Resource allocation in an organization is a critical process. Good business leaders do not "allocate" resources to their people, they create systems that allow the best ideas to "attract" resources (Hamel, 1999). The analogy here is the open-market economy we know as capitalism. Capital in an open market flows to those enterprises that create value better. There is no chief executive officer of the global economy who decides to invest 5 percent of global capital in General Electric stock and 8 percent in municipal bonds. Capital is a pull system, not a push system, and good business leaders try to create that same dynamic when allocating resources within their organization.

The five components of the VOICE model—Vision, Opportunity, Incentives, Communication, and Entrepreneurship—are practices of good organizations and good business leaders. Most important, these five practices evoke commitment from people in an organization. Good business leaders understand that employee commitment to the goals and values of the enterprise is the seminal ingredient to creating value for the organization and its owners.

## Summary

What do the best business leaders do best? That was the question posed at the outset of this discussion. I have tried to answer that question by defining the best business leaders as those who can create and sustain both economically and socially viable enterprises.

Figure 2.6 summarizes the answers to the three dimensions of effective business leaders—who they are, what traits they possess, and what practices they establish.

The definition of good business leaders has changed over the past 10 years—dramatically. Figure 2.6 reflects that change. For much of the 20th century, good business leaders displayed a militaristic, command-and-control style. The executives in an organization possessed *the* information and they were expected to have *the* answers. We have entered an explosive information-driven economic era. In today's complex, global enterprises, the best business leaders recognize that no one mortal individual can know everything necessary to run a successful organization. Giving peo-

**Figure 2.6. What the Best Business Leaders Do Best.**

| | |
|---|---|
| *Who* they are | The Three P's:<br>• Passion<br>• Performance<br>• Principle |
| What *traits* they possess | The Seven Key Traits:<br>• Business Acumen<br>• Customer Orientation<br>• Results Orientation<br>• Strategic Thinking<br>• Innovation and Risk Taking<br>• Integrity<br>• Interpersonal Maturity |
| What *practices* they establish | The Five VOICE Practices:<br>• Vision<br>• Opportunity<br>• Incentives<br>• Communication<br>• Entrepreneurship |

ple a voice in an enterprise and gaining their commitment distinguishes the very best business leaders today from those business executives who are still going through the motions. Is it more demanding on the individual business executive to do the things reflected in Figure 2.6? Yes. It is much easier to be a command-and-control business leader who tells others what to do. But good business leaders recognize the value in the protocol outlined here. They also recognize that demanding though it may be, it's not rocket science.

## References

Bass, B. M. (1990). *Bass & Stogdill's handbook of leadership: Theory, research and managerial applications* (3rd ed.). New York: Free Press.

Bennis, W. G., & Nanus, B. (1985). *Leaders: The strategies for taking charge.* New York: HarperCollins.

Bray, D. W., Campbell, R. J., & Grant, D. L. (1974). *Formative years in business: A long-term AT&T study of managerial lives.* New York: Wiley.

Collins, J. C., & Porras, J. I. (1996). Building your company's vision. *Harvard Business Review, 74*(5), 65–77.

Fleishman, E. A. (1953). The description of supervisory behavior. *Personnel Psychology, 37,* 1–6.

Hamel, G. (1999). Bringing Silicon Valley inside. *Harvard Business Review,* 77(5), 70–84.

LaFasto, F. M., & Larson, C. E. (1989). *Team work* (Vol. 10). Thousand Oaks, CA: Sage.

Rucci, A., Kirn, S., & Quinn, R. (1998). The Employee-customer-profit chain at Sears. *Harvard Business Review, 76*(1), 82–97.

Rucci, A., Ulrich, D., & Gavino, M. (2000). *The VOICE Model.* Unpublished manuscript.

Schlesinger, L. (1994). Putting the service-profit chain to work. *Harvard Business Review,* 72(2), 164–174.

Yukl, G., & Van Fleet, D. (1992). Theory and research on leadership in organizations. In M. Dunnette & L. Hough (Eds.) *Handbook of Industrial & Organizational Psychology,* pp. 147–197. Palo Alto, CA: Consulting Psychologists Press.

Mary C. Gentile, PhD, Director
www.GivingVoicetoValues.org

**Giving *Voice* to Values**

# Exercise: A Tale of Two Stories

In your lives thus far, you have likely encountered situations at school, with friends, in jobs or clubs, when your values conflicted with what you were asked to do. Often it is not easy to align your own personal values and purpose with those of your classmates, co-workers, friends, etc. This exercise is designed to help you identify and develop the competencies necessary to achieve that alignment.

***Objectives***

1. To reflect on your previous experiences, successful and less so, at effectively voicing and acting on your values in your lives.
2. To discover which conditions and problem definitions empower you to effectively voice your values, and which tend to inhibit that action.

***Instructions*[1]*:***

*Part I*

- Recall a time in your experiences in a summer job, an internship, a student club, a student team project, etc. when your values[2] conflicted with what you were expected to do in a particular, non-trivial decision, and you spoke up and acted to resolve the conflict.
- Consider the following 4 questions and write down your thoughts and brief responses:
    - What did you do, and what was the impact?
    - What motivated you to speak up and act?
    - How satisfied are you? How would you like to have responded? (This question is not about rejecting or defending past actions but rather about imagining your Ideal Scenario.)
    - What would have made it easier for you to speak/act?
        - Things within your own control
        - Things within the control of others

[1] During this exercise, you are expressly cautioned not to violate any obligations of confidentiality that you may have.

[2] In this exercise, a "values conflict" refers to a disagreement that has an ethical dimension to it. That is, I might disagree with your idea about the best way to promote a new club or program , but there is usually not an ethical component to that decision. However, if one promotion plan was honest about the club or program's mission and the other wasn't, for example, even this disagreement might be appropriate here.

*Part II*

- Recall a time in your experiences in a summer job, an internship, a student club, a student team project, etc. when your values conflicted with what you were expected to do in a particular, non-trivial decision, and you did *not* speak up or act to resolve the conflict.
- Consider the following 4 questions and write down your thoughts and brief responses:
  - What happened?
  - Why didn't you speak up or act? What would have motivated you to do so?
  - How satisfied are you? How would you like to have responded? (This question is not about rejecting or defending past actions but rather about imagining your Ideal Scenario.)
  - What would have made it easier for you to speak/act?
    - Things within your own control
    - Things within the control of others

Last Revised: 07/01/2010

HARVARD | BUSINESS | SCHOOL

9-307-059
REV: MAY 15, 2007

# Ethics: A Basic Framework

Markets are sometimes described as "amoral," but market participants frequently make ethical judgments about the people and practices they encounter in the marketplace. Indeed, most market actors prefer doing business with companies and individuals they can trust, and few—at least in a free and open society—willingly submit to treatment they regard as unethical. Wronged, injured, slighted, or ignored, many will take their business elsewhere, and some will actively seek redress through the courts, media, legislature, or other channels. Some will even "reward" or "punish" companies for their conduct toward third parties—for example, investors who favor good corporate citizens or customers who shun human rights violators.

A growing body of research points to these and other links between ethics and performance. Researchers have found, for example, that greater creativity is associated with fair rewards, mutual helpfulness, and honest information;[1] that employees are more likely to share knowledge in an environment of trust;[2] that avoiding misconduct and practicing good corporate citizenship contribute to a positive reputation;[3] and that firms convicted of wrongdoing often experience lower returns in succeeding years.[4] Of course, these findings do not prove that ethics always "pays." Indeed, such a conclusion would be mistaken. But this and other research does show that a company's ethics has important implications for its functioning as an organization, its ability to manage risk, its reputation in the marketplace, and its standing in the community.[5]

Despite these findings, ethical analysis has not traditionally been a defined part of management decision making. In most well-run companies, financial, legal, and competitive analyses are explicit and routine. Ethics, by contrast, is often left to instinct or "gut feel" and managed on an *ad hoc* basis as problems arise. As social science research indicates, many people make ethical judgments on the basis of instinct and emotion.[6] If they use reason and analysis at all, they do so after the fact—to justify their instinctual response rather than to formulate or test their judgment.

Instinct, of course, is an important guide to action and should rarely be ignored. But people's instincts frequently differ, and few people have such well-honed instincts that they automatically see the ethical issues involved in, say, a complex financial restructuring, a new business model, or a technology breakthrough. While instinct alone may work well enough in relatively simple, familiar situations, a more structured approach to identifying and addressing ethical issues is essential for business leaders today. This note outlines one such approach.

---

Professor Lynn Sharp Paine prepared this note as the basis for class discussion. The note reflects contributions from Professors Joseph L. Badaracco, Jr., Joshua D. Margolis, Thomas R. Piper, Sandra Sucher, and other members of the Leadership and Corporate Accountability teaching group.

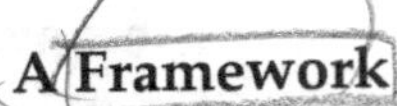

## A Framework

Scholars have long debated the definition of ethics.[7] It has been defined as narrowly as "the study of right and wrong" and as broadly as "the general inquiry into what is good."[8] Our framework draws from only a small part of this vast territory. It involves four fundamental questions that an actor—individual, company, or group—should consider when evaluating a possible course of action:

- Is the action consistent with the actor's basic duties?
- Does it respect the rights and other legitimate claims of the affected parties?
- Does it reflect best practice?
- Is it compatible with the actor's own deeply held commitments?

These questions elicit different types of ethical norms or standards. The first two questions bring out basic requirements—the ethical minimum that would be expected of anyone in the situation. The third and fourth raise considerations that are somewhat more discretionary though nonetheless important for companies and individuals who view themselves as leaders, given that leadership, almost by definition, means doing more than the minimum. Effective use of this framework requires an understanding of four concepts from ethical theory, each associated with one of the questions:

**Duties** A basic moral duty is a requirement to act—or not act—in a certain way. Duties are typically owed to *other parties*—the company, colleagues, customers, the general public—though duties to oneself are also important. A distinction is sometimes drawn between "perfect" duties, which involve specific obligations to particular parties (e.g., to keep a promise), and "imperfect" duties, which are more general and open-ended (e.g., a duty of charity). Although any competent actor is presumed to be capable of fulfilling basic duties, specialized knowledge and expertise are often required. Many basic moral duties have been written into law or otherwise codified. For example, duties to respect property, refrain from fraud, and avoid certain injuries to others are enforced by many legal systems, and similar provisions are found in many codes of business conduct. Basic duties are not always explicit; they may also reside in tacit understandings of what human beings owe to one another. Because basic duties reflect widely held expectations, actions that breach these duties may give rise to criticism or blame. They may also subject the actor to demands for an apology or compensation for injuries caused by the offending action.

**Rights** Moral duties go hand in hand with moral rights. A right is often the converse of a duty. For example, one party's property right corresponds with other parties' duty not to steal. Similarly, one party's right to know typically corresponds with another party's duty to inform. A right is thus an entitlement to certain behavior from other people.[9] Rights are sometimes categorized as "positive" if they require others to commit resources or take affirmative action (e.g., the right to education) and "negative" if they require others to forbear from certain actions (e.g., the right to privacy). Even though rights and duties are correlated, it is sometimes useful to focus on the rights side of the equation as rights are sometimes better defined than the related duties. Like basic duties, basic rights are often written into law or formal codes such as the Universal Declaration of Human Rights. Like failure to fulfill basic duties, failure to respect basic rights may be cause for blame, and rights violators may be penalized or required to compensate for harm caused by their actions.

**Best practice** Beyond basic rights and duties, most ethical systems also posit certain principles or standards of excellence. In ethical theory, these are sometimes referred to as "ideals," "values," or "aspirations." They might also be termed "best practice" standards since they represent conduct that is desirable but not necessarily obligatory. The distinction between behavior that is ethically required (the "musts") and behavior that is good but not mandatory ("shoulds" or "good-to-dos") is not always clear. One test is how the behavior would be received. Conduct that exemplifies best practice will often elicit praise or admiration even though its absence would not merit criticism or blame. For instance, honoring an agreement that it is not binding may earn the actor "moral credit" even if failure to carry out the agreement would have been excused. Similarly, a company that provides information beyond the requirements of law and basic honesty may garner praise for its candor even though nondisclosure would not have been blameworthy.

**Commitments** Most individuals and organizations take on moral commitments that stand outside—or go beyond—the publicly defined rights, duties, and standards that apply to all. These self-chosen, or subjective, commitments may be rooted in an individual's personal values and beliefs, the culture and practices of the organization, or the needs of the larger society. For example, a manager may believe deeply in honesty—telling it "straight" when most others would spin or shade the truth. Or a company may define itself around a commitment to the environment, employee development, or extraordinary service to the customer. Such commitments typically represent an important aspect of the actor's identity. Thus, although falling short on these commitments may not generate external criticism, it can be quite damaging to the actor's self-concept and may even lead to the actor's impaired functioning.

## Applying the Framework

This framework sounds simple, but applying it can be difficult. In using it to evaluate a possible course of action, challenges arise at each step in the process.

**Understanding the facts** A crucial first step is to understand the proposed course of action. This may seem obvious, but in many cases decision makers do not fully understand the nature or consequences of actions they are contemplating or even their own ultimate purpose in acting. Confident in their own good intentions and focused on their own narrow objectives, they often overlook collateral effects, alternative interpretations, and likely impacts on others. Yet, such considerations are integral to a reliable analysis. Without them, it is impossible to determine whether an action is harmful, fair, or even legal—or to predict its effectiveness in furthering the actor's own aims. Understanding key aspects of the action—its intended purpose, its proper description, and its likely consequences—is thus an essential step in the analytic process.

A useful tool for this purpose is what is sometimes called "stakeholder analysis" or "stakeholder impact assessment."[10] Stakeholder analysis has two basic components: identifying the parties likely to be affected by the action (that is, those with a "stake" to consider); and, for each party, mapping the action's likely consequences—both positive and negative, short term and long. With the likely outcomes for various stakeholders thus arrayed, the proposed action can be more thoroughly and systematically evaluated against the relevant ethical standards (duties, rights, best practices, and commitments). This process may also reveal opportunities to mitigate unnecessary harms or enhance the planned action's benefits. The workbook provided in **Exhibit 1** can be used to guide this analysis.

**Identifying relevant standards** A second challenge is defining what ethical standards to apply. Because ethical norms are often tacit rather than explicit and because they derive from varied sources—reason, law, philosophy, religion, custom, and perhaps even biology—deciding on the appropriate standards in a given situation is not always straightforward.[11] One starting point will be the company's own code and relevant industry standards. Another useful point of reference is the Global Business Standards Codex, a compilation of standards commonly found in leading codes of conduct for business around the world.[12] Although the codex does not differentiate between basic duties and best practices, it provides a list of widely accepted standards to govern a company's dealings with its stakeholders, including precepts such as obey the law, forgo bribery and deception, disclose conflicts of interest, practice fair dealing, safeguard health, and protect the environment.[13] The creators of the codex found that most of the commonly occurring standards were elaborations of just eight basic principles. A summary of the standards associated with each is found in **Exhibit 2**.

Fiduciary principle: Act in the best interests of the company and its investors.

Property principle: Respect property and the rights of those who own it.

Reliability principle: Keep promises, agreements, contracts, and other commitments.

Transparency principle: Conduct business in a truthful and open manner.

Dignity principle: Respect the dignity of all people.

Fairness principle: Deal fairly with all parties.

Citizenship principle: Act as responsible members of the community.

Responsiveness principle: Be responsive to the legitimate claims and concerns of others.

While many of these principles—and their associated standards—have roots in numerous ethical traditions, their significance and interpretation can vary enormously across different social and cultural contexts. So it would be simplistic to call them "universal values." Still, given their widespread endorsement, they provide a useful point of reference.[14]

**Maintaining objectivity** All forms of analysis are vulnerable to the prejudices of their users. To correct for self-serving and other biases in ethical analysis, many "tests" of ethical judgment have been offered. Three of the best known and most useful are:

Visibility: *Would I be comfortable if this action were described on the front page of a respected newspaper?*

Generality: *Would I be comfortable if everyone in a similar situation did this?*

Legacy: *Is this how I'd like my leadership to be remembered?*

These tests evoke varied perspectives for evaluating our judgments.[15] The "visibility" test—also called the "transparency," "sunshine," or "newspaper" test—reminds us to consider how our actions may be viewed by others. The "generality" test asks us to consider what would happen if our actions became the general practice.[16] Would society benefit? Would we want to live in such a society? The legacy test appeals to the decision maker's own future self-evaluation. Although these tests are presented as hypothetical, their importance for leaders is often real—given that leaders' actions are frequently reported in the press, replicated by others, and even, in some cases, recorded in history.

As this discussion indicates, ethical analysis requires rigorous thought and careful deliberation. In many cases, it will also require research and information gathering—on law and regulation, codes of conduct, customary practice, expert opinion, stakeholder concerns, public opinion, and other matters. Of course, ethical analysis is, to some extent, situational across time and cultures. As with legal and economic analysis, reasonable people will disagree, and errors will be made. But the magnitude of the errors can be substantially lessened and better decisions made if the method is consistently and carefully applied.

**Exhibit 1** Action Planning: Ethical Analysis Workbook

Proposed action:

Principal actor(s):

Other assumptions:

Main objectives:

Assumed time frame:

| **Key stakeholders** (affected parties) | **Likely consequences** | | **Ethical standards** | | | |
|---|---|---|---|---|---|---|
| | Positive (short and long term) | Negative (short and long term) | Duties to this party | Rights of this party | Best practice toward this party | Commitments to this party |
| | | | | | | |
| | | | | | | |
| | | | | | | |
| | | | | | | |
| | | | | | | |
| | | | | | | |
| | | | | | | |
| | | | | | | |

**Exhibit 2** Widely Endorsed Standards of Corporate Conduct

| Principles | What they require | What they prohibit |
|---|---|---|
| Fiduciary | Diligence, candor, loyalty to company<br>Disclosure of conflicts of interest<br>Prudence, intelligence, best efforts | Unauthorized self-dealing<br>Self-benefit at expense of company<br>Negligence, carelessness, half-hearted effort<br>Bribery, inducing breach of fiduciary duty |
| Dignity | Protect human health, safety, privacy, dignity<br>Respect fundamental human rights<br>Affirmative action to develop human capacities<br>Special concern for the vulnerable | Coercion, humiliation, invasion of privacy<br>Injury to health, safety<br>Force, violence, harming the innocent<br>Violations of basic human rights |
| Property | Respect for others' property<br>Safeguarding own property<br>Responsible use of own property | Theft, embezzlement<br>Misappropriation of intellectual property<br>Waste<br>Infringement on others' property |
| Transparency | Accuracy, truthfulness, honesty<br>Accurate presentation of information<br>Disclosure of material information<br>Correction of misinformation | Fraud, deceit<br>Misrepresentation<br>Materially misleading nondisclosures |
| Reliability | Fidelity to commitments, keeping promises<br>Fulfilling contracts, carrying out agreements<br>Care in making commitments—not more than can deliver | Breach of promise<br>Breach of contract<br>Going back on one's word<br>Fraudulent promises |
| Fairness | Fair dealing (in exchange)<br>Fair treatment (opportunity, pay)<br>Due process (notice, opportunity to be heard)<br>Fair competition (conduct among rivals) | Preferential or arbitrary treatment<br>Unfair discrimination<br>Unfair competitive advantage<br>Suppressing competition |
| Citizenship | Respect for law and regulation<br>Share in maintaining the commons<br>Cooperation with public officials<br>Civic contribution<br>Recognizing government's jurisdiction | Illegality, indifference to the law<br>Freeloading, free riding<br>Injury, damage to society, the environment<br>Improper involvement in politics or government |
| Responsiveness | Readiness to listen<br>Responding to complaints and suggestions<br>Addressing legitimate concerns of others | Indifference to legitimate claims and claimants<br>Neglect of serious concerns |

Source: Based on Lynn S. Paine, Rohit Deshpandé, Joshua D. Margolis, and Kim E. Bettcher, "Up to Code: Does Your Company's Conduct Meet World-Class Standards?" *Harvard Business Review* (December 2005).

## Endnotes

[1] Teresa M. Amabile, "How to Kill Creativity," *Harvard Business Review* (September–October 1998): 77–87; "Mobilizing Creativity in Organizations," *California Management Review*, vol. 40, no. 1 (Fall 1997): 39–58.

[2] Anil K. Gupta and Vijay Govindarajan, "Knowledge Management's Social Dimension: Lessons from Nucor Steel," *Sloan Management Review* (Fall 2000): 71–80.

[3] See, for example, Charles J. Fombrun, *Reputation: Realizing Value from the Corporate Image* (Boston, Mass.: Harvard Business School Press, 1996), esp. p. 6; Grahame Dowling, *Creating Corporate Reputations: Identity, Image, and Performance* (Oxford, U.K.: Oxford University Press, 2001), pp. 49–63.

[4] Melissa S. Baucus and David A. Baucus, "Paying the Piper: An Empirical Examination of Longer-Term Financial Consequences of Illegal Corporate Behavior," *Academy of Management Review*, vol. 40, no. 1 (1997): 129–151.

[5] For a review of this research, see Lynn Sharp Paine, Value Shift: Why Companies Must Merge Social and Financial Imperatives to Achieve Superior Performance (New York, N.Y.: McGraw-Hill, 2003), Ch. 2.

[6] Jon Haidt, "The emotional dog and its rational tail: A social intuitionist approach to moral judgment," *Psychological Review* 108 (2001): 814–834.

[7] Although the terms "ethics" and "morality" are sometimes defined differently, they are frequently used as interchangeable synonyms. This note treats the terms as interchangeable.

[8] G.E. Moore, *Principia Ethica*, orig. 1903 (Cambridge, U.K.: Cambridge University Press, 1968), p. 2. For an overview of definitions, see, for example, *The Definition of Morality*, eds. G. Wallace and A.D.M. Walker (London: Methuen & Co Ltd, 1970).

[9] On rights as compared to interests, see Ronald Dworkin, *Taking Rights Seriously* (Cambridge, Mass.: Harvard University Press, 1978).

[10] A 1964 document is often cited as the origin of the term "stakeholder," but use became widespread after the 1984 publication of R. Edward Freeman, *Strategic Planning: A Stakeholder Approach* (Boston, Mass.: Pitman Publishing, 1984). Interpretations and usages have since proliferated, and the term has even given rise to a theory of the firm. For a roundup, see Thomas Donaldson and Lee E. Preston, "The Stakeholder Theory of the Corporation: Concepts, Evidence, and Implications," *Academy of Management Review*, vol. 20, no. 1 (1995): 65–91. Although the stakeholder theory of the firm has been criticized on various grounds, most critics acknowledge that stakeholders' claims cannot be ignored. See, for example, Elaine Sternberg, "Stakeholder Theory Exposed," *Corporate Governance Quarterly*, vol. 2, no. 1 (March 1996).

[11] See, for example, the research of Frans B.M. de Waal, research professor in psychobiology, Yerkes Regional Primate Research Center, Emory University, Atlanta, Georgia.

[12] Lynn S. Paine, Rohit Deshpande, Joshua D. Margolis, and Kim E. Bettcher, "Up to Code: Does Your Company's Conduct Meet World-Class Standards," *Harvard Business Review* (December 2005).

[13] Compare, for example, recently promulgated codes such as the OECD Guidelines for Multinational Enterprises, OECD Policy Brief (June 2001); Caux Round Table Principles for Business (1994); United Nations Global Compact (1999). See also Muel Kaptein, "Business Codes of Multinational Firms: What Do They Say," *Journal of Business Ethics*, vol. 50, no. 1 (March 2004).

[14] Widespread endorsement of these principles should perhaps be unsurprising. Although the world's ethical traditions vary widely, scholars tell us that some themes appear repeatedly over time and across traditions. Calls for honesty, fairness, reciprocity, and mutual assistance can be found in virtually all traditions, as can injunctions against deception, betrayal, theft, injustice, violence, and indifference to others. The recurrence of these themes suggests that humans may be biologically programmed for morality (as for language) and that certain ethical norms may have survival value for groups that embrace them. See, for example, Sissela Bok,

*Common Values* (Columbia, Mo.: University of Missouri Press, 1995); H.L.A., Hart, *The Concept of Law* (Oxford, U.K.: Clarendon Press, 1961), pp. 187–191 (on basic standards of conduct necessary for any society's functioning).

[15] Other frequently cited tests include the "golden rule," the "mirror test," and the "sleep test." For different formulations of the "golden rule" in different cultures, see Sissela Bok's entry on this topic in *The Oxford Companion to Philosophy*, ed. Ted Honderich (Oxford, U.K.: Oxford University Press, 1995), p. 321. For different versions of the "mirror" test, see Wendy Fischman, Becca Solomon, Deborah Greenspan, and Howard Gardner, *Making Good: How Young People Cope with Moral Dilemmas at Work* (Cambridge, Mass.: Harvard University Press, 2004), pp. 178–179.

[16] The generality test is closely related to the "universalizability" test. See, for example, R.M. Hare, "The Structure of Ethics and Morals," in *Essays in Ethical Theory* (Oxford, U.K.: Clarendon Press, 1989); Marcus Singer, *Generalization in Ethics* (New York, N.Y.: Knopf, 1961).

Mary C. Gentile, PhD, Director
www.GivingVoicetoValues.org

**Giving *Voice* to Values**

# Starting Assumptions for *Giving Voice to Values*

Before we begin to practice possible approaches and scripts for voicing our values in the workplace, it is useful to be explicit about our starting assumptions. You may or may not be certain that you share all these assumptions but in order to gain the most from this curriculum, it is useful to approach it *as if you do*. This is the "story line," if you will, behind this work:

1. **I want to do this.**
   Most of us want to find ways to voice and act on our values in the workplace, and to do so effectively.

2. ***I have* done this.**
   Despite the fact that research and our own experiences reveal many individual and organizational inhibitors, most of us have, in fact, *chosen* to voice and act on our values on some occasions.

3. **I can do this more and better.**
   We have the potential to expand our capacity, our effectiveness and our likelihood to voice and act on our values by acknowledging that we have such a choice, and by practicing what we would say and do if we made that choice.

4. **It is easier for me to do this in some contexts than others.**
   Developing the "muscle" for voicing our values does not diminish the importance of selecting and developing organizational cultures and policies and incentives that *encourage* such choices. In fact, our effort to promote the development of such cultures, policies and incentives is, in itself, an instance of voicing values. And the more such organizational enablers are in place, the more likely it is that individuals will choose to voice their values. It is a virtuous circle.

5. **I am more likely to do this if I have practiced how to respond.**
   There are certain frequently heard "reasons and rationalizations" for NOT voicing and acting on our values. But there are also possible responses or re-framings that we can use to counter these "reasons and rationalizations." If we familiarize ourselves with these responses in advance, we are more likely to be able to access them when needed and to potentially shift a conversation or change a mind.

Prior reflection on responses to value conflicts can expand our confidence in the degrees of freedom we have in any given decision situation.

6. **My example is powerful.**
Just as we want to voice and act on our values, we can assume that many of our colleagues do as well. If we can access credible responses to frequently heard reasons for not voicing and acting on our values, we may encourage and empower others to join us.

7. **Mastering and delivering responses to frequently-heard rationalizations can empower others who share my views to act, but I cannot assume I know who those folks are.**
The responses we develop and practice for frequently-heard "reasons and rationalizations" are intended to strengthen our own confidence in voicing and acting on our values, as well as that of others who share our value conflict but are unable to find a way to explain their reluctance. However, we cannot assume we know who feels the conflict and who does not simply by observing their behavior because, as we have already acknowledged, we all have chosen to suppress these "felt" conflicts at some points in our past.

8. **The better I know myself, the more I can prepare to play to my strengths and be protected from my weaknesses.**
The greater our self-knowledge, the more likely we are to be able to anticipate and manage our responses to value conflicts. Prior reflection on our own personalities and behavioral tendencies under pressure enables us to *play to our strengths* and to *put mechanisms in place to protect us from our weaknesses*. Research tells us that often these "mechanisms" need to be external (incentives, deterrents, automatic review processes, transparency, a pre-established network of sounding boards, etc.). *Internal awareness of self-bias is important but not enough to prevent us from falling prey to it:* we need to go beyond awareness to action and/or external mechanisms.

9. **I am not alone.**
We can utilize our personal support networks as sounding boards; reach out to our colleagues to build a network of allies or to gather supporting information; and engage in strategic use of the managerial hierarchy. However, we must consider carefully which approach is most appropriate in a particular situation.

10. **Although I may not always succeed, voicing and acting on my values is worth doing.**
Just as with any other managerial action, we do not always succeed at what we set out to achieve. We are more likely to voice our values if we have decided that the cost of not doing so, and/or the benefit of doing so, is important enough to us that we would pursue them whether or not we were successful. In order to get to this place of clarity, we need to spend some serious time thinking about our own identity, personal purpose and definition of success and failure. It is also important to reflect upon the risks associated with voicing our values, so that we make this decision with our eyes open and prepared to handle the risks.

11. **Voicing my values leads to better decisions.**
It is often difficult to be certain that a course of action is "right," but we are more likely to come to the best decision if we feel empowered to voice our concerns about value conflicts and discuss them with others.

**Giving *Voice* to Values**

**12. The more I believe it's possible, the more likely I will be to do this.**
We are more likely to voice and act on our values when we believe it is possible to do so effectively. If we pay attention to positive examples of such voice and action and spend time developing support mechanisms and practicing the development and delivery of responses to frequently heard reasons and rationalizations for unethical actions, we can expand our sense of what's possible -- another virtuous circle.

Last Revised: 02/28/2010

Mary C. Gentile, PhD, Director
www.GivingVoicetoValues.org

**Giving *Voice* to Values**

## *GIVING VOICE TO VALUES*: BRIEF INTRODUCTION

Most of us want to bring our "whole selves" to work. Yet, experience and research demonstrate that many of us will encounter values conflicts in our careers, when the way we want to live and the things we want to accomplish seem in conflict with the expectations of our clients, our peers, our bosses and/or our organizations. The Giving Voice to Values curriculum is designed to help individuals learn to recognize, clarify, speak and act on their values when those conflicts arise.

The focus here is POST-decision making. It is not about deciding what the right thing *is*. Rather it is about how a manager raises these issues in an effective manner; what he/she needs to do and say in order to be heard; and how to try to correct an existing course of action when necessary.

**Distinctive features of the *Giving Voice to Values* Curriculum include:**

1. A focus on **positive examples** of times when folks *have* found ways to voice, and thereby implement, their values in the workplace;
2. An emphasis on the importance of finding an **alignment** between one's individual sense of purpose and that of the organization (which involves self-assessment and focus on individual strengths);
3. The opportunity to **construct and practice responses** to the most frequently heard reasons and rationalizations for *not* acting on one's values;
4. The opportunity to build commitment by providing repeated opportunities for participants to **practice** delivering their responses and to learn to provide **peer feedback and coaching** to enhance effectiveness.

Research and interviews reveal that there are many different ways to voice our values: looking for a win/win solution; changing the boss's mind through persuasion and logic; going over the boss's head within the organization; building coalitions of like-minded employees; and so on. But the pivotal moment is deciding to speak.

It's also important to understand that since there are so many different ways to voice our values, we can look for the approach that not only seems most likely to be effective in our particular situation, but also the one that is most comfortable, given our own personal style of communication and personality. Finally, there are things we can do to make it more likely that we will actually voice our values and that we will do so effectively: namely, pre-scripting, practice and coaching.

The point here is that just because we are addressing a question of values and ethics does not mean that we need to preach. Often, the very fact that a situation has an ethical component to it leads us to feel that we must gear ourselves up to be saints or even martyrs; in reality, we often just need to be competent and skillful. We can approach the communication challenge with the same analytical and personal capabilities that we would use in any other situation, whether it is a convincing our professor to give us an extension on our final paper or negotiating a later curfew. And as with other communication challenges, we will want to consider the needs and desires and emotional investments of the individuals to whom we are speaking, as opposed to focusing exclusively on our own. Re-framing "voice" as "dialogue," which includes a goodly dollop of "listening," is another important piece of the recipe.

It's also important to use the communication style with which we are most skilled and comfortable. For example, if our most effective style of communication is story-telling and the use of metaphor, we would likely want to play to our strengths, whether the topic is a moral conflict or not. Or, if we are uncomfortable with confrontation, we may choose to raise our objections through a line of careful questioning rather than assertion. Even if we are not convinced that our personal style will be most effective in a particular situation, we are most likely to speak if we start from the strengths we have, rather than attempting to be an entirely different type of person at a time of stress.

And of course, the power and influence of our context should not be underestimated. It's very hard to stand up against the majority or against an authority in any situation, let alone an ethically charged one. Nevertheless, we all know of times when we have seen individuals resist these pressures; we probably can think of some times when we have done so ourselves. Research and experience suggest that an explicit attempt to test our ideas with a diverse set of colleagues, and also perhaps to seek support from such a group both inside and outside the organization, may help us resist some of the unconscious influence. It may even help us find new ways of expressing our values that would not have occurred to us if we didn't seek out different perspectives.

### Reasons and Rationalizations

When we encounter values conflicts in the workplace, we often face barriers that appear in the form of "reasons and rationalizations" for pursuing a particular course of action that can confound our best attempts to fulfill our own sense of organizational and personal purpose. These are the objections you hear from your colleagues when you try to point out an ethical problem in the way things are being done. Sometimes you don't even hear them because they are the unspoken assumptions – seeming truisms – of the organization.

It is extremely difficult to make a strong argument against the "prevailing winds" if you feel you are in the minority; or if you don't feel you have the time to come up with a workable alternative; or if you don't want to take the chance to present a half-baked response. So this curriculum is about creating a time and space to be in the majority, with sufficient time to come up with a fully-baked and pre-tested response to some of the most common challenges you are likely to face in your workplace.

In order to develop this ability we want to consider the challenging situation carefully and answer the following questions:

- What are the main arguments you are trying to counter? What are the *reasons and rationalizations* you need to address?
- What's at *stake* for the key parties, including those who disagree with you? What's at *stake* for you?
- What *levers* can you use to influence those who disagree with you?
- What is your most *powerful and persuasive response* to the reasons and rationalizations you need to address? To whom should the argument be made? When and in what context?

Interestingly, these questions are not asking us to apply ethical analysis. Rather they are all about understanding the reasons and motivations – both rational and emotional, organizational and personal, ethical and perhaps unethical – that guide the behavior and choices of those with whom we want to communicate.

**Giving *Voice* to Values**

What can make this approach particularly useful for tackling values-based conflicts is that, after a while, we will begin to recognize familiar categories of argument or reasons that we typically hear from someone defending an ethically questionable behavior. And, similarly, there are some useful questions, persuasive arguments and ways of framing our own role/purpose, and that of our organization, which can help us respond persuasively to these frequent arguments.

Finally, the very act of recognizing and naming the argument can reduce its power because it is no longer unconscious or assumed; we have made it discussable and even put it into play with equally, or hopefully stronger, counter-arguments. Choice becomes possible, and that is what this note is all about.

Let's take a moment to identify a few of the familiar categories of values conflict and categories of rationalization or argument, as well as some possible types of response – by way of illustration.

Rushworth Kidder suggests that most ethical dilemmas fall into four categories or patterns:

- "Truth versus loyalty"
- "Individual versus community"
- "Short term versus long term"
- "Justice versus mercy"[1]

You will note that Kidder is talking here about conflicting values, not values versus a lack of values. Many times, we *do* face situations where our own values are conflicted or torn. But sometimes, the conflict exists more in the way the dilemma is described or framed Thus, being prepared to recognize the ways that the framing of a choice may call different values into play can be useful.

For example, a colleague in our company sales team may use an appeal to personal loyalty as a way to persuade us to violate our commitment to integrity, when he or she asks us to keep silent about their deceptive sales tactics. But recognizing the pattern in this values conflict – that is, "truth versus loyalty" – may enable us to feel more prepared and certain of our response. The conflict moves from the particular and the immediate moment into a broader, more general context, and we begin to see it more clearly at this distance. Once the pattern is clear, we might recognize that our colleague is not showing the same loyalty to us (by respecting our personal integrity) that he or she is asking *from* us.

We can also consider the kinds of argument or rationalization that we often encounter in values conflicts. Some of the most common arguments include:

- Expected or Standard Practice: "Everyone does this, so it's really standard practice. It's even expected."
- Materiality: "The impact of this action is not material. It doesn't really hurt anyone."
- Locus of Responsibility: "This is not my responsibility; I'm just following orders here."
- Locus of Loyalty: "I know this isn't quite fair to the customer but I don't want to hurt my reports/team/boss/company."

As we begin to recognize these categories of argument, we will become more adept at drawing upon responses to each of them. For example, the appeal to "expected or standard practice" is often an exaggeration. If everyone actually were doing "it" (whatever "it" is), what would be the consequences for business practice and customer

[1] Rushworth M. Kidder, *Moral Courage: Taking Action When Your Values Are Put To the Test* (New York: William Morrow, HarperCollins Publishers, Inc., 2005), page 89.

trust? If the practice is really accepted, why are there so often laws, rules and/or policies against it? Would you be comfortable if everyone knew you were doing this? Who wouldn't you want to know? And so on.

With regard to the "materiality" argument, it becomes important to recognize that determinations of materiality are often ambiguous. Rather than being objective, they can depend on the method of measurement being employed.[2] Additionally, some practices are considered fraudulent, regardless of their relative size; that is, some things can't be just a little wrong.[3]

The question of "responsibility" is another well-considered topic in ethics literature, and numerous guidelines have been developed for assessing whether or not we are required to act.[4] The point here, though, is that this argument is often used when we know we are uncomfortable with a decision or action but are afraid of the consequences of voicing and acting upon that judgment. Therefore, the individual using this argument has already acknowledged that they don't like the situation, and this provides an opening for further discussion.

Finally, as noted earlier, the question and definition of loyalty can be framed in multiple ways. For example, are we "loyal" when we protect the financial bonus of our team this quarter or when we protect their long-term reputation and productivity?

We can also identify patterns of reasoning and levers that can be useful to understand in our efforts to voice our values. For example:

- Thinking in the **long run as well as the short run**.
- Considering the situation in terms of the group and the firm's **wider purpose**, rather than in terms of the immediate transaction alone. For example, what behavior enables them to serve their customers best; to manage themselves most efficiently; to manage themselves in the most honest manner; to align incentives of the firm, the sales team and the customers, etc.?
- Considering the **assumed definition of "competitive advantage."** This definition sometimes seems to follow the old joke about two lawyers pursued by a bear in the woods. One lawyer says to the other, "We'll never be able to outrun that bear," and the other replies, "I don't have to outrun that bear; I just have to outrun you." Implicit in this view of competitiveness is the assumption that the point of business is conquest, narrowly defined as outrunning the competitors (whether they are external or internal). This model often results in shortsighted, narrow conceptions of managerial purpose. It can be valuable to suggest an alternative model for competitiveness, based upon overall and long-term excellence, rather than merely "outrunning" the competition. This conception can also allow for consideration of *how* we achieve results, as well as whether we do so.
- Positioning oneself as an **agent of "continuous improvement"** as opposed to the source of complaint. For example, how can we improve this system of incentives and goals to maximize performance while discouraging "gaming" the system?
- Positioning oneself as a source of **actionable alternatives** rather than "thou shalt not's:"
- Pointing out **addictive cycles** that can cause greater and greater pressures and risks, leading to larger and larger values conflicts.
- Considering who we need and can attract as an **ally** in our efforts.
- Considering the **costs to each affected party** and looking for ways to recognize and mitigate these in order make our arguments more appealing.

---

[2] Mary C. Gentile, "Discussions about Ethics in the Accounting Classroom: Student Assumptions and Faculty Paradigms," *Giving Voice to Values* curriculum, www.GivingVoiceToValues.org .

[3] "One Off Decisions" case, *Giving Voice to Values* curriculum, www.GivingVoiceToValues.org .

[4] "Reporting" module, page 11, *Giving Voice to Values* curriculum, www.GivingVoiceToValues.org .

- Assuming our audience members are **pragmatists** (as opposed to idealists or opportunists) and looking for ways to make it feasible for them to do the "right thing." This does not mean that they will never pay a price for their choices (sometimes such choices do mean sacrifice, at least in the short run), but it means that they will not feel as if they have been exploited for doing so. For example, if we want to ask our group to forego inappropriate revenue recognition it might help them to see that we are trying to address the problem at a systemic level, as well. After all, it is the organizational incentives that can encourage such choices.
- Assuming that our audience members are pragmatists, we will need to **counter the commonly held assumption of unethical behavior**: pragmatists often expect the lowest common denominator of behavior from those around them. In order to motivate individuals to step beyond this lowest common denominator, it is useful to share examples of effective managers who have made choices based on their sense of responsibility.

The point in identifying and delineating these different categories of argument and rationalization, as well as the categories of values dilemmas, is to help us recognize them when we encounter them; to understand the ways of thinking that produce them; and to be practiced in responding to them.

9.8.2010

Reading 1-2

# An Ethical Hero or a Failed Businessman? *The Malden Mills Case Revisited*

**Penelope Washbourne**

## Introduction

At the annual meeting of the Society for Business Ethics in Boston in 1997 the guest speaker was Aaron Feuerstein, the acclaimed CEO of Malden Mills, who brought tears to the eyes of skeptical academics with his tales of the mill fire in 1995 and his generous actions towards his employees. I had written a case about him during the winter of 1996 and suggested him as a guest speaker for the annual meeting. After the meeting, I was given a guided tour of the gleaming rebuilt factory in Lawrence, Mass., and was duly impressed by the state of the art manufacturing technology used to make that cozy fleece, Polartec, which is made from recycled plastic. Aaron Feuerstein's star continued to shine in the business press, and even in 2004, as a hero who paid his employees for a number of months after the fire destroyed their jobs.

As many noted then and now, here was a true man of virtue, an ethical giant in a business world of massive layoffs such as those at AT&T and Sunbeam, and when compared with colossal failures in leadership in many huge corporations.

I taught this case over the years, with video clips from the national media, in my business ethics courses and was subsequently told by students that the case had made a powerful impression on them. Maybe it was the pictures of those desperately anxious mill workers with their tears and gratitude responding to Feuerstein's announcement after the fire that he was going to continue to pay his workers for another month. "You're a saint" said one. Or maybe it was Feuerstein's own tears that affected my students?

The case touched a deep nerve: here was a business man who put the care of his workers above the bottom line. My goal in writing and teaching about this case was to demonstrate that it is better to teach business ethics with examples of ethical leadership than to continue to focus on, as most of our case books do, the multiple failures in moral leadership in corporate life. Even formerly exemplary companies can fall under an ethical cloud.

Subsequently, though I read that Malden Mills had gone bankrupt, since the tenth year anniversary of the fire was in 2005, I decided to take another look at what the effect had been on the local community of Aaron Feuerstein's actions after the fire. My reading of the events that have taken place since the fire raises an important dilemma for teaching this tale of ethical virtue. What has been the aftermath? It would be nice to say that the gleaming new mill saved the jobs in the community and that Aaron Feuerstein is still in charge of his grandfather's firm, well loved by his workers and local politicians for preserving the one remaining industry in an area of high unemployment.

It would be nice to say that not only is virtue its own reward, but also that it is indeed rewarded by the world. For Aaron Feuerstein and his family firm, unfortunately this is not the case. The actual story is more complex than that, as is often the case in real life.

To describe it briefly: Aaron borrowed money to rebuild the mill, beyond the money he would finally receive from the insurance company. He built a large facility, counting on the expansion of his Polartec fleece lines and the continuation of his brand of upholstery fabrics. His debt was more than his final insurance settlement, the upholstery business proved a failure and he decided to get out of it, cheap competition and an unseasonably warm winter cut into his Polartec sales and he had to declare bankruptcy in 2001. The firm remained under bankruptcy protection until 2003, but Aaron lost control of the company and GE Capital, the main creditor with 16.6 percent, became its largest shareholder, with a dominant influence on the new board. In July 2004 the board hired a new executive. A new manufacturing operation has been opened in China. Jobs in Lawrence and nearby New Hampshire have declined. In the meantime, Aaron and his son Daniel with a group of investors and a commitment to keep jobs in the local communities, attempted to buy back the firm. Their offers were rejected.

How indeed will I teach this case now? Were Aaron's actions after the fire virtuous or reckless? Did his hope for the future and his commitment to the local community blind him to the economic realities of the industry at the time and cause him to overbuild, and so put the whole company in jeopardy? From a utilitarian perspective, did he do the right thing? What was the long-term effect of his actions on the community?

I decided that I had to get close to the source and elected to spend a few days in Lawrence, Massachusetts, and I was able to interview Aaron Feuerstein in his home in Boston. When I interviewed Aaron in November 2004, he said he felt he had failed.

## Lawrence, Massachusetts

In fall 2004, the main impression of Lawrence as a community to a visitor unfamiliar with depressed mill towns in New England was decay. The massive empty mill buildings along the Merrimack River have forlorn signs for "Space Available," as if the next high-tech boom was going to transform this now virtual ghost town into a thriving business community. Along the main street with its closed businesses, even the Goodwill center was shuttered. The one remaining open facility was a large Headstart center with its brightly colored plastic play structures. The impression was that this must be a city that is heavily funded with federal grant monies for low income families.

Though large trash receptacles ready for collection lined the narrow residential streets the day I was there, they did not contain the abandoned sofas and junk in the empty lots. The local community newspaper, printed in Spanish and English, spoke of the challenge of trash as a neighborhood problem. The mayor wanted to put awnings over the shops in the main streets, to attract business downtown. Among the nail salons and the few ethnic food establishments, one set of buildings, and one alone, remained a viable concern, Malden Mills Inc. Located next to the Arlington section of town, one of the poorest neighborhoods, the mill is the only sizable employer in Lawrence, Massachusetts.

Five hundred of its employees live in a five mile radius of the mill and many walk to work. It would be fair to say that the economic well-being of Lawrence and its nearby community in New Hamphire, depressed as they are, is intimately connected to the well-being of the one remaining manufacturing facility paying union wages at an average rate in 2004 of $12.50 an hour, with benefits. The unemployment rate in Lawrence has remained at two and a half to three times the state average for the last 20 years , between 10 and 15 percent since 1983. The academic standings of the local schools are the lowest in the state.

My trip to Lawrence answered my question: Why did Aaron Feuerstein feel and still feel today such a fierce loyalty and sense of obligation to the community of Lawrence and its neighboring towns? What did it mean to those communities that he decided to rebuild the mill and committed to pay his employees for several months after the fire? As he told me, the tears of the workers after the fire were not tears of gratitude towards him, but recognition that without the mill there was nothing left for them, their future, or their community.

## The 72,000 People of Lawrence and Their History

This city calls itself the "city of immigrants." It claims that 45 different nationalities and ethnicities have lived in Lawrence. It was founded as a mill town in 1842 to establish woolen and cotton mills and to exploit the new technology of water power along the swift-flowing rivers. The large labor pool required for the factories was imported, and consisted largely of women and immigrants, who lived in dormitories and boarding houses. At its peak, between 1890 and 1915, there were 90,000 residents in Lawrence.

Lawrence was the site of the famous "Bread and Roses" strike in 1912 when after nine weeks of a strike for better conditions during a harsh winter, the company bosses brought the state militia out to attempt to force the 30,000 strikers into submission and prevent them from shipping their children out to relatives and sympathetic families in other communities.

Thus, over the years, Lawrence became known for being in the forefront of the struggle for workers' rights and for the right to organize unions. Now earlier generations of Scots and Irish and Eastern European immigrants have been been replaced by Puerto Ricans and first-generation immigrants from Central America. Their mill jobs allow them the ability to function in their native languages, a rare option in high-paying employment where knowledge of English is often a necessity.

Though most of Lawrence's jobs have disappeared as the mills finally closed after World War II, Aaron Feuerstein's commitment to continuing his operation in this immigrant, unionized town is unique. It stems from a recognition of the value of his own family's history and his grandfather's legacy. As a Hungarian Jewish immigrant in New York City at the turn of the century, his grandfather sold dry goods and eventually moved to Massachusetts and began the family firm in 1907. Aaron remembers his roots and the history of earlier generations of immigrant labor who formed the economic engine that brought succeeding generations to a better way of life. His antipathy to shipping jobs South and to offshoring manufacturing jobs at the expense of domestic workers comes from a profound respect for the skills of those who worked hard to build a future for their families in this country.

Though Aaron had indeed laid off workers due to business conditions, nevertheless he believes we owe these workers in this community an opportunity to perform on the job, for themselves and the community. This is a relationship of mutual respect and obligation that has been carried through three generations of Feuersteins towards their union workers and their communities in Massachusetts and New Hampshire. Aaron spoke proudly of never having had a strike over the years and of having tough but fair negotiations with the unions during his tenure in the company.

Knowing of Aaron's commitment to keep jobs in the local community, the union leadership had hoped that the Feuersteins would be successful in their efforts to regain control of the company. Since the advent of the new company management, the union threatened a strike last fall in November 2004, but finally settled on a new contract.

Aaron had resurrected himself once before when he went bankrupt in the 1980s. His technological innovations captured a new market in fleece material which he branded under the name of Polartec for garments for outdoor enthusiasts. His workers had come through for him in that difficult time. Once again he believed he could resurrect his company from the ashes. Could he do it again?

Aaron's sense of failure at this point in his life (he was 80 in 2005), paternalistic though it may sound, may have to do with failing to live up to the legacy of the family firm that had been handed to him, failing the very community he had pledged to support with good jobs, and failing to protect them from the cost-cutting strategies in which wages are just an expense.

## The Business Strategy and Hope for Lawrence

When fleece was invented it filled a wonderful need in the market for garments that did not become wet with moisture and perspiration, as cotton did, but were wickable, allowing the person to stay warm. Aaron's strategy was to pursue research and development and create high-end, high-quality products that could be recognized as a brand: "Polartec." Since its first invention the number of different weights, colors, and features has exploded, with windproof features and even designs for children's outerwear. Aaron believed that Malden Mills could stay ahead of increasing competition of offshore manufacturers and the "commodification" of the industry by staying ahead of the innovation curve. Fleece was soon everywhere, not just in high-quality jackets for climbers and winter sports enthusiasts, but in regular articles of clothing for adults and children, as well as blankets and throws.

After the fire, even though one of his main customers, Lands' End, initially showed support and featured the story of the mill's fire and Aaron's actions towards his employees in its spring 1996 catalogue, Aaron eventually lost major customers, including Lands' End, which sought other suppliers. Along with the interruption in supply, apparently the Polartec brand did not have the power in the general market, except in specialized high-end products, to withstand the flood of cheaper goods coming from Asia.

After the fire another of his product lines, jacquard upholstery velvet, proved to be unsuccessful in earning a brand identity. Furniture manufacturers were unwilling to pay the premium for a branded fabric and in 1998, Aaron got out of that business. It represented about 50 percent of the company's business at the time of the fire, and its production lines were hard hit by the fire and took longer to resume operation than the polarfleece lines.

One business strategy implemented after the fire by one of the company's former executives, Cesar Aguilar, who spent an uncomfortable weekend in wet clothing as part of his military reserve training, is beginning to pay off for the company and for the community, however. Malden Mills is supplying warm winter clothing to the troops in Afghanistan and Iraq as well as conducting research into new lightweight electronic high-tech fabrics that soldiers can wear next to their skin and that can monitor their vital signs and be of assistance in determining injuries. Another innovation is a next-to-skin fabric that would prevent the growth of bacteria and odor for soldiers who are out in the field. The U.S. military approved $21 million for Polartec garments for 2005, a portion of which goes to the garment manufacturer. That figure includes $1.5 million for research.

The military contracts offer a ray of hope for the company. Not only must all products made for the U.S. Armed Services be made in the United States, but the innovations in new products designed for military use can be developed into commercial applications in the future. In addition, according to a company spokesman the military business is not seasonal, which makes it easier to balance the workload. The military contract currently represents about 20 percent of Malden Mills' business.

## What Went Wrong?

After a traumatic event such as the fire, one's decision-making capacity is impaired. I know this from personal experience, having escaped from the Oakland Hills fire in 1991 where almost 3,000 homes were destroyed and 24 people ultimately died. I think my interest in this case certainly was influenced by having had this common experience. After a fire, "post-traumatic distress" is an important factor. Aaron even witnessed his factory burning down. In the aftermath of the fire, the shock and sense of loss are enormous, and yet major decisions that have a long-term impact must be made immediately. Relations with family and friends are strained. In Aaron's case, he had a huge sense of responsibility for the injured workers, several of whom were badly burned, though luckily none died, and for those who risked their lives to save parts of the buildings that were not so heavily engulfed. In addition, the fire happened just before Christmas. Though some members of his board, which included members of his own family who worked in the company, opposed it, Feuerstein generously offered to pay his idled workers for the following month, even though he was not required to do so. He said he did not do it for the publicity, but because he was firmly convinced it was the right thing to do. But in hindsight, was it the right thing to do?

Feuerstein renewed his pledge to his 1,500 employees for another three months. As the news spread of his actions he received about $1 million in donations, from small to large checks from all around the country. By the end of a month some of his operations were up and running again as they shifted equipment undamaged by the fire to other locations. Some of the manufacturing facilities for Polartec had been spared.

Was Feuerstein's generosity to his employees a costly decision that ultimately put his company in jeopardy? It cost about $15 million. One view is that by itself it may not have been a foolhardy decision, given the growing business he was in. Sales of Polartec had been growing by 50 percent anually at the time of the fire. Aaron also knew that if his business was going to have a chance to rebuild, he was going to have to rely heavily on his workers to put in an extraordinary effort to get him up and running again.

After three months the remaining workers who were still out of work were supported by unemployment and special funds from the gifts that had been donated.

The outpouring of support, both financial and in the public arena, surprised Feuerstein. He was a private man, an owner of a small family firm, little known outside of New England, and now all of a sudden he was in front of the cameras, making statements about the state of American business. He was invited to sit behind Hillary Clinton at President Clinton's State of the Union Address in January 1996. The names of Malden Mills and Aaron Feuerstein were in all the press and created a flood of goodwill for the company.

He was lauded not only for paying his workers after the fire, but for his immediate commitment to rebuild the factory in the same location. As he said so frequently in interviews after the fire, he and his father had not moved the operation to the South as many other mills did in search of cheaper labor in the 1950s and 1960s, so why would he abandon Lawrence now? He continues to believe that highly skilled labor can produce the best quality products, which in turn can differentiate a company from its competition, and that there is still a place for manufacturing in this country. This commitment earned him enormous political support from the local politicians, the governor, Senators Kennedy and Kerry, and New Hampshire representatives.

## The Decision to Rebuild

At issue seems to be not the fact of rebuilding in Lawrence, but the manner in which Aaron Feuerstein proceeded on this project.

Aaron knew that he was "fully insured." What he did not know, what no claimant after a loss knows, is what the actual payout amount will be. He would not know that for many months of negotiations with the insurer. At the point of a claim, the relationship with the insurer turns from one of being, as it were, "in good hands" to one that is adversarial in nature.

The insurer tries to keep the settlement as low as possible and the claimant wants to replace the buildings that burned. The insurer AGI was a tough negotiator, settling well after the newly rebuilt factory had been completed in 1997. The final insurance settlement was about $300 million, covering only 75 percent of the $400 million in rebuilding costs that Feuerstein had borrowed to put his factory in operation.

Was Aaron's decision to rebuild in the immediate aftermath of the fire one of an emotion-driven "survival instinct"? The firm's famous clock tower had been saved during the fire. How could Aaron not see that as a symbol of the firm's commitment to rise from the ashes? Was the idea of renting or renovating facilities, or scaling down the size, never seriously considered? Was the promise of all that cash that would allow him to replace aging equipment with brand new machines, to build a new state of the art facility to deal with the overbearing heat in summer and accommodate the new computerized methodologies, a license to spend more than he should?

Even within the context of rebuilding it was clear that Aaron thought big and wanted the best. There was dispute among the members of the board and with his own son about the scale of the rebuilding. The insurance coverage did not specify that the buildings had to be rebuilt at all or require a minimal square footage, but Aaron opted for the best. He replaced almost all of the space that had been lost, anticipating that his Polartec sales would continue to grow, even though his son was advising him to scale back the square footage. He later admitted that maybe his building plans had been overly extravagant, even to the point of buying new equipment, whereas before the fire he would have bought used. While the mill was being rebuilt, he had leased space for some of his operations in neighboring towns, but now it was he who was to have excess space as the business turned down.

What was Aaron's failure? Did he fail to anticipate the great gap between his rebuilding costs and his final insurance settlement? Did he fail to anticipate that in spite of great attention and support on one level from all the media, months of interruption of his supply would enable his competitors to gain an edge and win customers? Was his attention so focused on recovery from the fire and its aftermath, the insurance claims, and the lawsuits against the company from injured employees, that he failed to see the business risks? Was he imprudent or unlucky that a warm winter depressed fleece sales just at the time his upholstery line was floundering? Was Aaron Feuerstein trying to singlehandedly buck the inexorable pressure on the costs of manufacturing and prices that eventually led the new board after the bankruptcy to a partnership with a mill in China? In 2004 this outsourced production was at about 10 percent of production, but that figure is likely to rise due to the expiration of the textile tariffs with China in January 2005.

## The Legacy

Under the special arrangements of the bankruptcy settlement, Aaron and his sons had an opportunity to bid on the firm for another year, but their bids were rejected by the current owners. His group of financial investors, along with the Import-Export Bank, which had guaranteed a loan, had plans to develop the excess mill space into mixed income housing units and retain jobs in the local area. Though Aaron at 79 had surgery on his heart in July 2004, his determination to regain control over the company remained undimmed. He feared it would become another commodity company and the original vision of investing in innovative products that require a highly skilled workforce would be lost. He did not want to run the mill as CEO, but he wanted to resurrect the legacy of the family firm, committed to the goal of continuing to provide high-quality, well-paying jobs to the people of Massachusetts and New Hampshire.

If it were dependent solely on the force of his personality, it would have happened. Aaron is an obstinate man. The local politicians were supporting him, hoping that he could be given the chance to preserve the jobs in the local area.

Since Aaron failed to regain control of the family firm, has he failed? He believes that he has. But as a former journalist at the *Boston Globe* assures him, "You have won, Aaron, no matter what happens!" His ethical legacy is independent of whether or not his family regains control of Malden Mills.

Though his enterprise may have failed, he rebuilt the mill in Lawrence and gave the community hope that there is a future for their families. The new owners currently repeat their commitment to the community, though they state that more jobs will probably be offshored in the future.

What Aaron did was indeed an example of virtue ethics since it was in his character to be concerned for his employees. Examples of his prior support for them, such as giving asssistance to help buy a house or send a child to college, were recounted by workers after the fire. However, what Aaron did in paying his workers after the fire was more a demonstration of Carol Gilligan's "Ethic of Care," shaped by the importance of preserving relationships. When faced with the decision of what he could do for his workers he asked himself the question, not what was his duty to do, but what was the most loving thing to do?

This act has called American business leaders to consider again the employment relationship between an enterprise and its workers, not as being exclusively an economic one, but also a personal and communal one. Aaron Feuerstein's acts, which put his workers' needs above his own economic self-interest, were grounded in his religious convictions as an orthodox Jew. He believes he has a responsibility to them as individuals and to the common good. He had the unique chance to show that rather than pursuing the course of the moral minimum, he chose the moral maximum. As he said to me, *"At the end of the day, at the Final Judgment, will it be enough to say, 'I have been the CEO of a company and made a lot of money?' After your basic needs are met, what is the point of all that activity, if not to do some good? . . . on Judgment Day what do you amount to?"*

In the retail outlet at Malden Mills among the colorful bolts of cloth and remnants are two images that caught my attention. One was a portrait of Aaron Feuerstein made out of different colored cotton spools, a diffuse image made by an employee.

The other was a wall hanging embroidered by children at a synagogue school as a gift in thanks to Aaron for his support of them. What is his legacy? He is clearly loved.

Aaron is a unique businessman: He lives modestly and his heavily thumbed Bible sits on his table beside his two volumes of Shakespeare's comedies and tragedies.

He reads them frequently.

Is this a tragic tale? Maybe, but for Shakespeare's best tragic heroes, their defeat at the hands of fate is not the end. The truth of their life lives on.

# Bend the Rules

## Problem-Solving Strategies for Quiet Leaders

EXCERPTED FROM

*Leading Quietly:*
*An Unorthodox Guide to Doing the Right Thing*

BY

*Joseph L. Badaracco, Jr.*

Harvard Business School Press
*Boston, Massachusetts*

ISBN-13: 978-1-4221-2363-8
2363BC

This chapter was originally published as chapter 6 of *Leading Quietly: An Unorthodox Guide to Doing the Right Thing,*
copyright 2002 Harvard Business School Publishing Corporation.



You can purchase Harvard Business School Press books at booksellers worldwide.
You can order Harvard Business School Press books and book chapters online at www.HBSPress.org, or by calling 888-500-1016 or, outside the U.S. and Canada, 617-783-7410.

CHAPTER SIX

# Bend the Rules

BENDING THE RULES isn't something we associate with responsible leadership. If anything, it's what politicians do, or devious lawyers, or kids trying to get around a curfew. Real leaders, according to the conventional view, obey the law and play by the rules—because they see it as their duty and it sets the right example. They know that when leaders fiddle with the rules, others do the same.

Yet things are often more complicated. Consider, for example, telling the truth. This is something we are all supposed to do, but we also recognize exceptions to this rule. Some are trivial: You may decide not to tell a friend what you *really* think of her new scarf. Other exceptions are profound: During World War II, some families in Europe hid Jews from the Nazis and lied about it.

Between the trivial and profound cases are countless everyday situations in which strict adherence to the rules may do more harm than good. The basic problem is that no one is smart enough to throw a net of rules over all the possibilities—the world is simply too varied and fluid, too ambiguous and uncertain. Hence, we inevitably find ourselves in some situations in which the rules don't apply and others in which following them is a mistake or even a cop-out.

Quiet leaders respond to these ambiguous situations in a particular way. They are reluctant, for a variety of good reasons, to break the rules, but they don't want to obey them mechanically and cause harm. So they look, imaginatively and creatively, for ways to bend the rules without breaking them. And, when they find a way to bend the rules, they seize the opportunity and use it to uphold their values and commitments.

But bending the rules is a tricky business that involves walking some very fine lines. To understand why, we will look at a situation that involved a volunteer, a homeless boy, and a frightening, late-night subway ride.

## A Night in Hell's Kitchen

Nick Russo, a community service volunteer, and Jerome, a homeless boy, met early on a Tuesday evening in July in Hell's Kitchen, an area on the west side of Manhattan long known for crime, prostitution, and police officers who looked the other way.

Russo usually spent Tuesday nights working at the Aimes Center, a shelter for homeless teenagers. Most of his other evenings, as well as his weekends, were consumed by his job as an investment banker. Russo had become a volunteer two years earlier after a friend persuaded him to spend a weekend painting several rooms at the shelter. Soon afterwards, he began contributing both money and time to the shelter, even though every visit saddened and hardened him.

One night, for example, he arrived and found an eighteen-year-old boy lying on the floor, barely able to speak. He had been in a drug-related fight three days before, and one of his lungs had been pierced by an ice pick. A doctor had patched him up, and the boy had felt okay at the time. But, just before Russo arrived, his lung collapsed again, and he was gasping for air. The staff asked Russo to take him to a nearby hospital where, after more than an hour pleading with the doctors to see him, the boy finally got treatment. Russo had met fifteen-year-old boys and girls who worked as prostitutes to support drug habits; sixteen-year-old girls with babies, and nowhere to live; and kids who spent a night or two in the shelter and then fled because their crack bosses had learned where they were.

Russo met Jerome right after finishing the assignment he liked least, escorting a teenager to a city youth shelter. This had to be done when the Aimes shelter was full or when a teenager would not follow the rules. The problem was that the city shelters were overflowing with homeless youngsters, so leaving a teenager there was usually a cruel tug-of-war. In addition, city officials sometimes tried to avoid taking in additional kids, hoping the private shelter would take them back. In these situations, volunteers had been instructed to tell the security guard the youth's name, hand over a file, and walk out of the office. This tactic would force the shelter to admit the youth, though they sometimes had to spend their first few nights sleeping on the office floor.

One Tuesday night at about ten o'clock, Russo walked away from a city shelter. He felt disgusted, with himself and the system. He had just asked a passerby for directions, when a boy who was sitting against a wall jumped up and said, "I'm going that way. Follow me." Russo looked at him, surprised and said, "What are you doing hanging around here?"

"Nothin'. Just about to go hang at the games," the boy replied, referring to a video arcade at the Port Authority Terminal. Russo vividly recalled the last time he walked through the terminal late at night: the smell of urine, the dim light, a teenager sitting against a wall shaking violently from drug withdrawal, and gangs walking around in cool paranoia.

"What's your name?" Russo asked.

"Jerome."

"Don't you think you ought to be back inside that office?"

Jerome answered, "No, I hate them people, but I got some friends in there that I's visitin'."

"Oh, I see," Russo paused. "How old are you?"

"Fourteen. Folks say I'm, like, short for my age."

Both of them knew fourteen was a bit of a stretch. Russo didn't think Jerome looked a day over eleven. He knew right away that Jerome was a runaway in trouble. He had learned from his time at Aimes that street kids started conversations with almost everyone and tried to act cool, even though they were hurting inside. Russo was astonished and appalled to see an eleven-year-old kid out so late, on his own, in New York City. The neighborhood where Jerome was hanging around was a war zone filled with crack addicts, prostitutes, the homeless, and the mentally ill.

Russo knew he was close to breaking one of the basic rules at Aimes. During his initial training, he and the other new volunteers had signed a statement saying they would not work the streets unless they were part of a supervised outreach group. Russo also knew that volunteers had been fired for breaking the rule.

Russo had missed dinner so he asked Jerome if he wanted some food. Jerome said no, but followed him into a Korean Deli anyway. The man behind the counter looked at Jerome and smiled. Like Russo, he knew that Jerome was a sad, smart, manipulative kid. Russo bought himself a sandwich and got two candy bars and an apple for Jerome.

As they walked to the subway stop, he told Jerome about his family and his job. Jerome answered that he wanted to go to Wall

Street and make some cash, too. But Russo's efforts to learn where Jerome lived and who was taking care of him went nowhere.

It was after eleven when they got on the subway. A few moments later, Russo was reminded that "Hell's Kitchen" wasn't just a roguish old name kept alive for tourists. A man shuffled into their mostly empty car, sat down right next to them, stared dumbly at his reflection in the window, and then opened a long switch-blade knife and placed it on the seat next to Jerome. Although Russo's heart began beating wildly, he kept talking, didn't look at the man, and began thinking frantically about how to escape. A minute or so later, the man got up, smirked at Russo as if to say "You were lucky, this time," and got off the train.

The incident petrified Russo and suddenly the prospect of leaving Jerome on the streets appalled him. For the first time, he told Jerome he was from Aimes—news that Jerome clearly didn't like hearing. "Yeah, I've been to that place," he muttered. When Russo offered to take him there, Jerome refused. "No, I got to play games with my brother. He's waiting for me." But Russo wouldn't give up, and continued trying to convince Jerome to come with him. Aimes seemed to be the only safe haven for Jerome that night.

For several minutes, he made small talk with Jerome while trying to figure out what to do. When the train stopped a few minutes later, however, Jerome got up. "This is where I get off," was all he said. "Come with me," Russo pleaded once last time, but Jerome just winked at him and stepped off the train. Russo never saw him again.

## Reflections and Regrets

By most standards, Nick Russo deserves credit for quiet leadership. His work at the Aimes Center came on top of the sixty to eighty hours he put in every week as an investment banker. His volunteer work earned him no points at his bank and meant that he started some days worn out and feeling down. At times, he felt his volunteer efforts were basically futile, but he didn't quit.

The episode with Jerome made him feel particularly bad. He thought he had made a serious mistake in letting Jerome walk away, but didn't know how he could have prevented it. What had gone wrong? Perhaps his judgment was off because he was tired or scared by the man with the knife. Perhaps he understood intuitively that there was no way to persuade Jerome to come with him. But none of this made Russo feel any better, nor did the fact that, when he decided not to get off the subway with Jerome, he was following the rules of the Aimes Center.

Russo was judging himself, quite severely, by the heroic standard of leadership. He didn't do all he could to take care of Jerome. He hadn't found him shelter, even for a single night. Instead of taking a risk and following Jerome off the subway, Russo sat and watched the boy walk away. The man with the switchblade had almost attacked Jerome—what other predators awaited him that night?

The heroic model is not, however, the right way to think about what Russo did. It defines his problem as straightforward—protecting Jerome and finding him shelter—and suggests that a real leader would have done much more than Russo did. But from the perspective of quiet leadership, Russo did the right thing and handled a very difficult situation in an exemplary way. What Russo did was bend the rules—carefully, judiciously, and responsibly.

During his training, Russo was told repeatedly that volunteers were not allowed to engage in outreach. One reason was that successful outreach required training and supervised experience, which volunteers did not have. Other reasons involved risks to the Aimes Center. The Center could be held responsible if volunteers were injured as a result of their outreach efforts. In addition, a teenager seeking attention might accuse a volunteer of abuse without any witnesses to say otherwise, or a volunteer could seem to be involved in a drug sale. If any of this happened, the shelter's reputation would become a plaything of the media, and both fundraising and recruiting would suffer. For all these reasons, shelters didn't need what Russo later called "uncontrolled, freelance yuppies" working the streets.

When Jerome first approached him, Russo could have simply walked away. In doing so, he would have been following the no-outreach rule. Instead, he did something much more difficult and impressive. He spent a couple hours with Jerome, trying all the while to balance Jerome's clear and urgent needs with his own unambiguous responsibilities to the Aimes Center. In the end, Russo exercised leadership—he bent the rules of the Center, in order to try to help Jerome, but he did not break them, because of possible risks to the Center. Russo was willing to take on the challenge of operating in a difficult gray area, rather than resorting to blind allegiance to the rules or heroic and risky efforts on behalf of Jerome.

The problem Russo faced was the most challenging one we have examined. For example, Frank Taylor's difficulty with the new server was a matter of money, a big sale, and office politics. The worst consequence Taylor faced was a lower year-end bonus. Jerome's problem, in contrast, might have involved life and death.

Ethical efforts are often best judged like Olympic diving. It is important to compare what people actually accomplish to the degree of difficulty they face. Russo's dilemma was a complicated leap from a high platform—he was a volunteer with little experience, he was able to buy only a little time, he was dealing with a street-smart kid, he was operating in dark, menacing circumstances, and he had to protect the reputation of the Aimes Center.

Russo might have made a tragic mistake by ignoring Jerome in the first place, and he might have made a tragic mistake by following him off the subway.

Unfortunately, despite this careful balancing act, Russo did not feel good about what he had done. For years, he regretted not doing more to help Jerome—regardless of the degree of difficulty or any other excuse. Nevertheless, Russo *had* demonstrated real leadership.

## Take the Rules Very Seriously

When quiet leaders find themselves in complex ethical dilemmas, they follow two guidelines. One tells them to take the rules very seriously, which Russo did. The other tells them to look, creatively and imaginatively, for ways to follow the spirit of the rules while, at the same time, bending them.

Russo was a serious, thoughtful, law-abiding citizen. He had completed the Aimes Center's training program and, during his two years as a volunteer, had carefully followed its rules and guidelines. The no-outreach rule of the Aimes Center had dominated his thinking during the time he spent with Jerome. He understood the reasons for it—the need for special training and the problems that freelance outreach could cause for the Center and for volunteers themselves. Perhaps the strongest indication of how profoundly Russo understood the no-outreach rule was his ultimate decision not to break it.

The conviction that laws and rules are there to be understood, respected, and followed distinguishes responsible individuals and quiet leaders from underage drinkers and white-collar crooks. Scofflaws view laws and rules as cobwebs to be swept aside. Quiet leaders obey them because of their strong moral weight. In a democracy, the law reflects the will of the people and the traditions of a society. And, when individuals join organizations, they agree, implicitly or explicitly, to follow its rules and policies.

All the quiet leaders we have discussed took the rules very seriously. Rebecca Olson followed the rules in her handling of the charges against Richard Millar—by consulting with several attorneys regarding the hospital's obligations to him—even though her strong instinct was simply to fire him. Elliot Cortez believed his company was doing something wrong in skirting federal regulations on marketing prescription drugs. Captain Jill Matthews was incensed because the inspectors had so blatantly and casually thumbed their noses at the rules.

There is a second compelling reason why quiet leaders may be willing to bend the rules but usually stop short of flagrantly violating them: They care about their own self-interest. Violating the law can lead to fines, jail time, damaged reputations, and cameo appearances on the local news. Violations of organizational policy can be career-limiting moves. This is why Frank Taylor was extremely reluctant to violate the ban on old-network connections: He thought other sales reps would use this against him. Elliot Cortez was concerned that, if his company was caught playing games, he might end up getting blamed for marketing drugs for the wrong purposes. When quiet leaders face difficult issues, they take the rules seriously in order to protect their reputations, networks, and career prospects.

Most of the time, taking the rules seriously is the only guideline a responsible person needs. But when situations are complicated, following the rules to the letter can be irresponsible and even lead to unfortunate results. Consequently, quiet moral leaders—like Nick Russo—take the rules seriously while, at the same time, looking hard for room to maneuver.

## Look for Wiggle Room

Quiet leaders do not think that rules are made to be broken. They see this notion for what it is: an unethical and shortsighted way to deal with serious problems. But they also know that following the rules sometimes leads to painful dilemmas and harmful results. Then quiet leaders try hard to find or create some room to maneuver, but they also do so *within* the boundaries set by the rules. In other words, they take the rules seriously, but they also look for wiggle room.

Quiet leaders do this because they understand that life seldom presents challenges and problems in the form of stark, either-or choices. Nick Russo did not want to abandon Jerome, nor did he want to break the rules of the Aimes Center. He knew that both of these were serious obligations. He didn't want to make good on one of them by failing to meet the other. So instead he simply talked with Jerome, invited him to get some food, and then took the subway with him.

Was this outreach? When he met Jerome, Russo was headed back to the Center, not looking for kids needing shelter. And Russo didn't approach Jerome; Jerome approached him. True, Russo could have told Jerome to leave him alone. But his initial instinct in talking with Jerome and getting him a meal was simply to find out what was going on. Russo was reacting, as many people would, to the shock of being approached, late at night, by a young child. He was not wearing his "volunteer hat," nor hatching any plans for taking Jerome to the Aimes Center.

Moreover, the Aimes Center was dedicated to helping teenagers, and they were the targets of its no-outreach policy. While Jerome had claimed to be fourteen, it seemed more likely that he was about eleven. Hence, the no-outreach policy probably did not apply, strictly speaking, to Jerome. Nor did some of the rationale behind it. For example, the policy had been designed to protect volunteers from violence, but Jerome was small and young. He posed no visible threat to Russo.

These may seem to be quibbles or loopholes, but they point to a larger issue. The no-outreach rule was simply a requirement the Aimes Center had introduced, three years earlier, to help avoid certain problems. It wasn't one of the Ten Commandments or part of the U.S. Constitution; it wasn't a city or state law; and it didn't express a fundamental ethical principle, like telling the truth or respecting others' rights. It was a blanket prohibition, a crude instrument for a complicated world. It hadn't stood the test of time. In all likelihood, the rule would be modified and refined in the future, precisely because of situations like the one Russo faced.

Moreover, if Russo had ignored Jerome's first advance, he would have violated another important policy of the Aimes Center. The only time the Center "abandoned" teenagers was when it left them in City welfare offices—which is what Russo had just done. Although such action put young people in the custody of public officials, the Center viewed this tactic as a last resort and a mark of failure. In other words, once the Center had a relationship with a teenager, it did everything it could to help. Wasn't Russo obligated to do the same with Jerome? By talking with Jerome and going on the subway with him, wasn't he respecting the basic mission of the Aimes Center, rather than following a recent, untested, internal regulation? In this case, which was more important?

But what if he had left the train with Jerome? At that point, Russo was thinking explicitly about how he could get Jerome off the streets. Following him into the Port Authority Terminal and trying to persuade him to go to the Aimes Center would have been freelance outreach. Moreover, the episode with the knife-wielding passenger demonstrated for Russo the basic rationale for the no-outreach policy. When volunteers broke this rule, they could put themselves in real danger and imperil the reputation and future of the Aimes Center.

So Russo drew a line. He decided that talking with Jerome, buying him a meal, and riding the subway with him only bent the rules, but getting off the train violated them. Should he have done a little less? Could he have done a little more? Those questions cannot be answered with precision—even in retrospect. As we have seen, Russo continued to feel he should have done more, but there's no way to know what the outcome might have been if he had. In uncertain, fluid circumstances, the quest for final answers is futile. What really matters is the careful balancing of competing obligations. Nick Russo worked hard at this, under extremely difficult circumstances. He performed extremely well in a very demanding test of leadership.

Like Russo, quiet leaders don't want to impale themselves on the horns of dilemmas. They look long and hard for ways to meet all their obligations and commitments rather than make hard choices among them. Instead of confronting dilemmas head-on, they prefer to use creativity and imagination to work around them. This is what Frank Taylor did to avoid choosing between meeting his client's needs and following the "Win-Win" policy. Garrett Williams did the same in looking for ways to treat his employees fairly while satisfying his boss's demand for a quick turnaround.

When people are under stress, their natural tendency is to grab hold of whatever source of security they can find, and security is often found in following the rules to the letter. It takes courage and determination to follow the example Russo set. He took all his obligations to the Center seriously, but he didn't shirk his duties as a caring human being.

Bend the Rules

## Entrepreneurial Ethics

Most of the time, there is nothing wrong with following just the first of the two guidelines described in this chapter. Taking the rules seriously is usually the safe, smart, and responsible thing to do. If most people didn't behave this way most of the time, the trains wouldn't run on time and society would fly apart. In difficult situations, however, both guidelines become important. Following either one can lead to serious problems.

One of these problems is evading responsibility by taking the rules too seriously. Saying simply "These are the rules and I have to follow them" can be a way of avoiding responsibility. Only moral bookkeepers, fitted out with green eyeshades, define ethics as a checklist of "do's and don'ts." This may seem responsible, but sometimes it just isn't. In some cases, as the French moralist La Rochefoucauld put it, "We are held to our duty by laziness and timidity, but our virtue gets the credit."[1]

For quiet leaders, taking the rules seriously doesn't mean treating them as a paint-by-numbers exercise. When things get complicated, quiet leaders take initiative, trust their creativity, and work hard to create room to maneuver. They approach ethical problems as entrepreneurs, not clerks.

This entrepreneurial approach often pays big dividends. In part, this is because of the astonishing fertility of the human imagination. The human talent for seeing things in a variety of ways is a valuable skill. Martha Nussbaum, a gifted interpreter of Aristotle's ideas, has written, "Moral knowledge . . . is not simply intellectual grasp of propositions; it is not even simply intellectual grasp of particular facts; it is perception. It is seeing a complex, concrete reality in a highly lucid and richly responsive way; it is taking in what is there, with imagination and feeling."[2] Quiet leaders approach problems with the conviction that practical-minded creativity can almost always create new possibilities for responsible action.

Imagination cannot, of course, perform miracles. In one Woody Allen story, he describes sitting in a café and trying to convince a despondent friend that a review referring to a "playwright of absolutely no promise whatsoever" could be interpreted in several different ways. Sometimes situations *are* black and white and individuals cannot avoid hard choices. Sometimes we have to make good on one commitment or one responsibility and let others slide. But, until their backs are firmly against the wall, quiet leaders search vigorously and creatively for ways to make good on all their obligations.

The other reason imagination often succeeds is that most situations have more levels and greater intricacy than appear at first glance. For example, when Frank Taylor drilled down into his problem, he realized that there were a variety of ways to define what it meant to "connect" a computer to a network. This wasn't because he was playing fast and loose, but because there simply was no standard, etched-in-stone definition of what computer specialists call "connectivity." Taylor's analysis and fact-finding had revealed the complexities of his problem, and this gave him more opportunities for creative maneuvering. In fact, Taylor's eventual solution to his problem—getting the law firm's new servers classified as a test site—was itself a creative way of maneuvering within the rules of his company. Without this imaginative recasting of his problem, Taylor would have had to break the rules against old-network hookups or lose an important sale for his company. In other words, wiggle room isn't just hokum. It reflects reality. The complexities of the world, examined carefully, usually offer room to maneuver. This is why creative, opportunistic approaches to difficult issues often pay off.

But simply following the second guideline and looking for wiggle room can lead to dangers of its own. This is the reason why the first guideline—take the rules very seriously—cannot be forgotten. Imagination needs boundaries, and the laws and rules provide them. Consider the case of a bank robber who walks up to a teller, takes out a vial of cooking oil, says that it's really nitroglycerin that could blow up the bank, and asks for the contents of the cash drawer. This may be very clever, but it shows what can happen when imagination and cleverness are unbounded by the rules.

Breaking the rules is an easy way out, as is following them robotically. In contrast, bending the rules is hard work. It involves exercising creativity *within* the boundaries set by the law, the rules, and prevailing ethical customs. It demands discipline and restraint, along with flexibility and imagination. Finally, it requires a measure of faith—faith that difficult, careful judgments about competing obligations will make a difference in the long run.

Russo never learned what happened to Jerome. Perhaps he got into trouble that night, perhaps he found his way to safety, perhaps the concern and compassion Russo showed Jerome made him more likely to go to a shelter or seek other help. The ultimate effects of small things are often unclear. In this respect, they resemble letters, as once described by Emily Dickinson—they are written thoughtfully, addressed carefully, and placed in the mailbox, but no one knows if they are read or received.

## Leadership and Cleverness

This approach to ethical situations runs counter to our standard image of what leadership is all about. We prefer leaders who defend their values clearly and forcefully. We associate cleverness, complexity, loopholes, and maneuvering with dubious characters, not role models. Like many other politicians, Ross Perot appealed to this sentiment in his presidential campaigns. One of his favorite phrases was "See, it's simple," after which he would compare some longstanding, complex national problem to his car or an old dog.

A better motto is Albert Einstein's. He said, "Everything should be as simple as possible, but no simpler." Quiet leaders do not bend the rules casually, nor do they view cleverness and maneuvering as ideal ways to deal with problems. But sometimes the complexities of situations give them no choice. Drilling down doesn't produce an answer, and they can't buy more time. They confront situations like the one Russo faced as Jerome walked toward him in Hell's Kitchen.

So they look for ways to bend the rules without breaking them. They do this after grappling with the complexities of a situation, not as a shortcut around them. Their aim is not to avoid responsibilities, but to find a practical, workable way to meet all of their responsibilities. An imaginative, entrepreneurial approach to ethical dilemmas can often help people avoid heart-wrenching choices and enable them to make good on all the commitments they hold dear.

# Notes

CHAPTER SIX

1. Duc de la Rochefoucauld, *Maxims*, 58.

2. Martha Nussbaum, *Love's Knowledge* (Oxford: Oxford University Press, 1990), 84.

Mary C. Gentile, PhD, Director
www.GivingVoicetoValues.org

**Giving *Voice* to Values**

# An Action Framework for *Giving Voice to Values* "The To-Do List"

***Giving Voice to Values* is about learning how to act on your values effectively – not about wondering whether you could.**

**Values**
Know and appeal to a short list of widely shared values: e.g., honesty, respect, responsibility, fairness and compassion.[1] In other words, don't assume too little – or too much – commonality with the viewpoints of others.

**Choice**
Believe you have a choice about voicing values by examining your own track record. Know what has enabled and disabled you in the past, so you can work with and around these factors. And recognize, respect and appeal to the capacity for choice in others.

**Normality**
Expect values conflicts so that you approach them calmly and competently. Over-reaction can limit your choices unnecessarily.

**Purpose**
Define your personal and professional purpose explicitly and broadly before conflicts arise. What is the impact you most want to have? Similarly, appeal to a sense of purpose in others.

**Self-Knowledge, Self-Image and Alignment**
Generate a "self-story" about voicing and acting on your values that is consistent with who you are and that builds on your strengths. There are many ways to align your unique strengths and style with your

[1] Rushworth M. Kidder, *Moral Courage: Taking Action When Your Values Are Put To the Test* (New York: William Morrow, HarperCollins Publishers, Inc., 2005), p. 47.

values. If you view yourself as a "pragmatist," for example, find a way to view voicing your values as pragmatic.

**Voice**

Practice voicing your values in front of respected peers, using the style of expression with which you are most skillful and which is most appropriate to the situation, and inviting coaching and feedback. You are more likely to say those words that you have pre-scripted for yourself and already heard yourself express.

**Reasons and Rationalizations**

Anticipate the typical rationalizations given for ethically questionable behavior and identify counter--arguments. These rationalizations are predictable and vulnerable to reasoned response.

# Wells

# SECTOR-BENDING: BLURRING LINES BETWEEN NONPROFIT AND FOR-PROFIT

*J. Gregory Dees and Beth Battle Anderson*

Traditional sector boundaries are increasingly breaking down. Everyone has seen the headlines about nonprofit hospitals, HMOs, or health insurers converting to for-profit status, and in some cases being acquired by for-profit chains. But many individuals could not tell you whether their own provider is a nonprofit or a for-profit entity. Most have heard about Edison Schools, a public corporation that manages over 130 public schools in 22 states and Washington, D.C., but few know that Nobel Learning Communities has started a chain of independent, for-profit schools, operating 170 schools in 15 states. And while for-profit health clubs try to stir up controversy over unfair competition from suburban YMCAs, Pioneer Human Services, a Seattle nonprofit serving substance abusers and ex-convicts, quietly provides metal bending operations for Boeing as a means of training and employing their at-risk clients. Further south in Los Angeles, students at Crenshaw High School planted a community garden, began selling produce at the local farmer's market, and now sell all-natural salad dressings and applesauce in regional supermarkets and via mail order. Company profits provide college scholarships for the student owners, and 25% of the produce is donated to the needy in their community.

What is going on here? On small and large scales, in local communities and across the country, for-profits and nonprofits are moving into new territories and exploring uncharted waters. While this kind of sector-bending is not entirely new—remember Goodwill Industries or Girl Scouts Cookies—it is certainly growing in popularity. Increasingly we are turning to business methods and structures in our efforts to find more cost-effective and sustainable ways to address social problems and deliver socially important goods.

Should we be troubled by this behavior? We should not. As with any new development, this one has its risks, but these can be identified, evaluated, and managed. We have entered a very healthy period of experimentation. Some of the experiments will fail, but others will succeed. These successes should allow us to use resources, particularly scarce philanthropic resources, more effectively to serve public purposes. In this way, boundary-blurring activities have the potential to increase the "independence" of the "independent sector." They may even lead us to change the way we think about "sectors." Instead of emphasizing legal forms of organization, such as nonprofit, for-profit, and governmental, perhaps we can focus on communities of practice that include different organizational forms serving a common purpose, such as the improvement of elementary and secondary education or the preservation of bio-diversity.

### The Definition of Sector-Bending

Before exploring some of the potential benefits, it is important to understand what we mean when we talk about "sector-bending." Sector-bending refers to a wide variety of approaches, activities, and relationships that are blurring the distinctions between nonprofit and for-profit organizations, either because they are behaving more similarly, operating in the same realms, or both. Some behaviors are more widespread than others; several have been a reality of the social sector for generations; and others represent relatively new phenomena. For simplicity, we define sector-bending around four broad types of behavior: Imitation, Interaction, Intermingling, and Industry Creation. Just as the boundaries between sectors are blurring, the lines between these categories are indistinct. In fact, behaviors falling within one category quite often lead to or are part of activities associated with another.

*Imitation and Conversion*: Nonprofit organizations are increasingly adopting the strategies, concepts, and practices of the business world. Anyone working in this field sees it regularly. Organizations in which "customer" and "marketing" once had negative connotations are hiring marketers or consultants, identifying their target markets, segmenting their customers, and developing strategies. Tools developed specifically for use in the business world, such as Porter's Five-Forces strategy framework or Kaplan's Balanced Scorecard, are being adapted and adopted by nonprofit organizations. As successful business entrepreneurs become increasingly interested in bringing their skills, as well as their wealth, into the social sector, this trend should continue. Even a highly charitable, community-oriented organization has like Habitat for Humanity has been influenced by the business experience of its founder Millard Fuller, a marketing entrepreneur and self-made millionaire. Habitat builds houses for those who otherwise could not afford a home of their own, but it requires its new homeowners to repay a modest mortgage. Many other nonprofits have become more business-like by finding ways to generate fees for services rendered. In the most extreme case, nonprofits are actually converting to for-profit status. This practice is most prominent in health care, but it also happens elsewhere. For instance, America Works, a welfare-to-work training program, started as a nonprofit and later converted to for-profit status.

*Interaction*: Another kind of blurring occurs as nonprofits and for-profits increasingly interact with each other as competitors, contractors, and collaborators. Many of these interactions stem directly from public policy shifts away from grant making toward contracting and reimbursement. But private innovations, such as private health insurance, have also played a major role as nonprofits are finding new corporate markets for their goods, services, and assets.

Competitors: For-profits are playing a greater role in arenas formerly dominated by nonprofit and public sector organizations, while nonprofits are entering the domains of business. In the former category, health care provision provides the most obvious example, though even there, the average observer may underestimate the extent of the activity. For example, how many know that the largest single provider of hospice care in the U.S. is VITAS, a for-profit that started as a nonprofit. But the emergence of for-profit players extends beyond the health care arena to a wide range of social services including education, day care centers, rehabilitation services, affordable housing, and even welfare-to-work. Anywhere a savvy business entrepreneur can find a way to make a profit in a market dominated by nonprofit or public agencies we can expect to see for-profits enter and compete directly with nonprofit providers.

In return, nonprofits are competing head-to-head with businesses. Much of this activity is not new. Sheltered workshops have long provided services and produced goods in competition with business suppliers. This concept is being extended as many social services organizations are starting businesses to provide employment and training opportunities for their clientele. These nonprofit-run businesses range from manufacturing to bakeries, restaurants, grounds maintenance, and translation services. Larger nonprofits are moving more aggressively into ventures that compete directly with businesses. The American Association of Retired People offers an alternative to for-profit insurance companies. Harvard Business School Press broke with the image of an academic publisher to aggressively compete with for-profit publishers of business books. The National Geographic has moved beyond the production of branded tour books and maps to having its own cable television channel, competing directly with the Discovery Channel as well as with one of its longtime distributors and collaborators, the nonprofit Public Broadcasting System. Museum catalogues and web sites compete directly with businesses selling similar items.

Contractors: Furthermore, given that nonprofits are engaging in more "business-like" activities, it is not surprising that for-profits are contracting with nonprofits for both "nonprofit-like" goods and services as well as goods and services that were traditionally provided by other businesses. Universities are contracting with corporations to conduct research. Family Services of America sells "employee assistance programs" to companies like Xerox to provide social services for Xerox employees. For-profit players who have become social services providers are also contracting with nonprofits to access their expertise and community relationships. For example, after winning one welfare-to-work government contract, Lockheed Martin hired nearly 30 nonprofit agencies to supply various services. In other arenas, Bay Area business parks, commercial developments, and public facilities contract with Rubicon Landscape Services, an operation run by a nonprofit agency providing employment, job training, and other social services for the economically disadvantaged. Similarly, nonprofits are outsourcing the provision of specialized or capital-intensive services to for-profit providers. Nonprofit charter schools contract with for-profit education management companies to run the whole school or just provide administrative services. Universities contract with technology companies to transfer curriculum to media suitable for distance learning.

Collaborators: Nonprofits and for-profits are also entering into strategic partnerships and joint ventures that aim to be mutually beneficial to both parties. The Nature Conservancy partners with Georgia Pacific to manage forestlands in environmentally sensitive ways. City Year, a youth-service nonprofit, helps teach Timberland employees about team building and diversity and provides an outlet for employee community service, while Timberland offers City Year business expertise, funding, and uniforms. Together they developed a new Timberland product line called City Year Gear. Share Our Strength, an anti-hunger organization, entered into an agreement with American Express to market and raise money for both organizations via a cause-related marketing campaign called the "Charge Against Hunger."

*Intermingling*: A step beyond the interaction of independent nonprofit and for-profit organizations is the intermingling of organizational structures that occurs in "hybrid organizations." Hybrid organizations, as we are using the term, are formal organizations, networks or umbrella groups that have both for-profit and nonprofit components. For-profit organizations may create nonprofit affiliates, and nonprofits sometimes establish for-profit subsidiaries or affiliates. Nonprofit affiliates of for-profits usually serve purposes and conduct activities that do not fit neatly into a for-profit structure. For instance, two prominent community development financial institutions, Grameen Bank in Bangladesh and Shorebank Corporation in Chicago, were set up as for-profit organizations but over time created nonprofit affiliates and for-profit subsidiaries to attract and deploy resources most efficiently. Nonprofit organizations such as the Girl Scouts and United Way long ago established for-profit subsidiaries to generate revenues for their programs by selling equipment and merchandise to local organizations and licensing the organization name and logos to vendors. Additionally, recently some nonprofits have been looking for for-profit business opportunities explicitly to help generate income for the nonprofit. For example, for this reason Children's Home & Aid Society of Illinois (CHASI) launched Ask4 Staffing, Inc., an affiliated for-profit corporation that provides staffing solutions to social service organizations.

*Industry Creation*: Finally, as these various forms of sector-bending have evolved, a few relatively new sector-blurring fields of practice have emerged or at least have taken on a distinctive identity. The emerging industries of community development finance, welfare-to-work training, eco-tourism, charter schools, and alternative energy production are all populated by for-profit, nonprofit, and hybrid organizations looking to harness market forces for social good. The charter school movement provides an interesting example. Charter schools are independent public schools that are often run and managed by parent/teacher partnerships, community based nonprofits, universities, for-profit companies, or hybrid forms of organization. Some charter schools are new schools while others have been converted from traditional public schools. In return for demonstrated results, these schools are granted the autonomy and flexibility to operate outside of the traditional rules and regulations of the public school system. This independence will ideally spur innovation while enhancing accountability and providing choice and competition that will lead to reform and educational improvements in the K-12 system in the United States.

**Potential Benefits of Sector-Bending**

Many have raised concerns about the increasing popularity of boundary blurring activities, though few have explained the potential benefits. This situation is not surprising given the relatively early stage of many of these experiments, the challenges of performance measurement, and the complexity of the issues. Only time will tell whether and to what extent these benefits will be realized, but the potential benefits of new social innovations and experiments are great and should not be neglected.

*More Effective and Appropriate Resource Allocation*: Both the emergence of for-profits delivering social goods and services and the increase of nonprofits generating earned income can lead to better resource allocation and more effective use of scarce philanthropic funds. At the sector level, the presence of for-profits can allow for a greater division of labor. If for-profits can generate even a minimal profit by serving clients who are willing and able to pay (directly or through a third party), then donor-supported nonprofits can concentrate on serving those who need philanthropic subsidies to cover the costs of serving them. In essence, for-profits would be freeing charitable dollars to be concentrated on those who need them most. This overall market structure functions more efficiently and encourages innovation amongst both for-profits and nonprofits. For-profits have the profit incentive to provide better services to those who can pay. If their quality declines too dramatically due to cost-cutting measures, the nonprofit offers an alternative. For nonprofits, the threat of losing profitable customers to for-profits should also enhance their performance and innovation.

Moreover, in health and human services industries, research has shown that nonprofits appear to be slower than for-profits both to grow to meet demand and to contract in response to changes in the environment and declines in demand. Thus, perhaps we need two layers of providers in these industries—for-profits to ensure responsiveness to market changes and nonprofits to preserve access for all, with limited wasted resources overall. Admittedly, for certain capital-intensive industries, there may not be room in some markets for more than one provider, whether for-profit or nonprofit. Hospitals in smaller communities provide a good example. In these cases, it may make sense for the leaders to consider hybrid structures, such as a for-profit hospital with an affiliated nonprofit clinic, to attract the necessary resources and meet the full spectrum of community needs.

At the organizational level, for nonprofits earning more commercial revenues, the revenues can serve as a source of leverage for philanthropic donations. Not only should donors not want to subsidize customers who can pay (either directly or through an interested third party), but they also should be attracted to the possibility of their dollars having greater social impact when combined with the revenues from earned income activities. Ideally, a greater pool of funds will be available to provide social goods and services for which nobody is able or willing to pay, either because these are true public goods or the clients are economically disadvantaged. And if a nonprofit organization can support all or the vast majority of its social mission activities via earned income, donors should shift their charitable dollars to other causes that are more in need of philanthropic subsidy. Again, a more efficient allocation of resources results in maximum social value creation overall.

Furthermore, the use of appropriate business tools has the potential to improve the effectiveness of nonprofit organizations. The discipline of identifying customers, defining how you will create value for them, developing strategies that reflect the organization's competencies and the competitive environment in which it operates, and pushing for more careful tracking of impact can have a very healthy impact on organizational performance even in philanthropic organizations. Of course these tools can be misused, as can any tools. Nonetheless, the potential for improving organizational effectiveness by importing and adapting tools from the business world is great.

*More Sustainable Solutions:* The blurring of sector boundaries has been accompanied by an increased interest in finding systemic and sustainable solutions to social problems. It is difficult to say which trend is driving the other, but they are certainly intertwined and complementary. Where appropriate, social entrepreneurs are looking to address underlying problems rather than meet needs, empower individuals rather than provide charitable relief, and create sustainable improvements rather than short-term responses. Business methods and approaches provide valuable tools for achieving these goals. Habitat for Humanity requires its new homeowners to pay mortgages. Grameen Bank provides small business loans, instead of grants, to economically disadvantaged villagers in Bangladesh. Pioneer Human Services employs ex-convicts and recovering drug addicts in various enterprises. Each of these approaches requires the individuals receiving help to take an active role in improving their own lives. They need not feel like objects of charity.

Even providing social services through employers enhances the potential for positive, lasting social impact. While the workers do not pay directly for services, they feel a sense of entitlement when these services are included in their benefits package. Covered workers are likely to be more comfortable seeking help for their troubled teen, failing marriage, or alcohol abuse problem than they would if they had to find an appropriate agency on their own and either pay for the care out of pocket or request charitable assistance. The spread of employer-sponsored social service programs represents a systemic approach to addressing a variety of underlying problems. All of these "business-like" strategies empower the individuals and increase the chances of lasting social impact, giving them an advantage over charitable efforts that offer temporary assistance to those willing to accept charity.

When it is possible, aligning social and economic value creation through business approaches provides the most sustainable kind of solution. This principle is not limited to human services. Many environmentally concerned for-profit and nonprofit organizations have recognized the value of this alignment. For instance, The Nature Conservancy has shifted from just buying and preserving lands to finding ways to generate both economic and social value through sustainable harvesting techniques and environmentally conscious development. Some of this work is done in partnership with corporations that are working to find sustainable ways to harvest timber. While these types of initiatives are challenging to implement and require a real sensitivity to the tensions between economic and social goals, they provide valuable opportunities for experimentation and learning. A small number of successes could easily make up for a number of failed ventures.

*Increased Accountability*: Shifting from a charitable to a customer relationship improves accountability and can bring increased market discipline to the social sector. Paying customers are more likely than non-paying clients to hold organizations accountable by providing direct feedback, expressing their complaints publicly, or taking their business elsewhere. Even third-party payers can provide greater market discipline than most donors. They have greater legal standing to complain and often also have greater incentives to hold providers accountable and better information on performance. They tend to have a more direct obligation to and relationship with the service recipients, and the recipients themselves have a sense of entitlement since the service was paid, not charitable. Thus, employers can act based on input from their employees on the value and quality of the social goods and services delivered; public agencies can expect the same from their constituents.

This improved (though still imperfect) market discipline clearly holds true for for-profits and for nonprofits charging fees for the delivery of social goods and services. For other nonprofit activities, market discipline is only beneficial if the earned income strategies are aligned with effectively serving the organization's mission. For example, the success or failure of a hospital gift shop, a Save the Children brand tie, or a co-branded Starbucks coffee sampler from countries in which CARE operates reveals nothing about the nonprofit organizations' ability to achieve their social missions. These ventures are all subject to market forces, but the market is responding to products and services that are distinct from the organizations' mission-based activities. While these ventures may contribute value to the organizations in other ways, the market feedback will not help them assess or improve their creation of social value.

In other cases, the benefits of market discipline can extend into more commercial activities such as nonprofits' operating businesses to employ their clientele. The success or failure of these businesses, and the feedback from customers, can provide valuable information regarding the effectiveness, strengths and weaknesses of their job training and employment programs, much more so than merely asking the trainees if they were satisfied with the training. Thus, for mission-related activities, the value of market feedback can help overcome some of the performance measurement and accountability concerns in the nonprofit sector.

*Greater Financial Strength and Capacity*: Boundary-blurring activities have the potential to help build a social sector with greater financial strength and capacity than currently exists. For-profits entering the social sector increase the sector's access to capital, allow for faster growth and increased flexibility, and increase the capacity of the sector overall. For nonprofits, if earned income and other business methods can provide more diverse and sustainable revenue streams, then the financial strength of the organization will be improved. Granted, earned income streams are not necessarily more sustainable than donations or grants, and diversification can lead to fragmentation and loss of focus. But developing an appropriate earned income strategy can free up and even create new capacity, in the form of both financial and human resources, to be dedicated to direct delivery on the mission.

Overall, healthy competition among organizational forms has the potential to improve the effectiveness of the social sector. The diversity of options gives clients, paying customers, and funders a choice. Keeping in mind the genuine risks outlined below, we should let these experiments flourish and have the participants decide what works best for them. Some of the experiments will fail, and others may even prove detrimental in the short term. We should work to reduce the chances of irreparable harm, but acknowledge that progress has its costs. We must allow enough time for learning and for making adjustments.

**Risks and Concerns**

Though we are attracted to the potential benefits from sector-bending activities, we are not endorsing all activities or encouraging every organization to pursue sector-bending approaches. Bridging sectors is challenging and necessarily creates some tensions within organizations and the sectors. Increased commercial activity is not appropriate or feasible for every nonprofit, nor is a shift to providing social goods and services suitable or desirable for every for-profit. Not every individual or organization, no matter how successful and competent in certain arenas, will be adept at merging social goals with business activities or at operating in different political and cultural environments. In addition to the practical challenges, sector-bending activities pose some inherent risks. Without addressing the specific risks associated with each type of activity described earlier, we have identified three broad categories of significant, cross-cutting concerns: threats to direct social performance, potential loss of indirect social benefits, and further bifurcation of society into haves and have-nots. As we move forward with this boundary blurring experimentation, these areas must be vigilantly monitored and managed.

*Threats to Direct Social Performance*: Perhaps the greatest concern about the blurring of sector boundaries is that, despite the potential benefits mentioned above, these activities will actually result in a decline in social value created. Three specific concerns pose potential threats to direct social performance: business approaches may cause mission drift; profit emphasis may lead to lower quality services overall; and blurring of sectors may provoke a decline in advocacy by nonprofits.

Mission Drift: Business structures and methods could pull social-purpose organizations away from their original social missions. Social service organizations that intended to serve the very poor may find that it is easier to generate fees or contracts by serving clients who are less disadvantaged than to raise funds to subsidize their charity work. Similarly, a homeless shelter that starts a business to train and employ shelter residents may find that it is too difficult and costly to make this option available to the homeless who are hardest to employ. An environmental group that wants to produce products using nuts from a rain forest cooperative may discover that the cooperative cannot deliver enough high-quality nuts to meet demand and switch to other suppliers. A university attracted by lucrative funds from licensing practical developments emerging from its labs may shift resources away from the humanities and basic sciences toward applied sciences. Though, in theory, generating this kind of fee income should help an organization serve its intended audience through cross-subsidy or just by covering overhead expenses, the relative ease of bringing in commercial fees or the market pressures exerted on earned income activities may slowly draw an organization away from its mission. On a practical level, it may be easier to grow and fund an organization by giving up on its original mission and target audience. Strong leaders, engaged funders, active boards, and clear mission statements should help keep organizations focused, but these mechanisms are not perfect and mission drift could well occur despite them. The situation is made worse by the lack of clear performance measures in this sector as it is difficult for customers, payers, donors, and sometimes even board members and managers to recognize when certain activities are actually causing a decline in social impact.

Lower Quality Services: Moreover, many people worry that the presence of a profit motive or a strong emphasis on efficiency will lead service providers to cut corners, lowering both costs and quality. Various studies have looked at this issue in sectors where nonprofit and for-profit players compete directly. The results are inconclusive, as some studies have found differences in quality while others have not. However, even if research overwhelmingly found lower quality of care on average in for-profit versus nonprofit providers of health care and social services, one could not fairly conclude that having for-profit players is a bad thing unless the industry has excess capacity or the service quality has fallen below some morally acceptable minimum. For instance, we are familiar with a small nonprofit hospice for people with AIDS that offers very high quality care and is reluctant to expand for fear that the quality will decline. Yet many people in that community are on waiting lists for AIDS-related hospice care. Is it better to maintain very high quality and stay small, or would it be more socially desirable to lower quality but expand capacity to serve more of the people in need? If a for-profit enters the market and offers to provide a lower quality of care but serves the unmet need, is that a bad thing? It is bad *only if* the quality is so low that the customers would have been better off receiving no care at all. When quality is costly, as it is in many social services, providers may have to make a trade-off between the quality of care provided and the number of people served. While a profit incentive may pull a for-profit provider towards quantity rather than quality, if demand is greater than current supply, this bias may actually be socially desirable and superior to offering high quality care to a small number of people while others get no care at all.

Charter schools represent a case where quality is more crucial. These schools are replacing existing capacity rather than serving an unmet need. Thus, the question is whether these schools improve on the public schools they replace. We must monitor this situation with careful oversight and standards. Even so, we need realistic benchmarks. These experiments should be judged a failure only if they are not successful at delivering a better education than the existing alternatives. Since for-profit charter school operators want to maintain their contracts and even expand their markets, they have every incentive to perform at a high level and should be expected to do so. The challenge, again, is in finding the right measures, but parents and school boards face this same challenge in assessing public schools. Quality measurement problems should not automatically wed us to the *status quo* or rule out experimentation.

Decline in Advocacy by Nonprofits: Finally, advocacy is one of the crucial functions that nonprofit organizations can play. It is natural to worry that if nonprofits are contracting and collaborating with for-profits, it may compromise their roles as advocates and critics. Yet nonprofits have been striking this balance for quite some time when receiving corporate donations, gifts from wealthy individuals with their own business interests, or even grants and contracts from government agencies. Very few nonprofits are supported totally by grassroots fundraising. It is a matter of selecting the right partners and being clear on the terms of engagement. It is possible that nonprofits that have traditionally engaged in both service delivery and advocacy may have fewer resources to dedicate to advocacy if they are trying to compete with for-profit service providers or develop other streams of earned income. However, if successful, earned income activities should actually generate or free up other resources for advocacy activities. And even if there is some decline on these fronts, nonprofits dedicated solely to advocacy will not face these concerns and may even gain from a greater perceived need for their presence.

Corporate collaborations such as McDonald's and Environmental Defense Fund working together to address waste management issues have raised concerns that nonprofits are jeopardizing their legitimacy as watchdogs and social advocates by becoming too cozy with the business sector. But we cannot have it both ways. We cannot urge businesses to be environmentally conscious and socially responsible and then deprive them of access to the best resources for addressing our concerns. Groups particularly concerned about their independence need to limit their financial dependency on the corporations they should be watching and tailor their sector-bending activities to avoid conflicts of interest. Some nonprofits will, and should, always exist as advocates primarily working outside of and against the system. But as long as it is done carefully, having some advocates also work across sectors with for-profits and government agencies should enhance the success and overall social impact of their efforts.

The risk of reduced social impact is real, but it is unclear how serious it is. Little empirical data is available to help us assess the potential magnitude of this problem. Do new commercial revenues help an organization achieve its social objectives or do they pull the organization away from its mission, provide incentives for objectionably low levels of quality, and undercut its role as an independent advocate? We do not know for sure. However, we do know that these risks are not unique to boundary-blurring activities. Mission drift is a real issue for philanthropic organizations as they work to attract and satisfy different donors with agendas that may not perfectly match their original mission. We also know that donor-supported nonprofit organizations can be slow to respond, inefficient, and wasteful. Is the risk worse with sector-bending activities? The answer is unclear. Finally, we also know that many nonprofits do not serve the most needy or address the toughest social problems. It is an open question whether boundary-blurring activities will pull those who do away from these difficult populations and issues. But while these concerns are legitimate and need to be monitored and managed, in some instances, sector-bending activities' risks to direct social impact have been exaggerated. In others, it is just too early to tell.

*Undermining Indirect Social Benefits:* In addition to directly serving social objectives, many nonprofit organizations facilitate the creation of social capital in communities, and the nonprofit sector provides an outlet for expressing charitable impulses. It is conceivable that sector-bending activities on the part of nonprofits endanger both of these roles.

Nonprofits as Creators of Social Capital: Community-based nonprofits, particularly those with high levels of volunteer involvement, can serve as vehicles for building social capital—trusting connections between community members who might otherwise not have any contact with one another. Some observers are worried that sector-blurring activities in nonprofits will change the character of the interactions they spawn in a way that undermines social capital creation. Goodwill and mutual concern will be replaced by more arms-length business relationships. On a more practical level, as business skills become more valued, the level of volunteer engagement may decline, as might the diversity of the volunteers and board members.

While social capital should not be undervalued, one must consider how organizations create social capital and the types of organizations that create significant amounts before expressing major concerns about the effects of sector-bending activities on this front. Organizations can create social capital by offering a venue for members of the community to get acquainted through some common interests or activities. Only a small proportion of nonprofit organizations do this now. Many of them are professional organizations with limited volunteer activities. These professionally staffed nonprofits may not play this role any better than, or even as well as, a local grocery store, diner, neighborhood bar, or professional sports team. Nonprofits that do create a great deal of social capital include membership organizations, clubs, churches, amateur sports leagues, and service organizations with large numbers of volunteers. For many of these organizations, sector-bending is not a serious risk and is unlikely to drive out their social capital building activities. Will the local Rotary Club, Junior League, or little league become too business-like and drive out voluntary participation by their members? It seems unlikely. They may try to generate revenues through quasi-commercial events, such as candy sales or auctions, but these events are unlikely to undermine their capacity to build social capital.

Nonetheless, for the few organizations in a community that create social capital broadly, it is possible that moving away from a charitable economic model to one based more on business principles could result in a change in the organizational model that reduces the opportunities for volunteers and others to interact. However, such a consequence is certainly not inevitable. A church that uses business methods to start a day care center to serve its members may create new social capital by inviting members to volunteer at the center or bring their business knowledge to a diverse board that includes some of the parents served. A for-profit charter school can still have an active PTA that facilitates interactions between parents and teachers. Habitat's mortgage requirement does not reduce the social capital created by a house-building project. The sale of Girl Scouts cookies, if handled well, can foster positive relationships amongst the girls, their parents, and their neighbors (and sometimes even between parents and co-workers!).

Furthermore, the intelligent adoption of business practices could make many nonprofit organizations even more effective in creating social capital. For instance, marketing techniques may allow the organization to reach new audiences, increasing the diversity of participants and improving it social capital creation. Professionalization, the increasing emphasis on placing credentialed professionals in key service positions, is probably a greater threat to social capital creation than is commercialization. It would be a mistake to conflate the two, especially given that many social sector professionals, such as teachers, social workers, doctors, nurses, and environmental scientists, have been vocal opponents of bringing businesses or business methods into their domains.

Charitable Character of the Nonprofit Sector: The nonprofit sector provides a variety of ways in which people can express their charitable impulses. If it became sufficiently widespread, sector-bending could reduce the opportunities to give back by leading organizations away from relying on donations and volunteers. However, we need to be careful. The nonprofit sector has long been dependent on fee-based income for much of its revenue. Of course, the prevalence of fees varies widely from one sub-sector to another. However, if charging fees is corrupting to the charitable character of the sector, we have already crossed that bridge. Imagine colleges being prevented from charging tuition or performing arts groups being prohibited from charging for tickets. Could they raise enough in donations to provide the quality of services that they now provide? It seems unlikely. In any case, many nonprofit organizations, such as major universities, have found ways to blur sector boundaries and still provide opportunities for alumni to get involved and to give back.

Admittedly, some studies have suggested that increases in earned income tend to slow the growth rate in donations and, in extreme cases, may lead to a decline in donations. While intriguing, this finding should not be worrisome. This correlation is open to a number of explanations. It could reflect a conscious decision by the organization to pursue a strategy of being less dependent on contributions. The shift to earned income could also be designed to compensate for the anticipated loss of a major grant that was due to expire. The leaders of the organization may have had less time to dedicate to fundraising as they were launching an earned income strategy. Or they may simply have failed to market their new earned income plans effectively to their donors. In any case, at the sector level, increased earned income by some organizations should result in more efficient use of donations overall. If one organization successfully shifts to a heavy emphasis on earned income, its donors can shift their funds to other organizations that require a greater philanthropic subsidy.

Neither the rise of earned income nor the entrance of for-profits into the social sector has reduced the number of nonprofits looking for donations or volunteers. Vast opportunities still exist for donors and volunteers to experience the psychological benefits of supporting their favorite causes. Moreover, the rise of "venture philanthropy" and other forms of engaged philanthropy that explicitly draw on individuals' business skills and expertise appears to be attracting a new breed of donors to the sector who are interested in contributing significant time and money to generating social impact. These donors do not seem to be discouraged by earned income strategies. Indeed, many of them welcome them.

It would also be a mistake to assume that charity is somehow morally or socially preferable to commerce. Being the recipient of someone's charity can be demeaning, making recipients feel helpless and powerless. Many individuals are too proud to seek or accept charitable assistance except as a last resort. By comparison, as we described when discussing the potential benefits of sector-bending, treating clients as customers can be empowering, giving them standing to complain and a sense of ownership and accomplishment. Protecting the charitable purity of the sector is not necessarily a good thing.

The blurring of sector boundaries does not have to undermine the indirect social benefits associated with the nonprofit sector. In fact, in some cases, these types of activities may actually enhance them. Yet given the concerns that have been expressed regarding the decline of social capital in US communities, social sector leaders should pay close attention to the indirect social impacts of boundary blurring activities and consider these effects as they pursue the direct creation of social value.

*Bifurcation into Haves and Have-Nots*: With respect to sector-bending activities, one of the powerful benefits mentioned above was the potential unbundling of activities to allow philanthropic resources to be devoted to activities and individuals that are in the greatest need of charitable support. However, this benefit has a potential dark side. It could result in two classes of service in the social sector: one for those who can pay or are eligible for third-party payment and the other for those who need charitable assistance. This market differentiation could reinforce class differences in society at large. Again, this bifurcation is not a necessary consequence of sector-bending activities, but it is a possible consequence. Creative social sector leaders can take steps to avoid this consequence using some of the very business structures and methods that might have contributed to it. Better marketing to those who are willing and able to pay can increase the amount of money available to cross-subsidize those who cannot afford to pay. Clients can be offered the same services with a sliding price scale or with "scholarship" opportunities. Thus, sophisticated sector-bending organizations may be able to use business methods to improve their ability to serve all of their clients seamlessly, without any publicly apparent difference between those who can and cannot pay. However, doing so will require a diligent effort. Social entrepreneurs, funders, and public policymakers must be careful to consider and monitor all of the effects of these activities to assure that sector blurring does not lead to greater class divisions.

Given that many of the effects of sector-bending activities are uncertain, the impact of business practices on the decisions and activities of nonprofits should continue to be monitored closely in hopes of developing better mechanisms for measuring social performance and assessing the impact of various innovations. In fact, business methods may actually be able to help address some of the challenges of managing and measuring these risks. As we have already described, marketing techniques can help nonprofits attract resources and penetrate target markets more effectively; accounting tools may be adapted to measure performance; developing customer, as opposed to charitable, relationships should enhance customer market discipline and accountability. We are not proposing that business methods are the ultimate solution for addressing some of the shortcomings already inherent in the nonprofit structure, and we recognize that the adoption of business techniques will cause additional complications and implementation issues. But we are not convinced that sector-bending activities significantly increase the risks of poor performance, declining societal benefits, or further class division. We embrace transparency and evaluation as tools to help us assess these experiments, but we do not see a case for inhibiting activities that further blur the lines between nonprofit and for-profit.

**Pitfalls to Avoid in Making Assessments**

Though the risks are real, they seem manageable if we are realistic in our assessment of them. In evaluating the potential social impact and assessing the risks of sector-bending activities, we encourage researchers, public policy makers, and sector leaders to be careful to avoid three very natural pitfalls.

*Focusing on Individual Organizations Rather than the Sector or Society*: What happens within individual firms is certainly relevant to assessing the impact and risks of sector-bending activities. Understandably, much of the research takes this organization-level focus. However, for policy purposes, the emphasis should be on the overall performance of the sector and the overall impact on society, not just on performance by individual organizations. As we pointed out above, the fact that donations decline in a nonprofit organization that increases its earned income does not imply that donations decline overall in the sector. The donations may just flow to a more appropriate use, an area of greater need. This outcome represents a positive result.

Moreover, if for-profits or more commercial nonprofits are shown to offer lower quality services than more philanthropic nonprofits, this finding does not imply that users of the services are hurt by the presence of these lower quality providers. Lower quality services may serve excess demand that cannot be served by the limited capacity of high-quality providers. They may even represent a more cost-effective way of serving an unmet need. Not every car needs to be a Rolls Royce, and not every drug rehabilitation center needs to be comparable to the Betty Ford Center.

Finally, a study may show that a hospital provides less charitable care or does less research or provides less education after it converts from nonprofit to for-profit status. This conclusion neglects the fact that at the time of conversion, a fair price must be paid for the net assets of the nonprofit hospital and the proceeds must stay in the nonprofit sector. Usually a new health-related foundation is created. The social impacts of the old nonprofit hospital should be compared to the performance of the new for-profit hospital in combination with the new foundation that has been created. The issue is whether the conversion served society well, not whether the new for-profit hospital alone serves society as well as its nonprofit predecessor.

*Assuming What is Must Be*: Another danger is to assume that the kinds of average differences that are documented in descriptive studies must be the case. Consider again the decline in donations that may accompany an increase in fee-based revenue. If the organization could still put donations to good use, this decline may just reflect poor marketing to donors. Better marketing might correct the situation. This kind of effect may also reflect the tendency of major donors, such as leading foundations, to move on after a certain period of time. That practice could be changed, not by the nonprofit, but by the foundations. Similar reasoning applies to the issue of quality differences. Even if we found that on average nonprofit hospices provide better care than for-profits, we should not assume that this must be true in all cases. In many samples, even with statistically significant differences, the comparison groups will overlap. Some for-profits are likely to out perform some nonprofits, despite the statistical differences. If we believe it is socially desirable to improve the performance of for-profit hospices, we might look at the high performing for-profits to see if there are practices that can be profitably transferred to those that are not performing as well. Indeed, we could do the same across high performing and low performing nonprofits. We cannot neglect the different incentives and operating environments associated with different organizational structures, but we should use research findings productively to help improve overall performance. Structure does matter, as we will acknowledge below, but it alone may not determine behavior and impact.

*Comparing New Forms Against a Fictional Ideal*: Finally, it is natural to compare some of the new sector-bending structures to some kind of ideal organization built on principles of charity and funded exclusively through philanthropy. As we already mentioned, the nonprofit sector was never purely charitable. Many of the sector-bending changes are simply extensions of past behaviors into new arenas. It has been argued that people can trust nonprofits more because of the "non-distribution constraint" - nonprofits cannot pay profits out to those in a controlling position. However, this constraint is a crude and often ineffective instrument. It may inhibit certain forms of self-enrichment, but it is no guarantee against corruption and it does not ensure effective performance. We have enough examples of corrupt behavior in the sector to recognize that corruption is not unique to the for-profit sector (or government). The non-distribution constraint eliminates an incentive to maximize profits, but it does not replace that incentive with anything in particular. Power, politics, and money play important and potentially corrupting roles in any sector. People are people, and no one sector is morally superior. The attitude of moral superiority sometimes apparent in the nonprofit sector just serves as a barrier to creative problem solving.

Because of the non-distribution constraint, complacency, inefficiency, and waste can be serious problems in nonprofit organizations. At least for-profit organizations depend on the voluntary choices of customers to pay for their product to help assure they are creating value in an efficient way. In the more "pure" philanthropic nonprofits, donors are the primary payers, and they are rarely in a strong position to evaluate the efficiency and effectiveness of the organization. Few of them invest any serious effort in an assessment process. A nonprofit can survive, even thrive, and yet be very inefficient and ineffective in creating social value and serving its mission. In the absence of reliable impact measures, a common condition, who would know? In comparing sector-bending activities with more "traditional" nonprofits, we need to use an honest benchmark, not some ideal.

**Implications: Organizational Structure Still Matters**

If nonprofits and for-profits are engaging in increasingly similar activities and practices, are we moving into a world in which organizational structure doesn't matter? Not at all. Nonprofit and for-profit organizations will continue to co-exist and have distinct characteristics. Every social sector actor should be aware of these differences, and the associated strengths and weaknesses, in order to choose the best structure or combination of structures given a particular mission and operating environment. Different structures are tools with different qualities. Following are a few of the central distinctions:

*Potential Profitability*: For-profits are limited to engaging in activities that will yield sufficient profits for their investors. Even social-purpose businesses that raise funds from socially oriented investors must have an economic model that can generate at least modest profits to be sustainable. Nonprofits are not only freed from this constraint but are actually prohibited from distributing any profits. Surpluses can be created by nonprofits, but they must be used to further the mission of the organization.

*Access to Resources*: For-profits can use equity ownership to raise capital and reward performance, are generally better able to access debt markets, and if successful, can be "self-sustaining." Nonprofits can solicit donations and attract volunteers, but they have fewer options for incentive pay, no access to equity, and limited access to debt.

*Market Discipline*: Both for-profits and nonprofits are subject to market forces, but capital and consumer market discipline is much stricter and more effective in the for-profit sector. Nonprofits cannot create wealth for investors, and their missions often cannot be served by simply creating consumptive value for customers. Donors are rarely in a position to assess value creation or efficiency. Moreover, social performance is hard to measure in timely and reliable ways and is also subject to differences in individual values, further blunting the effects of market discipline for both for-profit and nonprofit operators who truly have a social mission.

*Governance and Control*: Boards of directors govern both for-profits and nonprofits, but investors own for-profits and, at least in theory, control the boards. Given the absence of investor-owners, the lack of strict market discipline, and the difficulty of performance measurement, the accountability of a nonprofit rests heavily on their boards and managers. For-profits are directly accountable to their investors. They can curb profit maximization and pursue social objectives if they maintain control by seeking out socially oriented investors and keeping their business closely held. Many businesses operate in this manner, although this approach greatly restricts the pool of available capital, offsetting some of the benefits of being a for-profit.

*Culture and Norms*: While not mandated by the particular organizational form, there are certain norms associated with each sector. Many nonprofit employees, and even some donors and volunteers, are uncomfortable with the language and practices of business and may be skeptical of the values and motives of people trying to introduce business concepts. Nonprofits also often rely heavily on "psychic income" to compensate for traditionally lower salaries. The sector overall also seems to have a bias towards smaller organizations, local autonomy, and consensus-driven decision-making.

*Taxes.* Under current tax laws, for-profits are generally subject to both income and property taxes on both the state and federal levels. Nonprofits are broadly exempt from these taxes as long as the property is used primarily for the nonprofit's social purposes and the income is generated from activities related to their primary mission. Nonprofits are subject to Unrelated Business Income Tax (UBIT) for ongoing activities that are not substantially related to their social purpose, though it is often difficult to differentiate taxable and nontaxable activities, and even then, there are significant opportunities for cost and revenue-shifting to minimize taxation.

We mention taxes here because current tax policy creates distinctions between nonprofit and for-profit structures that cannot be ignored. However, the complex interactions between tax policy and sector-bending activities are beyond the scope of this paper. That said, we are compelled to address briefly the common complaint that tax exemptions and ease of avoiding UBIT give nonprofits engaging in business activities an unfair competitive advantage. These concerns are exaggerated. Most nonprofits have inherent disadvantages with regard to social mission costs, size inefficiencies, difficulty attracting people with valuable business skills, and limited access to capital. We suspect these inefficiencies more than make up for the difference in tax status. If for-profits find that nonprofits have a clear competitive advantage, then perhaps the for-profit competitor has chosen the wrong organizational form. Indeed, if nonprofit status provides such an advantage, why haven't we seen more for-profits converting to nonprofit status to gain this advantage? Conversions, in fact, usually run in the other direction.

Thus nonprofits should not be prevented from engaging in potentially socially beneficial business-like activities merely because we have not determined how to monitor and tax them effectively. In any case, the limited profitability of many nonprofit business activities is unlikely to generate significant taxes. Moreover, any tax losses from nonprofit business activities could be made up by for-profits entering the social sector. They are bringing social sector activities into a taxable structure. All things considered, sector-bending could well increase overall tax receipts.

Given the above distinctions and the abundance of social issues and problems that need to be addressed, it is reasonable to assume that different organizational structures will continue to both be necessary and evolve as time progresses.

---

*J. Gregory Dees is adjunct professor of social entrepreneurship and nonprofit management at Duke University's Fuqua School of Business. He heads the Center for Advancement of Social Entrepreneurship (CASE) at Duke. Beth Battle Anderson, senior research associate at Fuqua, is managing director of CASE.*

HBR.ORG
Harvard Business Review

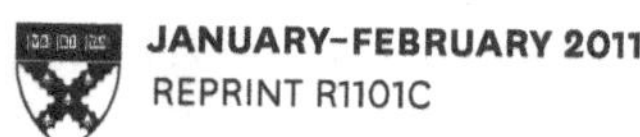


THE BIG IDEA

# Creating Shared Value

**How to reinvent capitalism—and unleash a wave of innovation and growth** ***by Michael E. Porter and Mark R. Kramer***

## The Big Idea

**Capitalism is under siege....** Diminished to set policies that sap economic growth.... The purpose of the corporation must be

# CREATING SH

trust in business is causing political leaders
**Business is caught in a vicious circle....**
redefined around

# ARED VALUE

How to reinvent capitalism—and unleash a wave of innovation and growth *by Michael E. Porter and Mark R. Kramer*

**THE CAPITALIST SYSTEM** is under siege. In recent years business increasingly has been viewed as a major cause of social, environmental, and economic problems. Companies are widely perceived to be prospering at the expense of the broader community.

Even worse, the more business has begun to embrace corporate responsibility, the more it has been blamed for society's failures. The legitimacy of business has fallen to levels not seen in recent history. This diminished trust in business leads political leaders to set policies that undermine competitiveness and sap economic growth. Business is caught in a vicious circle.

A big part of the problem lies with companies themselves, which remain trapped in an outdated approach to value creation that has emerged over the past few decades. They continue to view value creation narrowly, optimizing short-term financial performance in a bubble while missing the most important customer needs and ignoring the broader influences that determine their longer-term success. How else could companies overlook the well-being of their customers, the depletion of natural resources vital to their businesses, the viability of key suppliers, or the economic distress of the communities in which they produce and sell? How else could companies think that simply shifting activities to locations with ever lower wages was a sustainable "solution" to competitive challenges? Government and civil society have often exacerbated the problem by attempting to address social weaknesses at the expense of business. The presumed trade-offs between economic efficiency and social progress have been institutionalized in decades of policy choices.

Companies must take the lead in bringing business and society back together. The recognition is there among sophisticated business and thought leaders, and promising elements of a new model are emerging. Yet we still lack an overall framework for guiding these efforts, and most companies remain stuck in a "social responsibility" mind-set in which societal issues are at the periphery, not the core.

The solution lies in the principle of shared value, which involves creating economic value in a way that *also* creates value for society by addressing its needs and challenges. Businesses must reconnect company success with social progress. Shared value is not social responsibility, philanthropy, or even sustainability, but a new way to achieve economic success. It is not on the margin of what companies do but at the center. We believe that it can give rise to the next major transformation of business thinking.

A growing number of companies known for their hard-nosed approach to business—such as GE, Google, IBM, Intel, Johnson & Johnson, Nestlé, Unilever, and Wal-Mart—have already embarked on important efforts to create shared value by reconceiving the intersection between society and corporate performance. Yet our recognition of the transformative power of shared value is still in its genesis. Realizing it will require leaders and managers to develop new skills and knowledge—such as a far deeper appreciation of societal needs, a greater understanding of the true bases of company productivity, and the ability to collaborate across profit/nonprofit boundaries. And government must learn how to regulate in ways that enable shared value rather than work against it.

Capitalism is an unparalleled vehicle for meeting human needs, improving efficiency, creating jobs, and building wealth. But a narrow conception of capitalism has prevented business from harnessing its full potential to meet society's broader challenges. The opportunities have been there all along but have been overlooked. Businesses acting as businesses, not as charitable donors, are the most powerful force for addressing the pressing issues we face. The moment for a new conception of capitalism is now; society's needs are large and growing, while customers, employees, and a new generation of young people are asking business to step up.

The purpose of the corporation must be redefined as creating shared value, not just profit per se. This will drive the next wave of innovation and productivity growth in the global economy. It will also reshape capitalism and its relationship to society. Perhaps most important of all, learning how to create shared value is our best chance to legitimize business again.

## Moving Beyond Trade-Offs

Business and society have been pitted against each other for too long. That is in part because economists have legitimized the idea that to provide societal benefits, companies must temper their economic success. In neoclassical thinking, a requirement for social improvement—such as safety or hiring the disabled—imposes a constraint on the corporation. Adding a constraint to a firm that is already maximiz-

## Idea in Brief

The concept of shared value—which focuses on the connections between societal and economic progress—has the power to unleash the next wave of global growth.

An increasing number of companies known for their hard-nosed approach to business—such as Google, IBM, Intel, Johnson & Johnson, Nestlé, Unilever, and Wal-Mart—have begun to embark on important shared value initiatives. But our understanding of the potential of shared value is just beginning.

There are three key ways that companies can create shared value opportunities:

- By reconceiving products and markets
- By redefining productivity in the value chain
- By enabling local cluster development

**Every firm should look at decisions and opportunities through the lens of shared value. This will lead to new approaches that generate greater innovation and growth for companies—and also greater benefits for society.**

## Societal needs, not just conventional economic needs, define markets, and social harms can create internal costs for firms.

ing profits, says the theory, will inevitably raise costs and reduce those profits.

A related concept, with the same conclusion, is the notion of externalities. Externalities arise when firms create social costs that they do not have to bear, such as pollution. Thus, society must impose taxes, regulations, and penalties so that firms "internalize" these externalities—a belief influencing many government policy decisions.

This perspective has also shaped the strategies of firms themselves, which have largely excluded social and environmental considerations from their economic thinking. Firms have taken the broader context in which they do business as a given and resisted regulatory standards as invariably contrary to their interests. Solving social problems has been ceded to governments and to NGOs. Corporate responsibility programs—a reaction to external pressure—have emerged largely to improve firms' reputations and are treated as a necessary expense. Anything more is seen by many as an irresponsible use of shareholders' money. Governments, for their part, have often regulated in a way that makes shared value more difficult to achieve. Implicitly, each side has assumed that the other is an obstacle to pursuing its goals and acted accordingly.

The concept of shared value, in contrast, recognizes that societal needs, not just conventional economic needs, define markets. It also recognizes that social harms or weaknesses frequently create *internal* costs for firms—such as wasted energy or raw materials, costly accidents, and the need for remedial training to compensate for inadequacies in education. And addressing societal harms and constraints does not necessarily raise costs for firms, because they can innovate through using new technologies, operating methods, and management approaches—and as a result, increase their productivity and expand their markets.

Shared value, then, is not about personal values. Nor is it about "sharing" the value already created by firms—a redistribution approach. Instead, it is about expanding the total pool of economic and social value. A good example of this difference in perspective is the fair trade movement in purchasing. Fair trade aims to increase the proportion of revenue that goes to poor farmers by paying them higher prices for the same crops. Though this may be a noble sentiment, fair trade is mostly about redistribution rather than expanding the overall amount of value created. A shared value perspective, instead, focuses on improving growing techniques and strengthening the local cluster of supporting suppliers and other institutions in order to increase farmers' efficiency, yields, product quality, and sustainability. This leads to a bigger pie of revenue and profits that benefits both farmers and the companies that buy from them. Early studies of cocoa farmers in the Côte d'Ivoire, for instance, suggest that while fair trade can increase farmers' incomes by 10% to 20%, shared value investments can raise their incomes by more than 300%. Initial investment and time may be required to implement new procurement practices and develop the supporting cluster, but the return will be greater economic value and broader strategic benefits for all participants.

ILLUSTRATION: LORENZO PETRANTONI

## The Roots of Shared Value

At a very basic level, the competitiveness of a company and the health of the communities around it are closely intertwined. A business needs a successful community, not only to create demand for its products but also to provide critical public assets and a supportive environment. A community needs successful businesses to provide jobs and wealth creation opportunities for its citizens. This interdependence means that public policies that undermine the productivity and competitiveness of businesses are self-defeating, especially in a global economy where facilities and jobs can easily move elsewhere. NGOs and governments have not always appreciated this connection.

In the old, narrow view of capitalism, business contributes to society by making a profit, which supports employment, wages, purchases, investments, and taxes. Conducting business as usual is sufficient social benefit. A firm is largely a self-contained entity, and social or community issues fall outside its proper scope. (This is the argument advanced persuasively by Milton Friedman in his critique of the whole notion of corporate social responsibility.)

This perspective has permeated management thinking for the past two decades. Firms focused on enticing consumers to buy more and more of their products. Facing growing competition and shorter-term performance pressures from shareholders, managers resorted to waves of restructuring, personnel reductions, and relocation to lower-cost regions, while leveraging balance sheets to return capital to investors. The results were often commoditization, price competition, little true innovation, slow organic growth, and no clear competitive advantage.

In this kind of competition, the communities in which companies operate perceive little benefit even as profits rise. Instead, they perceive that profits come at their expense, an impression that has become even stronger in the current economic recovery, in which rising earnings have done little to offset high unemployment, local business distress, and severe pressures on community services.

It was not always this way. The best companies once took on a broad range of roles in meeting the needs of workers, communities, and supporting businesses. As other social institutions appeared on the scene, however, these roles fell away or were delegated. Shortening investor time horizons began to narrow thinking about appropriate investments. As the vertically integrated firm gave way to greater reliance on outside vendors, outsourcing and offshoring weakened the connection between firms and their communities. As firms moved disparate activities to more and more locations, they often lost touch with any location. Indeed, many companies no longer recognize a home—but see themselves as "global" companies.

These transformations drove major progress in economic efficiency. However, something profoundly important was lost in the process, as more-fundamental opportunities for value creation were missed. The scope of strategic thinking contracted.

Strategy theory holds that to be successful, a company must create a distinctive value proposition that meets the needs of a chosen set of customers. The firm gains competitive advantage from how it configures the value chain, or the set of activities involved in creating, producing, selling, delivering, and supporting its products or services. For decades businesspeople have studied positioning and the best ways to design activities and integrate them. However, companies have overlooked opportunities to meet fundamental societal needs and misun-

### WHAT IS "SHARED VALUE"?

**The concept of shared value can be defined as policies and operating practices that enhance the competitiveness of a company while simultaneously advancing the economic and social conditions in the communities in which it operates. Shared value creation focuses on identifying and expanding the connections between societal and economic progress.**

The concept rests on the premise that both economic and social progress must be addressed using value principles. **Value is defined as benefits relative to costs, not just benefits alone. Value creation is an idea that has long been recognized in business, where profit is** revenues earned from customers minus the costs incurred. However, businesses have rarely approached societal issues from a value perspective but have treated them as peripheral matters. This has obscured the connections between economic and social concerns.

In the social sector, thinking in value terms is even less common. Social organizations and government entities often see success solely in terms of the benefits achieved or the money expended. As governments and NGOs begin to think more in value terms, their interest in collaborating with business will inevitably grow.

derstood how societal harms and weaknesses affect value chains. Our field of vision has simply been too narrow.

In understanding the business environment, managers have focused most of their attention on the industry, or the particular business in which the firm competes. This is because industry structure has a decisive impact on a firm's profitability. What has been missed, however, is the profound effect that location can have on productivity and innovation. Companies have failed to grasp the importance of the broader business environment surrounding their major operations.

### How Shared Value Is Created

Companies can create economic value by creating societal value. There are three distinct ways to do this: by reconceiving products and markets, redefining productivity in the value chain, and building supportive industry clusters at the company's locations. Each of these is part of the virtuous circle of shared value; improving value in one area gives rise to opportunities in the others.

The concept of shared value resets the boundaries of capitalism. By better connecting companies' success with societal improvement, it opens up many ways to serve new needs, gain efficiency, create differentiation, and expand markets.

The ability to create shared value applies equally to advanced economies and developing countries, though the specific opportunities will differ. The opportunities will also differ markedly across industries and companies—but every company has them. And their range and scope is far broader than has been recognized. *[The idea of shared value was initially explored in a December 2006 HBR article by Michael E. Porter and Mark R. Kramer, "Strategy and Society: The Link Between Competitive Advantage and Corporate Social Responsibility."]*

### Reconceiving Products and Markets

Society's needs are huge—health, better housing, improved nutrition, help for the aging, greater financial security, less environmental damage. Arguably, they are the greatest unmet needs in the global economy. In business we have spent decades learning how to parse and manufacture demand while missing the most important demand of all. Too many companies have lost sight of that most basic of questions: Is our product good for our customers? Or for our customers' customers?

In advanced economies, demand for products and services that meet societal needs is rapidly growing. Food companies that traditionally concentrated on taste and quantity to drive more and more consumption are refocusing on the fundamental need for better nutrition. Intel and IBM are both devising ways to help utilities harness digital intelligence in order to economize on power usage. Wells Fargo has developed a line of products and tools that help customers budget, manage credit, and pay down debt. Sales of GE's Ecomagination products reached $18 billion in 2009—the size of a *Fortune* 150 company. GE now predicts that revenues of Ecomagination products will grow at twice the rate of total company revenues over the next five years.

In these and many other ways, whole new avenues for innovation open up, and shared value is created. Society's gains are even greater, because businesses will often be far more effective than governments and nonprofits are at marketing that motivates customers to embrace products and services that create societal benefits, like healthier food or environmentally friendly products.

#### BLURRING THE PROFIT/NONPROFIT BOUNDARY

**The concept of shared value blurs the line between for-profit and nonprofit organizations. New kinds of hybrid enterprises are rapidly** appearing. For example, WaterHealth International, a fast-growing for-profit, uses innovative water purification techniques to distribute clean water at minimal cost to more than one million people in rural India, Ghana, and the Philippines. Its investors include not only the socially focused Acumen Fund and the International Finance Corporation of the World Bank but also Dow Chemical's venture fund. Revolution Foods, a four-year-old venture-capital-backed U.S. start-up, provides 60,000 fresh, healthful, and nutritious meals to students daily—and does so at a higher gross margin than traditional competitors. Waste Concern, a hybrid profit/nonprofit enterprise started in Bangladesh 15 years ago, has built the capacity to convert 700 tons of trash, collected daily from neighborhood slums, into organic fertilizer, thereby increasing crop yields and reducing $CO_2$ emissions. Seeded with capital from the Lions Club and the United Nations Development Programme, the company improves health conditions while earning a substantial gross margin through fertilizer sales and carbon credits.

**The blurring of the boundary between successful for-profits and nonprofits is one of the strong signs that creating shared value is possible.**

## THE CONNECTION BETWEEN COMPETITIVE ADVANTAGE AND SOCIAL ISSUES

There are numerous ways in which addressing societal concerns can yield productivity benefits to a firm. Consider, for example, what happens when a firm invests in a wellness program. Society benefits because employees and their families become healthier, and the firm minimizes employee absences and lost productivity. The graphic below depicts some areas where the connections are strongest.

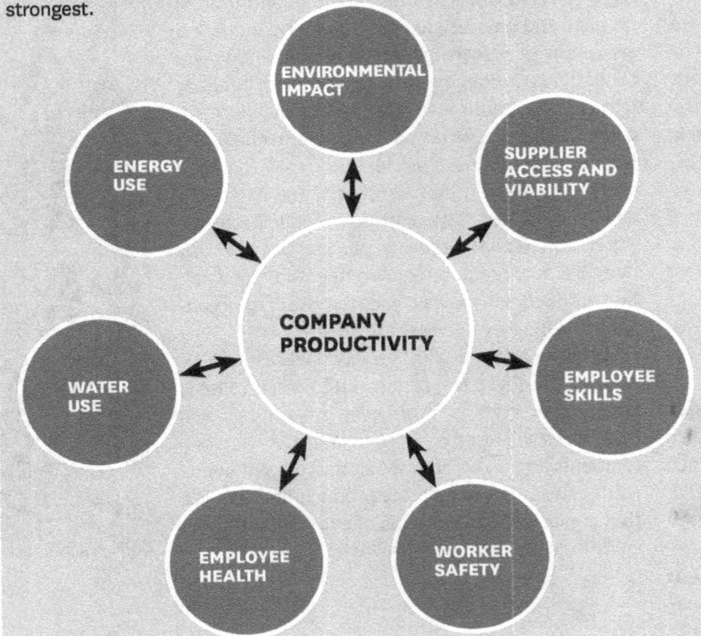


Equal or greater opportunities arise from serving disadvantaged communities and developing countries. Though societal needs are even more pressing there, these communities have not been recognized as viable markets. Today attention is riveted on India, China, and increasingly, Brazil, which offer firms the prospect of reaching billions of new customers at the bottom of the pyramid—a notion persuasively articulated by C.K. Prahalad. Yet these countries have always had huge needs, as do many developing countries.

Similar opportunities await in nontraditional communities in advanced countries. We have learned, for example, that poor urban areas are America's most underserved market; their substantial concentrated purchasing power has often been overlooked. (See the research of the Initiative for a Competitive Inner City, at icic.org.)

The societal benefits of providing appropriate products to lower-income and disadvantaged consumers can be profound, while the profits for companies can be substantial. For example, low-priced cell phones that provide mobile banking services are helping the poor save money securely and transforming the ability of small farmers to produce and market their crops. In Kenya, Vodafone's M-PESA mobile banking service signed up 10 million customers in three years; the funds it handles now represent 11% of that country's GDP. In India, Thomson Reuters has developed a promising monthly service for farmers who earn an average of $2,000 a year. For a fee of $5 a quarter, it provides weather and crop-pricing information and agricultural advice. The service reaches an estimated 2 million farmers, and early research indicates that it has helped increase the incomes of more than 60% of them—in some cases even tripling incomes. As capitalism begins to work in poorer communities, new opportunities for economic development and social progress increase exponentially.

For a company, the starting point for creating this kind of shared value is to identify all the societal needs, benefits, and harms that are or could be embodied in the firm's products. The opportunities are not static; they change constantly as technology evolves, economies develop, and societal priorities shift. An ongoing exploration of societal needs will lead companies to discover new opportunities for differentiation and repositioning in traditional markets, and to recognize the potential of new markets they previously overlooked.

Meeting needs in underserved markets often requires redesigned products or different distribution methods. These requirements can trigger fundamental innovations that also have application in traditional markets. Microfinance, for example, was invented to serve unmet financing needs in developing countries. Now it is growing rapidly in the United States, where it is filling an important gap that was unrecognized.

### Redefining Productivity in the Value Chain

A company's value chain inevitably affects—and is affected by—numerous societal issues, such as natural resource and water use, health and safety, working conditions, and equal treatment in the workplace. Opportunities to create shared value arise because societal problems can create economic costs in the firm's value chain. Many so-called externalities actually inflict internal costs on the firm, even in the absence of regulation or resource taxes. Excess packaging of products and greenhouse gases

**By reducing its packaging and cutting 100 million miles from the delivery routes of its trucks, Wal-Mart lowered carbon emissions and saved $200 million in costs.**

are not just costly to the environment but costly to the business. Wal-Mart, for example, was able to address both issues by reducing its packaging and rerouting its trucks to cut 100 million miles from its delivery routes in 2009, saving $200 million even as it shipped more products. Innovation in disposing of plastic used in stores has saved millions in lower disposal costs to landfills.

The new thinking reveals that the congruence between societal progress and productivity in the value chain is far greater than traditionally believed (see the exhibit "The Connection Between Competitive Advantage and Social Issues"). The synergy increases when firms approach societal issues from a shared value perspective and invent new ways of operating to address them. So far, however, few companies have reaped the full productivity benefits in areas such as health, safety, environmental performance, and employee retention and capability.

But there are unmistakable signs of change. Efforts to minimize pollution were once thought to inevitably increase business costs—and to occur only because of regulation and taxes. Today there is a growing consensus that major improvements in environmental performance can often be achieved with better technology at nominal incremental cost and can even yield net cost savings through enhanced resource utilization, process efficiency, and quality.

In each of the areas in the exhibit, a deeper understanding of productivity and a growing awareness of the fallacy of short-term cost reductions (which often actually lower productivity or make it unsustainable) are giving rise to new approaches. The following are some of the most important ways in which shared value thinking is transforming the value chain, which are not independent but often mutually reinforcing. Efforts in these and other areas are still works in process, whose implications will be felt for years to come.

**Energy use and logistics.** The use of energy throughout the value chain is being reexamined, whether it be in processes, transportation, buildings, supply chains, distribution channels, or support services. Triggered by energy price spikes and a new awareness of opportunities for energy efficiency, this reexamination was under way even before carbon emissions became a global focus. The result has been striking improvements in energy utilization through better technology, recycling, cogeneration, and numerous other practices—all of which create shared value.

We are learning that shipping is expensive, not just because of energy costs and emissions but because it adds time, complexity, inventory costs, and management costs. Logistical systems are beginning to be redesigned to reduce shipping distances, streamline handling, improve vehicle routing, and the like. All of these steps create shared value. The British retailer Marks & Spencer's ambitious overhaul of its supply chain, for example, which involves steps as simple as stopping the purchase of supplies from one hemisphere to ship to another, is expected to save the retailer £175 million annually by fiscal 2016, while hugely reducing carbon emissions. In the process of reexamining logistics, thinking about outsourcing and location will also be revised (as we will discuss below).

**Resource use.** Heightened environmental awareness and advances in technology are catalyzing new approaches in areas such as utilization of water, raw materials, and packaging, as well as expanding recycling and reuse. The opportunities apply to all resources, not just those that have been identified by environmentalists. Better resource utilization—enabled by improving technology—will permeate all parts of the value chain and will spread to suppliers and channels. Landfills will fill more slowly.

For example, Coca-Cola has already reduced its worldwide water consumption by 9% from a 2004 baseline—nearly halfway to its goal of a 20% reduction by 2012. Dow Chemical managed to reduce consumption of fresh water at its largest production site by one billion gallons—enough water to supply nearly 40,000 people in the U.S. for a year—resulting in savings of $4 million. The demand for water-saving technology has allowed India's Jain Irrigation, a leading global manufacturer of complete drip irrigation systems for water conservation, to achieve a 41% compound annual growth rate in revenue over the past five years.

**Procurement.** The traditional playbook calls for companies to commoditize and exert maximum bargaining power on suppliers to drive down prices—even when purchasing from small businesses or subsistence-level farmers. More recently, firms have been rapidly outsourcing to suppliers in lower-wage locations.

Today some companies are beginning to understand that marginalized suppliers cannot remain productive or sustain, much less improve, their quality. By increasing access to inputs, sharing technology, and providing financing, companies can improve supplier quality and productivity while ensuring access to growing volume. Improving productivity will often trump lower prices. As suppliers get stronger, their environmental impact often falls dramatically, which further improves their efficiency. Shared value is created.

A good example of such new procurement thinking can be found at Nespresso, one of Nestlé's fastest-growing divisions, which has enjoyed annual growth of 30% since 2000. Nespresso combines a sophisticated espresso machine with single-cup aluminum capsules containing ground coffees from around the world. Offering quality and convenience, Nespresso has expanded the market for premium coffee.

## THE ROLE OF SOCIAL ENTREPRENEURS

**Businesses are not the only players in finding profitable solutions to social problems. A whole generation of social entrepreneurs is pioneering new product concepts that meet social needs using viable business models. Because they are not locked into narrow traditional business thinking, social entrepreneurs are often well ahead of established corporations in discovering these opportunities. Social enterprises that create shared value can scale up far more rapidly than purely social programs, which often suffer from an inability to grow and become self-sustaining.**

Real social entrepreneurship should be measured by its ability to create shared value, not just social benefit.

Obtaining a reliable supply of specialized coffees is extremely challenging, however. Most coffees are grown by small farmers in impoverished rural areas of Africa and Latin America, who are trapped in a cycle of low productivity, poor quality, and environmental degradation that limits production volume. To address these issues, Nestlé redesigned procurement. It worked intensively with its growers, providing advice on farming practices, guaranteeing bank loans, and helping secure inputs such as plant stock, pesticides, and fertilizers. Nestlé established local facilities to measure the quality of the coffee at the point of purchase, which allowed it to pay a premium for better beans directly to the growers and thus improve their incentives. Greater yield per hectare and higher production quality increased growers' incomes, and the environmental impact of farms shrank. Meanwhile, Nestlé's reliable supply of good coffee grew significantly. Shared value was created.

Embedded in the Nestlé example is a far broader insight, which is the advantage of buying from capable local suppliers. Outsourcing to other locations and countries creates transaction costs and inefficiencies that can offset lower wage and input costs. Capable local suppliers help firms avoid these costs and can reduce cycle time, increase flexibility, foster faster learning, and enable innovation. Buying local includes not only local companies but also local units of national or international companies. When firms buy locally, their suppliers can get stronger, increase their profits, hire more people, and pay better wages—all of which will benefit other businesses in the community. Shared value is created.

**Distribution.** Companies are beginning to reexamine distribution practices from a shared value perspective. As iTunes, Kindle, and Google Scholar (which offers texts of scholarly literature online) demonstrate, profitable new distribution models can also dramatically reduce paper and plastic usage. Similarly, microfinance has created a cost-efficient new model of distributing financial services to small businesses.

Opportunities for new distribution models can be even greater in nontraditional markets. For example, Hindustan Unilever is creating a new direct-to-home distribution system, run by underprivileged female entrepreneurs, in Indian villages of fewer than 2,000 people. Unilever provides microcredit and training and now has more than 45,000 entrepreneurs covering some 100,000 villages

By investing in employee wellness programs, Johnson & Johnson has saved $250 million on health care costs.

across 15 Indian states. Project Shakti, as this distribution system is called, benefits communities not only by giving women skills that often double their household income but also by reducing the spread of communicable diseases through increased access to hygiene products. This is a good example of how the unique ability of business to market to hard-to-reach consumers can benefit society by getting life-altering products into the hands of people that need them. Project Shakti now accounts for 5% of Unilever's total revenues in India and has extended the company's reach into rural areas and built its brand in media-dark regions, creating major economic value for the company.

**Employee productivity.** The focus on holding down wage levels, reducing benefits, and offshoring is beginning to give way to an awareness of the positive effects that a living wage, safety, wellness, training, and opportunities for advancement for employees have on productivity. Many companies, for example, traditionally sought to minimize the cost of "expensive" employee health care coverage or even eliminate health coverage altogether. Today leading companies have learned that because of lost workdays and diminished employee productivity, poor health costs them more than health benefits do. Take Johnson & Johnson. By helping employees stop smoking (a two-thirds reduction in the past 15 years) and implementing numerous other wellness programs, the company has saved $250 million on health care costs, a return of $2.71 for every dollar spent on wellness from 2002 to 2008. Moreover, Johnson & Johnson has benefited from a more present and productive workforce. If labor unions focused more on shared value, too, these kinds of employee approaches would spread even faster.

**Location.** Business thinking has embraced the myth that location no longer matters, because logistics are inexpensive, information flows rapidly, and markets are global. The cheaper the location, then, the better. Concern about the local communities in which a company operates has faded.

That oversimplified thinking is now being challenged, partly by the rising costs of energy and carbon emissions but also by a greater recognition of the productivity cost of highly dispersed production systems and the hidden costs of distant procurement discussed earlier. Wal-Mart, for example, is increasingly sourcing produce for its food sections from local farms near its warehouses. It has discovered that the savings on transportation costs and the ability to restock in smaller quantities more than offset the lower prices of industrial farms farther away. Nestlé is establishing smaller plants closer to its markets and stepping up efforts to maximize the use of locally available materials.

The calculus of locating activities in developing countries is also changing. Olam International, a leading cashew producer, traditionally shipped its nuts from Africa to Asia for processing at facilities staffed by productive Asian workers. But by opening local processing plants and training workers in Tanzania, Mozambique, Nigeria, and Côte d'Ivoire, Olam has cut processing and shipping costs by as much as 25%—not to mention, greatly reduced carbon emissions. In making this move, Olam also built preferred relationships with local farmers. And it has provided direct employment to 17,000 people—95% of whom are women—and indirect employment to an equal number of people, in rural areas where jobs otherwise were not available.

These trends may well lead companies to remake their value chains by moving some activities closer to home and having fewer major production locations. Until now, many companies have thought that being global meant moving production to locations with the lowest labor costs and designing their supply chains to achieve the most immediate impact on expenses. In reality, the strongest international competitors will often be those that can establish deeper roots in important communities. Companies that can embrace this new locational thinking will create shared value.

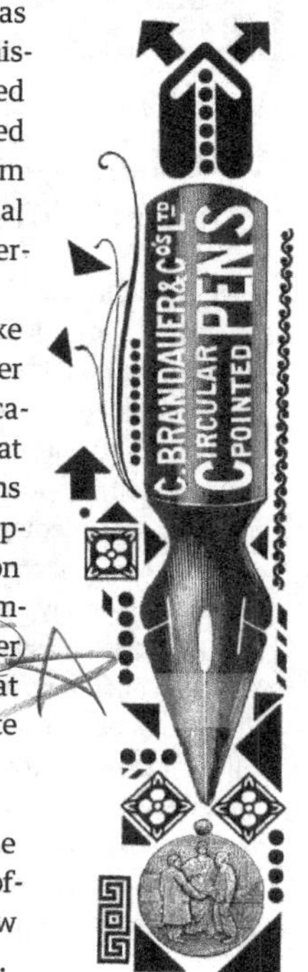


**AS THESE** examples illustrate, reimagining value chains from the perspective of shared value will offer significant new ways to innovate and unlock new economic value that most businesses have missed.

### Enabling Local Cluster Development

No company is self-contained. The success of every company is affected by the supporting companies and infrastructure around it. Productivity and innovation are strongly influenced by "clusters," or geographic concentrations of firms, related businesses, suppliers, service providers, and logistical infrastructure in a particular field—such as IT in Silicon Valley, cut flowers in Kenya, and diamond cutting in Surat, India.

Clusters include not only businesses but institutions such as academic programs, trade associations, and standards organizations. They also draw on the broader public assets in the surrounding community, such as schools and universities, clean water, fair-competition laws, quality standards, and market transparency.

Clusters are prominent in all successful and growing regional economies and play a crucial role in driving productivity, innovation, and competitiveness. Capable local suppliers foster greater logistical efficiency and ease of collaboration, as we have discussed. Stronger local capabilities in such areas as training, transportation services, and related industries also boost productivity. Without a supporting cluster, conversely, productivity suffers.

Deficiencies in the framework conditions surrounding the cluster also create internal costs for firms. Poor public education imposes productivity and remedial-training costs. Poor transportation infrastructure drives up the costs of logistics. Gender or racial discrimination reduces the pool of capable employees. Poverty limits the demand for products and leads to environmental degradation, unhealthy workers, and high security costs. As companies have increasingly become disconnected from their communities, however, their influence in solving these problems has waned even as their costs have grown.

Firms create shared value by building clusters to improve company productivity while addressing gaps or failures in the framework conditions surrounding the cluster. Efforts to develop or attract capable suppliers, for example, enable the procurement benefits we discussed earlier. A focus on clusters and location has been all but absent in management thinking. Cluster thinking has also been

## Creating Shared Value: Implications for Government and

**While our focus here is primarily on companies, the principles of shared value apply equally to governments and nonprofit organizations.**

Governments and NGOs will be most effective if they think in value terms—considering benefits relative to costs—and focus on the results achieved rather than the funds and effort expended. Activists have tended to approach social improvement from an ideological or absolutist perspective, as if social benefits should be pursued at any cost. Governments and NGOs often assume that trade-offs between economic and social benefits are inevitable, exacerbating these trade-offs through their approaches. For example, much environmental regulation still takes the form of command-and-control mandates and enforcement actions designed to embarrass and punish companies. Regulators would accomplish much more by focusing on measuring environmental performance and introducing standards, phase-in periods, and support for technology that would promote innovation, improve the environment, and increase competitiveness simultaneously.

The principle of shared value creation cuts across the traditional divide between the responsibilities of business and those of government or civil society. From society's perspective, it does not matter what types of organizations created the value. What matters is that benefits are delivered by those organizations—or combinations of organizations—that are best positioned to achieve the most impact for the least cost. Finding ways to boost productivity is equally valuable whether in the service of commercial or societal objectives. In short, the principle of value creation should guide the use of resources across all areas of societal concern.

Fortunately, a new type of NGO has emerged that understands the importance of productivity and value creation. Such organizations have often had a remarkable impact. One example is TechnoServe, which has partnered with both regional and global corporations to promote the development of competitive agricultural clusters in more than 30 countries. Root Capital accomplishes a similar objective by providing financing to farmers and businesses that are too large for microfinance but too small for normal bank financing. Since 2000, Root Capital has lent more than $200 million to 282 businesses, missing in many economic development initiatives, which have failed because they involved isolated interventions and overlooked critical complementary investments.

A key aspect of cluster building in developing and developed countries alike is the formation of open and transparent markets. In inefficient or monopolized markets where workers are exploited, where suppliers do not receive fair prices, and where price transparency is lacking, productivity suffers. Enabling fair and open markets, which is often best done in conjunction with partners, can allow a company to secure reliable supplies and give suppliers better incentives for quality and efficiency while also substantially improving the incomes and purchasing power of local citizens. A positive cycle of economic and social development results.

When a firm builds clusters in its key locations, it also amplifies the connection between its success and its communities' success. A firm's growth has multiplier effects, as jobs are created in supporting industries, new companies are seeded, and demand for ancillary services rises. A company's efforts to improve framework conditions for the cluster spill over to other participants and the local economy. Workforce development initiatives, for example, increase the supply of skilled employees for many other firms as well.

At Nespresso, Nestlé also worked to build clusters, which made its new procurement practices far more effective. It set out to build agricultural, technical, financial, and logistical firms and capabilities in each coffee region, to further support efficiency and high-quality local production. Nestlé led efforts to increase access to essential agricultural inputs such as plant stock, fertilizers, and irrigation equipment; strengthen regional farmer co-ops by helping them finance shared wet-milling facilities for producing higher-quality beans; and support an extension program to advise all farmers on growing techniques. It also worked in partnership with the Rainforest Alliance, a leading international NGO, to teach farmers more-sustainable practices that make production volumes more reliable. In the process, Nestlé's productivity improved.

## Civil Society

through which it has reached 400,000 farmers and artisans. It has financed the cultivation of 1.4 million acres of organic agriculture in Latin America and Africa. Root Capital regularly works with corporations, utilizing future purchase orders as collateral for its loans to farmers and helping to strengthen corporate supply chains and improve the quality of purchased inputs.

Some private foundations have begun to see the power of working with businesses to create shared value. The Bill & Melinda Gates Foundation, for example, has formed partnerships with leading global corporations to foster agricultural clusters in developing countries. The foundation carefully focuses on commodities where climate and soil conditions give a particular region a true competitive advantage. The partnerships bring in NGOs like TechnoServe and Root Capital, as well as government officials, to work on precompetitive issues that improve the cluster and upgrade the value chain for all participants. This approach recognizes that helping small farmers increase their yields will not create any lasting benefits unless there are ready buyers for their crops, other enterprises that can process the crops once they are harvested, and a local cluster that includes efficient logistical infrastructure, input availability, and the like. The active engagement of corporations is essential to mobilizing these elements.

Forward-thinking foundations can also serve as honest brokers and allay fears by mitigating power imbalances between small local enterprises, NGOs, governments, and companies. Such efforts will require a new assumption that shared value can come only as a result of effective collaboration among all parties.

## Government Regulation and Shared Value

**The right kind of government regulation can encourage companies to pursue shared value; the wrong kind works against it and even makes trade-offs between economic and social goals inevitable.**

Regulation is necessary for well-functioning markets, something that became abundantly clear during the recent financial crisis. However, the ways in which regulations are designed and implemented determine whether they benefit society or work against it.

Regulations that enhance shared value set goals and stimulate innovation. They highlight a societal objective and create a level playing field to encourage companies to invest in shared value rather than maximize short-term profit. Such regulations have a number of characteristics:

First, they set clear and measurable social goals, whether they involve energy use, health matters, or safety. Where appropriate, they set prices for resources (such as water) that reflect true costs. Second, they set performance standards but do not prescribe the methods to achieve them—those are left to companies. Third, they define phase-in periods for meeting standards, which reflect the investment or new-product cycle in the industry. Phase-in periods give companies time to develop and introduce new products and processes in a way consistent with the economics of their business. Fourth, they put in place universal measurement and performance-reporting systems, with government investing in infrastructure for collecting reliable benchmarking data (such as nutritional deficiencies in each community). This motivates and enables continual improvement beyond current targets. Finally, appropriate regulations require efficient and timely reporting of results, which can then be audited by the government as necessary, rather than impose detailed and expensive compliance processes on everyone.

Regulation that discourages shared value looks very different. It forces compliance with particular practices, rather than focusing on measurable social improvement. It mandates a particular approach to meeting a standard—blocking innovation and almost always inflicting cost on companies. When governments fall into the trap of this sort of regulation, they undermine the very progress that they seek while triggering fierce resistance from business that slows progress further and blocks shared value that would improve competitiveness.

To be sure, companies locked into the old mind-set will resist even well-constructed regulation. As shared value principles become more widely accepted, however, business and government will become more aligned on regulation in many areas. Companies will come to understand that the right kind of regulation can actually foster economic value creation.

Finally, regulation will be needed to limit the pursuit of exploitative, unfair, or deceptive practices in which companies benefit at the expense of society. Strict antitrust policy, for example, is essential to ensure that the benefits of company success flow to customers, suppliers, and workers.

A good example of a company working to improve framework conditions in its cluster is Yara, the world's largest mineral fertilizer company. Yara realized that the lack of logistical infrastructure in many parts of Africa was preventing farmers from gaining efficient access to fertilizers and other essential agricultural inputs, and from transporting their crops efficiently to market. Yara is tackling this problem through a $60 million investment in a program to improve ports and roads, which is designed to create agricultural growth corridors in Mozambique and Tanzania. The company is working on this initiative with local governments and support from the Norwegian government. In Mozambique alone, the corridor is expected to benefit more than 200,000 small farmers and create 350,000 new jobs. The improvements will help Yara grow its business but will support the whole agricultural cluster, creating huge multiplier effects.

The benefits of cluster building apply not only in emerging economies but also in advanced countries. North Carolina's Research Triangle is a notable example of public and private collaboration that has created shared value by developing clusters in such areas as information technology and life sciences. That region, which has benefited from continued investment from both the private sector and local government, has experienced huge growth in employment, incomes, and company performance, and has fared better than most during the downturn.

To support cluster development in the communities in which they operate, companies need to identify gaps and deficiencies in areas such as logistics, suppliers, distribution channels, training, market organization, and educational institutions. Then the task is to focus on the weaknesses that represent the greatest constraints to the company's own productivity and growth, and distinguish those areas that the company is best equipped to influence directly from those in which collaboration is more cost-effective. Here is where the shared value opportunities will be greatest. Initiatives that address cluster weaknesses that constrain companies will be much more effective than community-focused corporate social responsibility programs, which often have limited impact because they take on too many areas without focusing on value.

But efforts to enhance infrastructure and institutions in a region often require collective action, as the Nestlé, Yara, and Research Triangle examples show. Companies should try to enlist partners to share the cost, win support, and assemble the right skills. The most successful cluster development programs are ones that involve collaboration within the private sector, as well as trade associations, government agencies, and NGOs.

## Creating Shared Value in Practice

Not all profit is equal—an idea that has been lost in the narrow, short-term focus of financial markets and in much management thinking. Profits involving a social purpose represent a higher form of capitalism—one that will enable society to advance more rapidly while allowing companies to grow even more. The result is a positive cycle of company and community prosperity, which leads to profits that endure.

Creating shared value presumes compliance with the law and ethical standards, as well as mitigating any harm caused by the business, but goes far beyond that. The opportunity to create economic value through creating societal value will be one of the most powerful forces driving growth in the global economy. This thinking represents a new way of understanding customers, productivity, and the external influences on corporate success. It highlights the immense human needs to be met, the large new markets to serve, and the internal costs of social and community deficits—as well as the competitive advantages available from addressing them. Until recently, companies have simply not approached their businesses this way.

Creating shared value will be more effective and far more sustainable than the majority of today's corporate efforts in the social arena. Companies will make real strides on the environment, for example, when they treat it as a productivity driver rather than a feel-good response to external pressure. Or consider access to housing. A shared value approach would have led financial services companies to create innovative products that prudently increased access to home ownership. This was recognized by the Mexican construction company Urbi, which pioneered a mortgage-financing "rent-to-own" plan. Major U.S. banks, in contrast, promoted unsustainable financing vehicles that turned out to be socially and economically devastating, while claiming they were socially responsible because they had charitable contribution programs.

Inevitably, the most fertile opportunities for creating shared value will be closely related to a company's particular business, and in areas most important to the business. Here a company can benefit the most economically and hence sustain its commitment over time. Here is also where a company brings the most resources to bear, and where its scale and market presence equip it to have a meaningful impact on a societal problem.

Ironically, many of the shared value pioneers have been those with more-limited resources—social entrepreneurs and companies in developing countries. These outsiders have been able to see the opportunities more clearly. In the process, the distinction between for-profits and nonprofits is blurring.

Shared value is defining a whole new set of best practices that all companies must embrace. It will also become an integral part of strategy. The essence of strategy is choosing a unique positioning and a

**Not all profit is equal. Profits involving a social purpose represent a higher form of capitalism, one that creates a positive cycle of company and community prosperity.**

distinctive value chain to deliver on it. Shared value opens up many new needs to meet, new products to offer, new customers to serve, and new ways to configure the value chain. And the competitive advantages that arise from creating shared value will often be more sustainable than conventional cost and quality improvements. The cycle of imitation and zero-sum competition can be broken.

The opportunities to create shared value are widespread and growing. Not every company will have them in every area, but our experience has been that companies discover more and more opportunities over time as their line operating units grasp this concept. It has taken a decade, but GE's Ecomagination initiative, for example, is now producing a stream of fast-growing products and services across the company.

## HOW SHARED VALUE DIFFERS FROM CORPORATE SOCIAL RESPONSIBILITY

**Creating shared value (CSV) should supersede corporate social responsibility (CSR) in guiding the investments of companies in their communities. CSR programs focus mostly on reputation and have only a limited connection to the business, making them hard to justify and maintain over the long run. In contrast, CSV is integral to a company's profitability and competitive position. It leverages the unique resources and expertise of the company to create economic value by creating social value.**

| CSR | CSV |
| --- | --- |
| Values: doing good | Value: economic and societal benefits relative to cost |
| Citizenship, philanthropy, sustainability | Joint company and community value creation |
| Discretionary or in response to external pressure | Integral to competing |
| Separate from profit maximization | Integral to profit maximization |
| Agenda is determined by external reporting and personal preferences | Agenda is company specific and internally generated |
| Impact limited by corporate footprint and CSR budget | Realigns the entire company budget |
| Example: Fair trade purchasing | Example: Transforming procurement to increase quality and yield |

In both cases, compliance with laws and ethical standards and reducing harm from corporate activities are assumed.

A shared value lens can be applied to every major company decision. Could our product design incorporate greater social benefits? Are we serving all the communities that would benefit from our products? Do our processes and logistical approaches maximize efficiencies in energy and water use? Could our new plant be constructed in a way that achieves greater community impact? How are gaps in our cluster holding back our efficiency and speed of innovation? How could we enhance our community as a business location? If sites are comparable economically, at which one will the local community benefit the most? If a company can improve societal conditions, it will often improve business conditions and thereby trigger positive feedback loops.

The three avenues for creating shared value are mutually reinforcing. Enhancing the cluster, for example, will enable more local procurement and less dispersed supply chains. New products and services that meet social needs or serve overlooked markets will require new value chain choices in areas such as production, marketing, and distribution. And new value chain configurations will create demand for equipment and technology that save energy, conserve resources, and support employees.

Creating shared value will require concrete and tailored metrics for each business unit in each of the three areas. While some companies have begun to track various social impacts, few have yet tied them to their economic interests at the business level.

Shared value creation will involve new and heightened forms of collaboration. While some shared value opportunities are possible for a company to seize on its own, others will benefit from insights, skills, and resources that cut across profit/nonprofit and private/public boundaries. Here, companies will be less successful if they attempt to tackle societal problems on their own, especially those involving cluster development. Major competitors may also need to work together on precompetitive framework conditions, something that has not been common in reputation-driven CSR initiatives. Successful collaboration will be data driven, clearly linked to defined outcomes, well connected to the goals of all stakeholders, and tracked with clear metrics.

Governments and NGOs can enable and reinforce shared value or work against it. (For more on this topic, see the sidebar "Government Regulation and Shared Value.")

### The Next Evolution in Capitalism

Shared value holds the key to unlocking the next wave of business innovation and growth. It will also reconnect company success and community success in ways that have been lost in an age of narrow management approaches, short-term thinking, and deepening divides among society's institutions.

Shared value focuses companies on the right kind of profits—profits that create societal benefits rather than diminish them. Capital markets will undoubtedly continue to pressure companies to generate short-term profits, and some companies will surely continue to reap profits at the expense of societal needs. But such profits will often prove to be short-lived, and far greater opportunities will be missed.

The moment for an expanded view of value creation has come. A host of factors, such as the growing social awareness of employees and citizens and the increased scarcity of natural resources, will drive unprecedented opportunities to create shared value.

We need a more sophisticated form of capitalism, one imbued with a social purpose. But that purpose should arise not out of charity but out of a deeper understanding of competition and economic value creation. This next evolution in the capitalist model recognizes new and better ways to develop products, serve markets, and build productive enterprises.

Creating shared value represents a broader conception of Adam Smith's invisible hand. It opens the doors of the pin factory to a wider set of influences. It is not philanthropy but self-interested behavior to create economic value by creating societal value. If all companies individually pursued shared value connected to their particular businesses, society's overall interests would be served. And companies would acquire legitimacy in the eyes of the communities in which they operated, which would allow democracy to work as governments set policies that fostered and supported business. Survival of the fittest would still prevail, but market competition would benefit society in ways we have lost.

Creating shared value represents a new approach to managing that cuts across disciplines. Because of the traditional divide between economic concerns and social ones, people in the public and private sectors have often followed very different educational and career paths. As a result, few managers have the understanding of social and environmental issues required to move beyond today's CSR approaches, and few social sector leaders have the managerial training and entrepreneurial mind-set needed to design and implement shared value models. Most business schools still teach the narrow view of capitalism, even though more and more of their graduates hunger for a greater sense of purpose and a growing number are drawn to social entrepreneurship. The results have been missed opportunity and public cynicism.

Business school curricula will need to broaden in a number of areas. For example, the efficient use and stewardship of all forms of resources will define the next-generation thinking on value chains. Customer behavior and marketing courses will have to move beyond persuasion and demand creation to the study of deeper human needs and how to serve nontraditional customer groups. Clusters, and the broader locational influences on company productivity and innovation, will form a new core discipline in business schools; economic development will no longer be left only to public policy and economics departments. Business and government courses will examine the economic impact of societal factors on enterprises, moving beyond the effects of regulation and macroeconomics. And finance will need to rethink how capital markets can actually support true value creation in companies—their fundamental purpose—not just benefit financial market participants.

There is nothing soft about the concept of shared value. These proposed changes in business school curricula are not qualitative and do not depart from economic value creation. Instead, they represent the next stage in our understanding of markets, competition, and business management.

**NOT ALL** societal problems can be solved through shared value solutions. But shared value offers corporations the opportunity to utilize their skills, resources, and management capability to lead social progress in ways that even the best-intentioned governmental and social sector organizations can rarely match. In the process, businesses can earn the respect of society again.

**HBR Reprint** R1101C

**Michael E. Porter** is the Bishop William Lawrence University Professor at Harvard University. He is a frequent contributor to *Harvard Business Review* and a six-time McKinsey Award winner. **Mark R. Kramer** cofounded FSG, a global social impact consulting firm, with Professor Porter and is its managing director. He is also a senior fellow of the CSR initiative at Harvard's Kennedy School of Government.

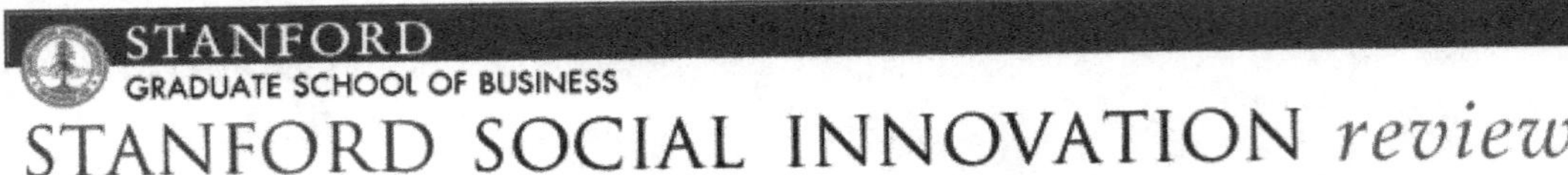


# The Hidden Costs of Cause Marketing

By Angela M. Eikenberry

Stanford Social Innovation Review
Summer 2009

Stanford Social Innovation Review
518 Memorial Way, Stanford, CA 94305-5015
Ph: 650-725-5399. Fax: 650-723-0516
Email: info@ssireview.com, **www.ssireview.com**

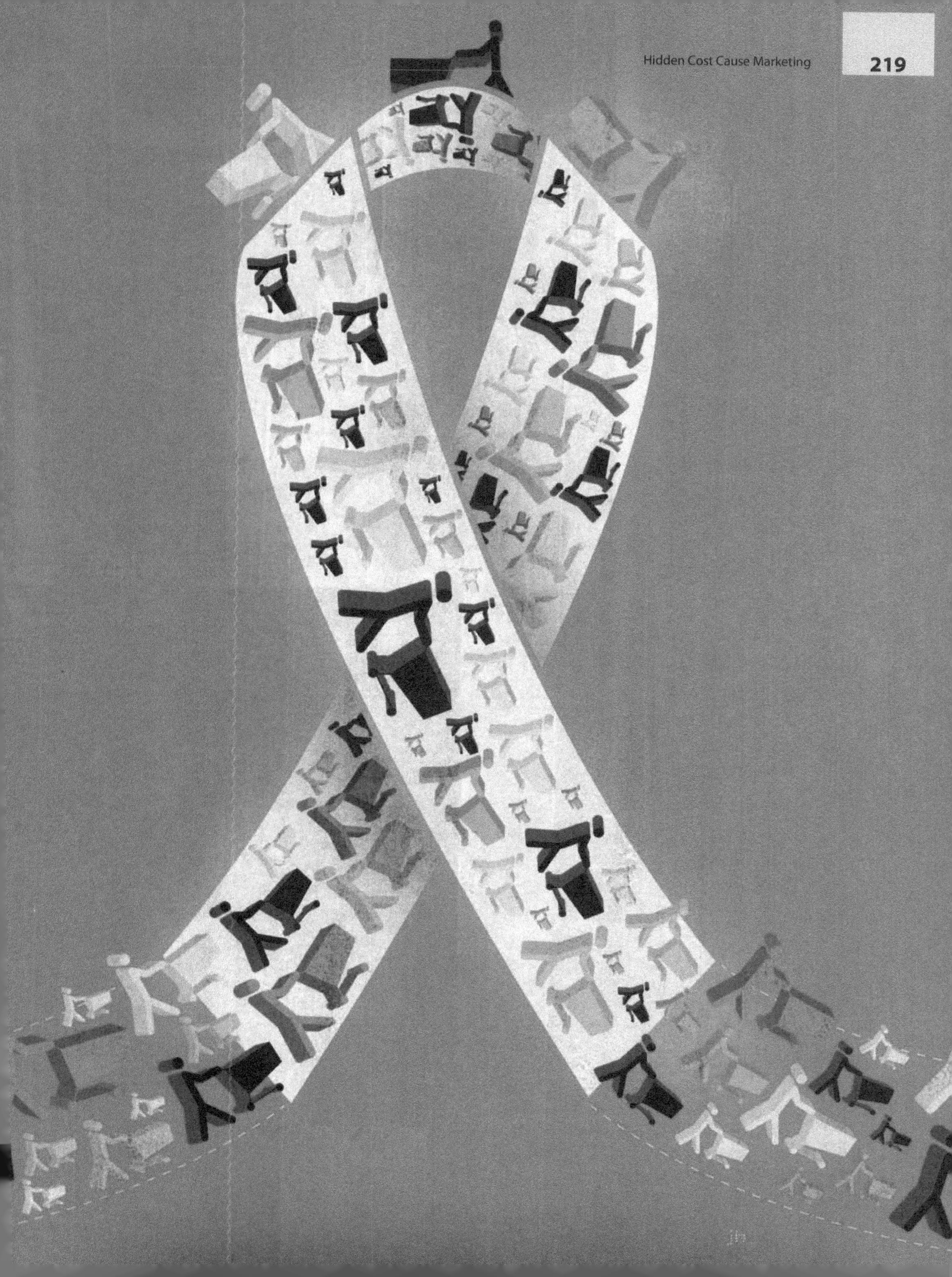

# The Hidden Costs of Cause Marketing

By Angela M. Eikenberry | Illustration by John Hersey

From pink ribbons to Product Red, cause marketing adroitly serves two masters, earning profits for corporations while raising funds for charities. Yet the short-term benefits of cause marketing—also known as consumption philanthropy—belie its long-term costs. These hidden costs include individualizing solutions to collective problems; replacing virtuous action with mindless buying; and hiding how markets create many social problems in the first place. Consumption philanthropy is therefore unsuited to create real social change.

I do my main charity work once a week—at the grocery store. Like some of you, this week I bought organic yogurt that not only is healthier for my family and the Earth, but also supports nonprofit environmental and educational organizations. I also picked up snack bars that promote peace (no kidding!) and salad dressing that funds various (unnamed) charities across the country. For all of this hard work, I rewarded myself with some Endangered Species Chocolate, which helps "support species, habitat, and humanity," according to the company's Web site. Delicious.

All of these purchases are examples of what my colleague Patricia Mooney Nickel of Victoria University and I call *consumption philanthropy*.[1] Also known in the business world as cause-related marketing or cause marketing, consumption philanthropy pairs the support of a charitable cause with the purchase or promotion of a service or product. (See "Flavors of Consumption Philanthropy" on page 53 for a description of the types of cause marketing.)

One example is the Product Red campaign, which California politician Robert Shriver has led and U2 lead singer Bono has promoted since its launch in 2006. By purchasing select Product Red-branded items from companies like Gap Inc., Apple Inc., Dell Inc., and Starbucks Corp., consumers can also support nonprofits like the Global Fund to Fight AIDS, Tuberculosis, and Malaria. The most well-known among the Red products, the Red iPod, costs $199, with $10 of that amount going to the Global Fund. So far, Red and its corporate partners have contributed more than $59 million to charity.

Consumption philanthropy seems like the ideal solution to many of the problems our society faces today. It allows charities to raise much-needed funds and to educate consumers. It helps corporations increase their profits, bolster their reputations, and distinguish their brands. And it lets consumers feel that they are making a difference in the world. On the surface, all seems rosy.

Yet lurking beneath this rosy surface are some disturbing consequences of combining consumption and philanthropy. I do not mean the often-cited risks of cause marketing, which include misalignment between the charity and the corporate sponsor, wasted resources, customer cynicism, or tainted images of charity. Most critiques of consumption philanthropy focus on these pesky problems of execution without questioning its basic underlying assumption—that consumption philanthropy, if done well, would do good for all.

I disagree with this assumption. Consumption philanthropy individualizes solutions to collective social problems, distracting our attention and resources away from the neediest causes, the most effective interventions, and the act of critical questioning itself. It devalues the moral core of philanthropy by making virtuous action easy and thoughtless. And it obscures the links between markets—their firms, products, and services—and the negative impacts they can have on human well-being. For these reasons, consumption philanthropy compromises the potential for charity to better society.

## Short-Term Fix

Strategies that combine consumption with philanthropy have skyrocketed in the last two decades. Among corporate sponsors, cause-marketing expenditures went from almost zero in 1983 to an estimated $1.3 billion in 2006, according to IEG Inc., a Chicago-based firm that tracks cause-related activities in the United States. At the same time, consumers increasingly demand that companies practice philanthropy and social responsibility. A 2004 Cone/Roper report found that 86 percent of American respondents were "very or somewhat likely to switch from one brand to another that is about the same in price and quality, if the other brand is associated with a cause."

As a growing body of research attests, consumption philanthropy does offer short-term benefits. Many corporations that sign on for cause-marketing campaigns enjoy higher sales and wider publicity for their products and services, improve their image with consumers, expand their markets, and boost employee morale. For example, cosmetics giant Avon Products Inc. says that cause marketing on behalf of early breast cancer detection and research has improved its relationships not only with its predominantly female customer base, but also with its predominantly female sales force.[2]

Meanwhile, charities gain legitimacy in the marketplace because they are seen "as viable partners in commercial ventures and not just as beggars pandering for the corporate dollar," write Australian marketing professors Michael Jay Polonsky and Greg Wood in their review of cause-related marketing.[3] Through cause-marketing campaigns, charities also generate revenues, attract volunteers, raise awareness of their cause, and receive extensive publicity. For instance, the Susan G. Komen Breast Cancer Foundation's partnership with Yoplait—Save Lids to Save Lives—has raised millions of dollars for the foundation while also increasing public awareness of breast cancer (and strengthening Yoplait's brand image).

Consumers also seem to win from participating in cause marketing. They get additional information about a charity or cause, as well as a convenient way to spend their disposable income on charitable causes. For example, consumers who were planning to buy chicken noodle soup or cereal anyway can choose to buy the "pink" Campbell's chicken noodle soup or "pink" Cheerios to meet their needs, while also providing funds for breast cancer research.

## Lone Rangers

Yet the long-term effects of consumption philanthropy are troubling. The first of these effects is that consumption philanthropy—which usually takes place as individual market transactions—distracts its participants from collective solutions to collective problems. This distraction steers people's attention and collective resources away from the neediest causes, the most effective interventions, and the act of critical questioning itself.

The growth of consumption philanthropy reflects many people's confidence in the power of the market (that is, the institutions, systems, and places where buyers and sellers exchange things) to deal with all sorts of social problems. That confidence stems from the ideology of neoliberal economics, which prevailed worldwide—at least before the current economic collapse. This ideology "views all aspects of human society as a kind of market," note management scholars Brenda Zimmerman and Raymond Dart.[4] For instance, in his 2005 book, *The Fortune at the Bottom of the Pyramid: Eradicating Poverty Through Profits*, University of Michigan management professor C.K. Prahalad portrays the world's poorest people as an untapped market niche whose salvation will come when they are fully integrated into the market. Likewise, in response to the 9/11 terrorist attacks, President Bush told Americans that our best, most patriotic recourse was to go shopping.

But one problem with relying on consumers to right the world's wrongs is that most consumers are not very interested in or capable of righting the world's wrongs. The primary goal of people in marketplaces is to make choices that fulfill their self-interested, individual material needs and desires. In this capacity, they generally have little impetus to consider "the public" or "the public good." Caught up in the transactions of buying and selling, they have little opportunity to question the fundamental principles of corporate organization. And unlike citizens who share in the collective authority, responsibility,

ANGELA M. EIKENBERRY is an assistant professor in the School of Public Administration at the University of Nebraska at Omaha, where she studies and teaches philanthropy, nonprofit management, and public administration theory. Her book, *Giving Circles: Philanthropy, Voluntary Association, and Democracy*, will be published in summer 2009.

## Flavors of Consumption Philanthropy

**Transactional.** This is the most widespread model of consumption philanthropy. For each unit of product or service a corporation sells, it contributes a portion of the proceeds to a social cause. Two examples are the pink products campaign that the Susan G. Komen Breast Cancer Foundation organizes and the Product Red campaign that Robert Shriver and Bono back. Through them, consumers can buy a product while also supporting breast cancer research or the HIV/AIDS, malaria, and tuberculosis battle in Africa. Both campaigns partner with multinational corporations in the United States and elsewhere.

**Promotion-Based.** Corporations promote a cause and make charitable contributions. The donations are not necessarily tied to business transactions and not necessarily monetary, but do promote both the cause and the corporation. An example is the partnership between the Anti-Defamation League and Barnes & Noble. Their Close the Book on Hate initiative provides instructional materials and lectures to promote racial and cultural tolerance.

**Licensing.** A charity such as the World Wildlife Fund licenses the use of its name and logo to a company such as Visa. The company then donates a percentage of every transaction associated with the logo to the charity.

and dignity of public life, individual consumers have little reason to wonder how larger political-economic structures might create social problems in the first place.

Recent research indeed shows that when money enters the picture, people's more charitable impulses often fall by the wayside. University of Toronto management professor Sanford DeVoe and his colleagues, for example, have shown in laboratory experiments that participants are less likely to volunteer for a charity after calculating how much money they earn per hour than they are after merely reporting their annual salary. Putting a price tag on time, it seems, makes people less willing to give their time away "for free." [5] (For more information, see "The Stingy Hour" in the winter 2008 issue of the *Stanford Social Innovation Review.*)

The research evidence also shows that individualized consumer approaches to philanthropy actually shift giving away from more collective approaches. Professors Karen Flaherty, currently at Oklahoma State University, and William Diamond of the University of Massachusetts Amherst found in a 1999 study that cause-marketing campaigns hinder future donations to charities because consumers think that their purchases *are* donations.[6] So when the plate passes for charitable contributions, respondents to cause-marketing campaigns feel that they've already given. Likewise, findings published in 2004 in the *Journal of Marketing* suggest that consumers who support socially responsible companies believe that they have already done their philanthropic share.[7]

Consistent with these findings, Zimmerman and Dart tell the story of a person who attended a book sale held by a nonprofit organization. The person bought a hot dog, a drink, and a couple of books at the event. When the nonprofit asked for donations, the attendee demurred, thinking that the purchases were a sufficient contribution to the organization.

Another less favorable implication of consumption philanthropy's reliance on the purchasing decisions of individual consumers is that it may disadvantage less attractive but nonetheless worthy causes. Consider the many pink ribbon campaigns for breast cancer, for instance. Since 1991, when the first pink ribbon was handed out at the Susan G. Komen Foundation's Race for the Cure, pink ribbons and products have flourished. Today, the Komen Foundation raises about $30 million a year through 130 corporate partnerships.

The sheer volume of pink products seems to lead many consumers to believe that breast cancer is the most pressing health problem facing women today. Yet the most recent (2004) data from the U.S. Centers for Disease Control and Prevention show that the leading cause of death among women in the United States is heart disease, not breast cancer. And although cancer is the leading cause of death for women ages 35-64, breast cancer is not the most common form of cancer among women (skin cancer is), nor is it the leading cause of death among women diagnosed with cancer (lung cancer holds this distinction). Because of the success of cause marketing for breast cancer, however, breast cancer-related organizations receive attention that is disproportionate to the scope of the disease.

As consumption philanthropy becomes ubiquitous, some observers worry that it may, in the long run, have exactly the opposite of its intended effect and will desensitize the public to social ills while decreasing other forms of philanthropic action. Accordingly, Matthew Berglind of Northwestern University and Cheryl Nakata of the University of Illinois at Chicago write in a 2005 *Business Horizons* article: "It is not difficult to imagine cause-related marketing campaigns interjecting themselves into the millions of purchase transactions that take place each day. In response, people may simply tune out and say 'no' because they cannot process each and every request or because they believe they have already donated enough." [8]

### Easy Virtue

One of the redeeming aspects of consumption philanthropy is that it makes philanthropy simple and convenient. As I do every weekend at the grocery store, shoppers can protect the Earth, promote world peace, and fund a network of otherwise unnamed charities without deviating from their routines in the least. In this way, consumption philanthropy can contribute to a more compassionate marketplace.

The other side of this easy virtue, however, is that it is *too* easy. Consumption philanthropy does not allow people to exercise their moral core. Philanthropy originated in the Greek ideal of *philanthropos* or "love of humankind." According to Aristotle's *Nicomachean Ethics*, philanthropy allows people to enact the all-important virtues of generosity, benevolence, kindness, compassion, justice, and reciprocity. Enacting these virtues, in turn, allows people to develo their character, cultivate their human potential, and strengthen their moral fiber.

Can consumption philanthropy achieve these same ends? Probably not. When people link their charitable donations to their preexisting consumption decisions, they need not exercise a deeper sense of moral responsibility. They need not take any extra steps (beyond, say, choosing a different brand of yogurt) or make any additional sacrifices. Instead, they need only to pursue their shopping needs and wants. Indeed, the consumer-philanthropist may even enjoy a cost savings for her seemingly virtuous effort. As a recent Project Red advertisement put it: "30 percent off for you, 5 percent to fight AIDS in Africa." One could argue that consumption philanthropy—especially if there is a charitable surcharge—represents effort, and the choice to buy a "socially responsible" product represents intention, but there is very little sacrifice, if any, required. And so consumption philanthropy becomes divorced from the experience of duty.

Perhaps a more disturbing feature of consumption philanthropy is that consumers need not be aware of the supposed beneficiary of their actions. The morality of philanthropy comes from acting for other people, according to scholars Warren Smith and Matthew Higgins.[9] Acting for other people, in turn, requires figuring out what they really need.

Yet consumption philanthropy sidesteps both this requirement and, more generally, contact with people in need. For example, a person who uses a charity-licensed credit card to pay for an expensive meal, and thereby sends a percentage of his purchase to a cause that fights hunger, may no longer feel obligated to find out who is hungry or why they are hungry. Without this knowledge, he may feel less empathy for poor people, and therefore less compelled to change the conditions that caused their plight.

More broadly, in the absence of people's active and effortful moral engagement, corporations and their profit-driven needs set the tone for acceptable ways of being philanthropic. As a result, people's genuine benevolent sentiments are co-opted for profit, and their care is reduced to a market transaction.

## Market Blindness

A third long-term negative consequence of consumption philanthropy is that it obscures the ways that markets produce some of the very problems—physical, social, and environmental—that philanthropy attempts to redress. In *Pink Ribbons, Inc.*, Samantha King describes the paradox of some pink ribbon products: labels on the outside that promote breast cancer awareness and research, but chemicals on the inside that cause the disease in the first place. (See the spring 2007 *Stanford Social Innovation Review* for a review of this book.) So consumers buy, say, a $6 SpongeBob Pink Pants toy to help fight cancer, not realizing that this product—a frivolous item—also likely creates the toxins and other environmental hazards that help cause cancer.

Consumption philanthropy seldom calls on consumers to question the labor that went into the creation of these products. Do these allegedly responsible corporations pay their workers a living wage? Do they create safe working conditions? Do they make fair contracts? Product Red may be donating money to fight disease in Africa, but it isn't doing enough to protect the workers who make its products, says Bristol, U.K.-based nonprofit Labour Behind the Label. Although Product Red partner Gap has worked diligently over the years to improve its ethical practices and image, for instance, the apparel company still runs afoul of both international regulations and activists: Two years ago, London's *Observer* found children making Gap clothing in sweatshops in India. Cause-marketing items may be no worse than ordinary products, but they appear to be no better, either.

Finally, consumption philanthropy rarely questions the act of consuming or the environmental havoc that more and more products wreak. Did the energy used to create that Endangered Species Chocolate bar destroy another acre of rain forest, and therefore hasten the endangerment of yet another species and the warming of the planet? Was that SpongeBob Pink Pants toy really worth the petroleum—and the environmental degradation that came with extracting, refining, and transforming it—that went into it? Rather than raising these questions about our purchases and their consequences, consumption philanthropy encourages people to buy more by making them feel better about it.

In short, consumption philanthropy lulls people into a false sense of doing good through their purchases, even as they are potentially doing harm through their purchases. Indeed, in many cases, consumption philanthropists are exacerbating the very harms they wish to reduce. At the same time, consumption philanthropy feeds the systems and institutions that contribute to many social problems in the first place.

Meanwhile, because consumption and philanthropy have become one and the same, the distance from which one would critique consumption and the market, and imagine alternatives, is eliminated. Philanthropy becomes depoliticized, stripped of its critical, social change potential. The result is that consumption philanthropy stabilizes, more than changes, the system (the market) that some would argue led to the poverty, disease, and environmental destruction philanthropists hope to eradicate. Consumption philanthropy is thus not about change, but about business as usual.

## Profit-Free Philanthropy

I cannot offer the solution to the problems of consumption philanthropy. But I hope at least to offer a starting point for dialogue about unexamined assumptions and the political nature of philanthropy. What are our assumptions and expectations of philanthropy? Should philanthropy create social change? If so, what type of change?

If we are concerned about solving societal problems, reinvigorating the moral core of philanthropy, and making markets protect—or at least not harm—human well-being, a market approach cannot be an appropriate avenue for philanthropy. The most benevolent philanthropic agenda would not be infused with consumption. Instead, it would give voice to those who suffer. This may be the best way to create social change.

Why amplify the voices of those who suffer? As we have seen in movements for workers' rights, African-Americans' civil rights, and women's and gender rights in the United States, when the aggrieved speak and the more powerful listen, policies, political processes, and public perceptions can change. Social movements are one of the principal ways in which "collectivities can give voice to their grievances and concerns about the rights, welfare, and well-being of *themselves*

and others."[10] And social movements—such as the American Revolution and the abolition of slavery—have brought about some of the most significant developments and changes in human history.

For philanthropy to give voice to those who suffer, it needs to support grassroots social movements. Since at least the 1950s, a small but persistent group of foundations and donors has practiced social change philanthropy through its unfettered support of nonprofit groups and grassroots associations. These nonprofit organizations and grassroots associations, in turn, support the movements that give voice to the marginalized. This is in line with Tracy Gary's challenge to donors, in *Inspired Philanthropy*, to practice a philanthropy that "has a role in changing the inequities of society" by joining donor interests and experiences with needs in the community. The National Committee for Responsive Philanthropy likewise calls on foundations to dedicate at least 25 percent of their grant dollars to advocacy, organizing, and civic engagement that promotes equity, opportunity, and justice.

Boston-based Haymarket People's Fund is committed to this vision of philanthropy. Founded in 1974, the fund supports groups that are working in the areas of racism, workers' rights, women's and gender rights, housing and homelessness, and environment and health issues. Its mission is explicitly to "strengthen the movement for social justice" by supporting "grassroots organizations that address the root causes of injustice," and its democratic funding practices transform the typically hierarchical relations between donors and recipients.

Other nonprofit organizations and philanthropic institutions could focus on cultivating more meaningful and diverse relationships with donors, rather than on raising funds through consumption. Through a more regular and deeper relationship with donors, these organizations and institutions can encourage philanthropists to pay attention to how their philanthropy fits into the larger movement to serve the public good. This will allow them to revive the moral core of their philanthropic acts, as well as to engage in political discourse about what role philanthropy should play in society.

To this end, fundraising experts Kay Sprinkel Grace and Alan Wendroff suggest that fundraisers move away from a *transactional* model of giving, whose emphasis is on cultivating donors of major gifts, and toward a *transformational* model of giving, whose "focus is on the impact of the gift and the renewing relationship, not just on the transaction."[11]

Changing philanthropy to give greater voice to those who suffer also means changing the current focus in corporate philanthropy. Rather than tying charity to profits, corporations should focus on their own responsibility to their employees (through means such as fair wages and healthy, satisfying work conditions), the environment (through means such as greener and more sustainable practices), and the global society (through means such as Fair Trade practices and loyalty to communities of operation). Corporations might also join other foundations and donors in funding grassroots efforts to improve communities. These alliances would be strategic partnerships not for profits, but for change from the bottom up.

Though many corporations will find it difficult to be socially responsible on all these dimensions, a few are already doing well on most of them. Two examples are Google Inc. and Whole Foods Market Inc. Google is well-known for its supportive and holistic labor practices: The company pays its employees well, gives them time to explore new projects and creative endeavors, and offers them amenities ranging from on-site roller hockey rinks to free food 24 hours a day. Google also values diversity. Likewise, the Google Foundation supports anti-poverty, alternative energy, and environmental efforts. Whole Foods is the largest corporation to purchase renewable energy credits and promotes the use of nonpolluting electricity sources. Several of its stores are 100 percent green-powered.

## TRUE BENEVOLENCE

Consuming more will not solve today's social and environmental problems. Indeed, consumption may very well create more of the kinds of problems that we had hoped philanthropy would fix. Relying on individual consumer choices, consumption philanthropy is unsuited to the scale or complexity of the problems it seeks to fix. Couched in market transactions, it neither acknowledges the voice of the transactions' beneficiaries nor gives philanthropists the satisfaction of mindful virtuous action. And caught in the mechanisms of the market, it obscures the fact that the market caused many of the problems that philanthropy seeks to redress.

For philanthropy to lead to social change—if that is indeed what we hope and expect it to do—I suggest we look to philanthropy as a tool to bring greater voice to those who have suffered or are marginalized, and for those who advocate for bettering society. This is not easy in today's society, although our current economic crisis is increasingly demonstrating the limitations of the market.

The time has come to question our assumptions and then to imagine alternative, more hopeful futures. Surely, genuinely philanthropic benevolence would call not for more consumption, but for the elimination of the conditions that make philanthropy necessary. ■

*Notes*

1 This work is based on an article by Patricia M. Nickel and Angela M. Eikenberry, "A Critique of the Discourse of Marketized Philanthropy," *American Behavioral Scientist*, 52(7), 2009: 974-89.

2 John Davidson, "Cancer Sells," *Working Woman*, 22(5), 1997: 36-39.

3 Michael Jay Polonsky and Greg Wood, "Can the Overcommercialization of Cause-Related Marketing Harm Society?" *Journal of Macromarketing*, 21(1), 2001: 12.

4 Brenda Zimmerman and Raymond Dart, "Charities Doing Commercial Ventures," Trillium Foundation, 1998.

5 Sanford E. DeVoe and Jeffrey Pfeffer, "Hourly Payment and Volunteering: The Effect of Organizational Practices on Decisions About Time Use," *Academy of Management Journal*, 50(4), 2007: 783-98.

6 Karen Flaherty and William Diamond, "The Impact of Consumers' Mental Budgeting on the Effectiveness of Cause-Related Marketing," *American Marketing Association Conference Proceedings*, 10, 1999: 151-52.

7 Donald R. Lichtenstein, Minette E. Drumwright, and Bridgette M. Braig, "The Effect of Corporate Social Responsibility on Customer Donations to Corporate-Supported Nonprofits," *Journal of Marketing*, 68(4), 2004: 16-32.

8 Matthew Berglind and Cheryl Nakata, "Cause-Related Marketing: More Buck Than Bang?" *Business Horizons*, 48(5), 2005: 443-53.

9 Warren Smith and Matthew Higgins, "Cause-Related Marketing: Ethics and Ecstatic," *Business & Society*, 39(3), 2000: 304-22.

10 David A. Snow, Sarah A. Soule, and Hanspeter Kriesi, "Mapping the Terrain," in *The Blackwell Companion to Social Movements*, Oxford, U.K.: Blackwell Publishing, 2004: 3-16.

11 Kay Sprinkel Grace and Alan Wendroff, *High-Impact Philanthropy: How Donors, Boards, and Nonprofit Organizations Can Transform Communities*, New York: John Wiley & Sons, 2001: 15.